Who
Owns
the
Land
?

STANLEY A.

Updated and Revised by

Who Owns the Land

ELLISEN

CHARLES H. DYER

THE ARAB/ISRAELI CONFLICT

Tyndale House Publishers, Inc.
WHEATON, ILLINOIS

Library of Congress Cataloging-in-Publication Data

Ellisen, Stanley A.
    Who owns the land? : the Arab-Israeli conflict / Stanley A. Ellisen ; updated and revised by Charles H. Dyer.—Rev. ed.
        p. cm.
Includes bibliographical references and index.
    ISBN 0-8423-8436-7 (pbk.)
    1. Arab-Israeli conflict.   2. Jews—History.   3. Zionism—History.   4. Israel—History.
5. Bible—Prophecies—Jews.   I. Dyer, Charles H., date.   II. Title.
DS119.7 .E4434 2003
231.7′6—dc21   2003009768

Printed in the United States of America

07   06   05   04   03
5   4   3   2   1

This
revised edition
is dedicated to
the memory of
Dr. Stanley A. Ellisen.
May a new generation
come to appreciate
his knowledge and
insight.

tents

pre

THE ADAGE "Truth is stranger than fiction" is eloquently demonstrated in the history of Israel. More than history, the story of the Jews is high drama—drama with a divine component. It's really the merging of two agendas, human and divine, widely diverging but oscillating throughout history. Few features of exciting drama are missing in this all-time box-office extravaganza.

Yet much of this drama's astounding plot has been hidden or veiled. Church historians have largely spurned the wandering Jews or relegated them to footnotes. For too long, conventional wisdom has justified the church's theft of Isaac's blessing, consigning the intended heirs to oblivion.

The determined Jews, however, have never accepted this verdict and are now demanding a rewriting of that history. In retrospect, we can see their powerful influence through Eastern and Western history, often so powerful as to sway world events. World War I, for instance, has been called a war without rationale—but factor in the Jews, and a flood of meaning rushes before us. The same could be said of the Renaissance, the discovery of America, and most conspicuously, World War II.

Fortunately, Jewish historians have preserved a vast literature on their people's tumultuous journey through the centuries. These portrayals are often full of sordid details. But as agonizing and gruesome as those details can be, they're essential for a true perspective of history. They are, in fact, indispensable if we're to discern rightly the explosive tensions in the Middle East today.

My interest in this intriguing drama began with a trip to the Middle East in 1952, shortly after the new state of Israel was established. I toured with a group from the American Christian Palestine Committee. The air was alive with optimism. But in visiting both sides of the barbed wire, our group could already detect a crisis in the making. Since that time, some bitter clashes have rent the land in what many have called a holy war, a situation that threatens to degenerate even further into a monumental struggle of race and religion. The Palestine question today tends to polarize not only Arabs and Jews, but East and West as well.

My purpose in writing this survey is to highlight that history from a biblical Christian perspective. Though both Jewish and Arab views have been amply stated and Christian writers have discussed an assortment of related issues, I believe a biblical viewpoint from a conservative perspective is still needed.

In these chapters, I will seek to tie the biblical account to the Jews' perilous journey through church history, showing the religious and social dynamics that have led to their determined stand in Palestine today. Related to that story is the growth and philosophy of Islam, which I have briefly traced to show the Arab point of view. The work is not intended to be a defense of either.

Though the story has been written for the general Christian public, I've included copious notes in order to substantiate many of the incredible events and views that have been presented. Because the literature is massive, I've sought to use the most original sources available in order to minimize the subjective element in an admittedly emotional sea of controversy. For this, I'm greatly indebted to a host of writers and researchers who have labored long and well, as the brief bibliography will attest.

I pray that this focus on the Lord's brethren will honor him and throw some light on their perilous journey through church history to this, their challenging rendezvous with destiny.

Stanley A. Ellisen
1991

face TO REVISED EDITION

MANY BOOKS have tried to explain the current crisis in the Middle East. Few have ever done so with the depth of wisdom and insight displayed by Dr. Stanley Ellisen. When the book went out of print, that wisdom was lost to all but the fortunate who stumbled on the work in school libraries or secondhand bookstores.

I want to express my profound gratitude to Evelyn Ellisen, John Van Diest, and Tyndale House Publishers for their foresight in seeing the value of this work for a new generation. I am honored to have been asked to take part in preparing this revised edition.

Charles H. Dyer
2003

CHAPTER 1

Contours
of Conflict

RABBI HAROLD KUSHNER tells of a youngster who came home from Sunday school after being taught the biblical story of Israel crossing the Red Sea. His mother asked him what he had learned and he told her: "The Israelites got out of Egypt, but Pharaoh and his army chased after them. They got to the Red Sea and couldn't cross it and the Egyptian army was getting closer. So Moses got on his walkie-talkie, the Israeli air force bombed the Egyptians, and the Israeli navy built a pontoon bridge so the people could cross." The mother was shocked. "Is that the way they taught you the story?" she asked. "Well, no," the boy admitted, "but if I told you what they told us, you'd never believe it."[1]

The same might be said of the whole history of Israel. Much of it is laced with the unbelievable. Modern Israel seems to share that heritage in remarkable ways. The unbelievable has almost become commonplace—and is usually accompanied by conflict. Few nations have found themselves so continuously in that maelstrom.

To appreciate the dilemma and catch the mood of the present drama, let's recall several significant datelines from modern times that have raised eyebrows around the globe, fastening world attention on this small slice of land.

London, November 2, 1917—The Balfour Declaration pledges British support for Zionists' goal of a Jewish homeland in Palestine.

September 29, 1922—The Balfour Declaration becomes part of the British Mandate and is ratified by the League of Nations.

October 11, 1938—Highly irritated, the World Congress of Arabs unites in Cairo to denounce and reject the document. They base their rejection on earlier promises made by the British to Sherif Hussein that Britain would help the Arabs establish independent states in the Middle East. The vagueness of these promises sets the stage for inevitable clashes in the following years.

Lake Success, New York, November 29, 1947—The United Nations votes by a two-thirds majority to partition Palestine and agrees that this should take place following the termination of Britain's Mandate over Palestine on May 15, 1948. The partitioning is designed to appease both sides, allowing both Jews and Arabs to establish independent states in the area. This decision is quickly (yet cautiously) accepted by the Jewish Agency, but is adamantly rejected by the Arab League. Arab leaders immediately prepare to take the whole land when the British haul down the Union Jack on May 15.

Jerusalem, June 7, 1967—Jordan's decision to join with Egypt and Syria in attacking Israel backfires and the old city of Jerusalem falls to the Jews for the first time in modern history. The fierce battle and costly triumph bring tears and cheers from Jews worldwide, permitting them to fulfill their ancient dream of "next year in Jerusalem." Arabs are shocked and bitter, especially Jordan's King Hussein. His grandfather, Abdullah, had lost the holy cities of Mecca and Medina to the Saudi dynasty, and now his dream of becoming caretaker of Jerusalem's shrines is also shattered.

United Nations, November 22, 1967—In a unanimous vote, the United Nations Security Council adopts Resolution 242, calling for Israel's withdrawal from territories it occupied in the Six-Day War. But it also calls for the "termination of all claims or states of belligerency," as well as acknowledgment of the territorial integrity of all states in the region. This is later reaffirmed in Resolution 338. Though most delegates see it as another step toward peace in the area, its promise is overshadowed by the Arabic Declaration at Khartoum on September 1, vowing "no peace with Israel, no negotiations with Israel, no recognition of Israel." Egyptian President Nasser makes it clear his struggle to rid Palestine of the Jews is not subject to compromise.

Gaza Strip, December 6, 1987—An Israeli businessman is fatally stabbed in Gaza City. Two days later, four Palestinians are killed in a traffic accident. Rumors spread that the deaths were in retaliation for the earlier murder. Riots break out, and a teenager is shot and killed after throwing Molotov cocktails at a patrol. The underdog Palestinians successfully snatch world sympathy long held by Israel's Holocaust victims.

Oslo, Norway, September 9, 1993—Following a series of secret negotiations between Israel and the Palestinians, Yasser Arafat sends a letter to Israeli Prime Minister Yitzhak Rabin that recognizes Israel's right to exist as a nation, accepts all UN Security Council resolutions, renounces terrorism, and commits to a peaceful resolution of their conflict. In response, Israel recognizes the PLO (Palestinian Liberation Organization) as the representative of the Palestinian people in all negotiations.

Camp David, Maryland, July 25, 2000—A fifteen-day summit between Yasser Arafat, Israeli Prime Minister Ehud Barak, and U.S. President Bill Clinton ends in failure. The peaceful resolution to the Arab–Israeli crisis that seemed so close at hand evaporates amid charges of intransigence and veiled threats of violence.

Jerusalem, September 28, 2000—The smoldering conflict between Israel and the Palestinians reignites when Ariel Sharon visits the Temple Mount. The Palestinians had been demanding sovereignty over all East Jerusalem, including *Haram es Sharif* (the Temple Mount). They see Ariel Sharon's walk as Israel's response, and they react with violent demonstrations. The al Aqsa *intifada* begins.

These datelines point out just some of the conflict and controversy that today beset Israel. Much of it is rooted in Israel's historic relations with the ancient world, the church, and the Arabs. In the following chapters, we'll look at a series of dramas in Israel's agonizing history in an effort to gain some perspective and hope to those who long for peace in the volatile Middle East.

CHAPTER 2

A Family Feud Rekindled

OUR GENERATION is witnessing a family feud that redefines the term. Today, this feud between the Jews and Arabs is grabbing headlines around the world. Jerusalem—often called the "Holy City" and "City of Peace"—has been witness to some of history's bloodiest massacres. That irony has returned to plague our generation, as the ancient city has again become the turbulent linchpin of world peace. And yet, peace in the explosive Middle East will need to satisfy the competing claims of both groups.

Both Jews and Arabs trace their national roots to the great patriarch Abraham, to whom God promised the land of Canaan, which includes modern-day Israel and the disputed territories. That promise has been their major bone of contention throughout history. Appealing to that promise and claiming property rights by virtue of long residency, each side makes its case on what appears to be legitimate ground. Neither is less adamant or eloquent in suing for divine and natural rights to the land.

To whom does this little strip of hillside really belong? World opinion is sharply divided, with arbiters at a standoff. Evangelical Christians wonder if a divine movement of cosmic proportions is shaping up. Stalking across our headlines are peoples with ancient ancestries—Jews, Arabs, Egyptians, Syrians, Lebanese, and now the Iraqis, with the Northern and Western giants glowering in the wings . . . the eerie stuff of which end-time prophecies are made. Throw in a dashing white horse, and Armageddon suddenly seems much more real.

The purpose of this book, however, is not to resolve the thorny political issues, but to suggest how we, as a community of believers, should respond to the dilemma. Should we rush to the defense of Israel against those who seem to resist the "fulfillment of prophecy"? Or should our sympathies be with the displaced Palestinians and their Arab cousins who have taken up their cause? As Christians, should we favor the Israelis who openly disdain the messiahship of Jesus, or lean toward the Arabs who at least respect him as a prophet but reduce him to a size smaller than Muhammad? Or should we simply keep our hands in our pockets and plead neutrality? Tough questions, admittedly. To arrive at legitimate answers, we must identify the major factors that make up this quarrel.

The answers to our questions must begin with a brief review of Jewish history from ancient times to the present. Few would doubt the immense influence of this people on our society. Though they constitute a very small percentage of the world's population (one-third of one percent), their influence on and contributions to the areas of science, medicine, education, religion, philosophy, business, politics, economics, the media, and communications have been remarkable.

Recall, for instance, Albert Einstein, the physicist; Baruch Spinoza, the philosopher; Rothschild, the family of financiers; Chaim Weizmann, the World War I chemist; Karl Marx, the philosopher and developer of dialectical materialism; Arthur Rubinstein and Vladimir Horowitz, the great pianists; Louis Marshall, the constitutional lawyer and jurist; the Marx brothers, comedians; Bernard Baruch, the financier and planner of the New Deal; and Felix Frankfurter, the liberal Supreme Court Justice. The field of practical psychology was almost a Jewish science until recently, dominated by such names as Sigmund Freud and the Adlers of Vienna and Prague.[2] Need we mention the many prominent names in the media and film industries today? Charles Singer has compiled a massive list of such Jewish giants in the various arts and sciences.[3] Few areas of life have escaped their phenomenal influence.

Still, far too often the church has treated them horribly. From the destruction of Jerusalem in the first century to recent times, the Jews were a people without a homeland, often living in practical isolation in a gentile jungle. What brought about their resurgence is a story of many miracles.

In this review, we'll briefly trace Jewish history from biblical times, highlighting the events that led to the fall of Jerusalem and the rise of the new state of Israel. We'll also look at the place of the Arabs, especially the role of the Palestinians in modern times.

THE DIVINE COVENANTS CONCERNING THE LAND

Two Old Testament covenants relate specifically to Israel's divine right to the land of Canaan. The first is the Abrahamic covenant described in Genesis. The second covenant occurred some six hundred years later when the Palestinian covenant was given to Moses (Deuteronomy 28–30).

The Covenant with Abraham

When God made his covenant with Abram (whom God later renamed Abraham), he guaranteed the patriarch that his descendants would receive the land as an "everlasting possession" (Genesis 12:7; 13:15; 17:8). In response to Abram's plea to make Ishmael the covenant heir, the Lord declared that his covenant promises were nonnegotiable. Ishmael, he said, would receive great blessings, but the covenant promises would go to and through Isaac (Genesis 17:18-21). To emphasize this, the Lord later met with both Isaac and Jacob to confirm the Abrahamic covenant (Genesis 26:3; 28:13).

The later prophets further appealed to this covenant to justify Israel's right to the land as they went in to claim it (Deuteronomy 1:8; 1 Chronicles 16:15-18; Nehemiah 9:8; Ezekiel 33:24). Though Abraham only "sojourned" in the land, his descendants were promised the land as an everlasting inheritance.

The Palestinian Covenant with Israel[4]

The Palestinian covenant was given to Moses nearly six hundred years later as Israel was about to cross Jordan into Canaan. With this covenant, the Lord confirmed his earlier promise to Abraham and itemized the conditions under which his people were to occupy the land. He emphasized that the land belonged to him; it was his special covenant land, which he was giving to his covenant people. Grounded in the Abrahamic covenant, this promise too was unconditional; it guaranteed that the land would eventually belong to Israel forever (Genesis 13:14-15; Psalm 105:9-11). But its benefits were conditional, dependent on Jewish obedience and conduct (Deuteronomy 28). Should Israel persist in disobedience, the Lord warned he would "[uproot] them from their land in anger and in fury and in great wrath" (Deuteronomy 29:28, NASB). As the Lord's covenant people, the Jews could occupy the covenant land only if they observed the covenant law. The land itself belonged to the Lord, whose name was Jehovah (YHWH or "Covenant Lord").

Though this Palestinian covenant promised discipline and dispersion for disobedience, it also promised restoration whenever the nation would return to the Lord. When "you return to the LORD your

God and obey Him . . . , then the LORD your God will restore you . . . and will gather you again from all the peoples where the LORD your God has scattered you" (Deuteronomy 30:2-3, NASB). Knowing the people's propensity for evil and how they would fail miserably in the following centuries, the Lord still assured them of their final return and restoration after being scattered to "the ends of the earth" (Deuteronomy 30:4, NASB).

These final words of Moses to the fledgling nation constituted both a divine warning and an encouragement: a warning that unbelief and rebellion would bring the Lord's judgment through a worldwide scattering; but a promise that repentance would bring final restoration to the land forever. Thus, the Abrahamic and Palestinian covenants were Israel's divine guarantee of the land and became the basis of the Jews' later claims.

THE DIVINE EXPULSION OF ISRAEL FROM THE LAND

With such clear promises of divine favor (Deuteronomy 7:6-8; 14:2), one might expect that this chosen people would mature under the Lord's tutelage to bless the world by holy and righteous living. Surely with the Lord's corrections they must have overcome their evil tendencies and triumphed in a burst of glory. Anything less would seem to thwart God's covenant purposes. Weren't they God's handpicked people?

They were his chosen people, but they never fully achieved his promised blessing. Such a grand finale failed to materialize—how well we know! The very opposite occurred, and all their fond dreams lay in ashes as the pages of the Old Testament closed with scarcely a benediction. Both the northern and southern kingdoms had become so thoroughly corrupted that righteousness had all but vanished from the land. Consequently, the Lord fulfilled his promise of judgment and removed his people from it.

To evict Israel from the land, the Lord used two of the most vicious nations of ancient history—a punishment in keeping with the vile idolatry it had adopted. The brutal Assyrians were the executioners who cleared out the northern kingdom of Israel in 722 B.C., and the savage Babylonians purged the southern kingdom of Judah in 586 B.C. In that final sweep of the south, the Lord allowed Nebuchadnezzar to demolish both Jerusalem and the sacred temple built by Solomon (Jeremiah 25:9; 52:12-13).

Thus began the period of Israel's dispersion among the Gentiles, often called the "times of the Gentiles" (Daniel 2; 7; Luke 21:24). The distinguishing feature of this period is Israel's subjection to gentile nations. Instead of the Lord ruling the world through Israel as he had proposed (Deuteronomy 28:13, 44), he now ruled Israel through the Gentiles. That period began with Nebuchadnezzar (605 B.C.) and continued through four projected world empires: Babylon, Persia, Greece, and Rome. It even extended to a brief period of revived Rome, just before Messiah's coming to set up his everlasting kingdom (Daniel 2:44). Though chosen to be the "head," Israel became the "tail" by spurning the Lord's leadership (Deuteronomy 28:13, 44). And in doing so, the nation lost its national sovereignty, and Jews were scattered among the nations.

GOD'S PURPOSE IN ISRAEL'S DISPERSION

How could this triumph of the heathen over God's covenant people possibly fulfill the Lord's purposes? Why would God allow pagan hordes to conquer the covenant land and seemingly derail his grand plan to use the seed of Abraham to bless the world? How do we interpret this apparent upset of the divine applecart? Did these world empires obstruct or frustrate the Lord's nicely laid covenant plans?

The answer, of course, is that those heathen nations inadvertently fulfilled an agenda other than their own. They unknowingly served a vital function in the Lord's plan for Israel by culling out the ungodly and making the faithful remnant fight to preserve their faith. Each of these proud empires dutifully played its part. The first kingdom, Babylon, trudged all the way from Mesopotamia to destroy Judah and to remove its remnant to Babylon.

Seventy years later, Persia returned the faithful to Jerusalem in order to rebuild the temple—right on schedule according to Jeremiah's prediction (Jeremiah 25:12; 29:10). Time and again, the Lord proclaimed that he was the one who raised and toppled world empires, in this case to chasten and restore his people Israel (Isaiah 45:1–4; 46:11).

Next, the Greeks conquered the world in 333 B.C. when Alexander the Great blazed through the Middle East, plunging all the way to India. A zealous "missionary" of Hellenism and a student of Aristotle, Alexander spread the gospel of Hellenistic culture, humanistic philosophies, and Zeus worship. (He was also seeking to avenge the Persians' devastation of Greek cities in the previous century.) This invasion from the west severely tested the remnant of Israel, forcing them to choose between this "new age" movement with its gods of freedom, and the stringencies of their ancient faith. Backed into a corner by Syrian legates after the partitioning of Alexander's empire, the faithful of Israel defied the intruders and rose to new heights of courage and trust in God. In the face of overwhelming odds, the Maccabees assembled a ragtag army and thrust back the Syrian hordes, finally winning a degree of independence. This inspiring reenactment of the David-versus-Goliath drama called the nation back to its faith and became a timeless inspiration to Israel, remembered even to this day in the eight-day celebration of Hanukkah.

The fourth kingdom to rule Israel was the "iron" kingdom of Rome (Daniel 2:40). This mighty empire unwittingly prepared the world for Messiah's coming. The caesars subdued and unified the globe, making it hostage to Rome; and Herod the Idumaean subjugated Judea under Rome's patronage. Both governments were strictly self-serving and ungodly, but the policies and programs they pursued readied the world for Messiah.

ISRAEL'S CONDITION WHEN JESUS APPEARED

How did these gentile powers prepare Israel for the coming of Messiah? Admittedly, their primary purpose was negative, but they forced the people to recognize their need for deliverance. They were an irritant, calling for a remedy. While the Greeks forced the Jews out of their narrow, cultural cocoon and gave the world a universal language into which the Hebrew scriptures were translated, the Romans provided a universal government with monitored peace and a road system that enabled easy travel—both important keys to the later spread of the gospel. But the greatest contribution to Israel was the energizing of its faith. These pagan empires challenged the Jews' faith, forcing them to fight for it, to appreciate it. The tattered flock of Israel—with little more than godly resolve—steeled itself to stand up to the pagan onslaughts of Hellenism.

These events also stirred their dreams of a promised deliverer. The people recalled the prophecies of a mighty champion, a Son of David. As Israel watched the conquering Alexanders, Caesars, and Herods who trounced the righteous in their way, the faithful longed for their promised hero. They dimly saw this greater David waiting in the wings, preparing to come with vengeance to smash their foes. They knew that the likes of Goliath, Haman, and Antiochus Epiphanes would fall before him (Isaiah 9:7; 63; Micah 5:4; Luke 1:71-74), and these hopes fired their courage and awakened visions of supremacy over the nations. Such dreams became national dogma.

In the coming of Jesus, however, the Jewish people failed to find the militant Messiah they had envisioned.

This man was simply not the Messiah they had in mind. Rather than dashing to their side to slay Goliath with David's sword, Jesus came gently with healing balm to save the sick and erring. Instead of rising up against Rome, he appeared to join with Rome against the faithful. He welcomed Roman tax collectors and religious outcasts on the basis of simple faith and repentance. He stormed through their temple like a bull in a china shop, violating their lucrative ritual system. He even "desecrated" the Sabbath by performing works of mercy on such sacred days. Worst of all, he forgave sins and accepted the praise of God. Recognizing that God is One, he claimed to be One with God (Deuteronomy 6:4, cf. John 10:30). Often he confronted them as the "Son of God" of whom the Psalmist spoke (Psalm 2:7, 12). In all this, he seemed to ignore their political bondage and offered little sympathy concerning their gentile oppressors.

For this, he faced only rejection from the religious leaders of Israel. And the astounding climax came when these religious leaders joined their political enemies to rid the land of this would-be Messiah. Mark tells us the "Pharisees went out and immediately began taking counsel with the Herodians against Him, as to how they might destroy Him" (Mark 3:6, NASB). These sworn enemies temporarily forgot their squabbling when they judged that the fate of the nation depended on their destroying this pretender (John 11:49-50). In so doing, they showed their allegiance with Rome rather than with the prophesied Messiah. At Jesus' crucifixion, they accepted responsibility for his death, saying, "His blood be on us and on our children!" (Matthew 27:25, NASB). The final words of the chief priests at Jesus' trial were: "We have no king but Caesar" (John 19:15).

Not a pretty picture, especially for the chosen people. The affair seemed unreal, sordid, like a half-remembered nightmare. Could the trial and death of Jesus have been some clever Passover plot, a hoax perpetrated by this Nazarene and his followers? Might Jesus and his little band have been overzealous to fulfill prophecy?

Or could it have been a genuine case of mistaken identity? Could the chosen people themselves have made a mistake of cosmic proportions? A look into the following centuries provides some appalling, but revealing clues.

3

The Jews in Worldwide Dispersion

BEFORE HIS DEATH, Jesus gave his disciples some startling predictions about Israel's future: Dark days lay ahead. Jerusalem and its newly refurbished temple would be leveled and the Gentiles would again desolate the city. Those who survived would be led away captive into all the world (Matthew 24:2; Luke 19:44; 21:24). Daniel the prophet had long before prophesied this, noting that it would occur shortly after the Messiah would "be cut off" (Daniel 9:26, NASB). Jesus predicted the coming fulfillment of that prophecy, saying it was "because you did not recognize the time of your visitation" (Luke 19:44, NASB). Israel had been visited by heaven and failed to recognize its divine Visitor.

THE DISPERSION UNDER ROME
Jerusalem's Destruction in A.D. 70

The prophecy about Jerusalem was fulfilled less than forty years later through the ruthless power of Rome. After a three-year campaign against stubborn resistance, the Romans subjected Jerusalem to four months of unprecedented anguish and bloodshed. Flavius Josephus, a Jewish historian who was himself part of the story, recorded the details of the gory drama. Josephus is generally regarded as a traitor to his nation, having shifted his allegiance to Rome as the tide turned against the zealot cause. He was, however, thoroughly acquainted with the Roman siege of Jerusalem and sought to preserve a historical record of the catastrophe. His writings are our main source of that history, aside from confirmations from the Dead Sea Scrolls, and are generally regarded as basically accurate, with some obvious biases.[5]

Two Roman generals directed this siege in A.D. 67 after a climate of rebellion developed among Jewish youths who were frustrated by unemployment and Roman oppression. To quell the uprising, Emperor Nero sent his most successful generals, Flavius Vespasian and his son Titus, along with fifty thousand crack troops. Even with that force, it took two years to conquer Galilee and Judea and to draw a noose around the strongholds surrounding Jerusalem. In the meantime, zealots in Jerusalem split into several warring factions, bringing a state of civil war to the desperate city. This alone exacted a heavy toll of lives.

Turmoil also raged in Rome in A.D. 68. Following Nero's exile, a train of aspirants sought to rule and unify the empire, but were met with little success. In the fall of 69, Vespasian saw his chance for the throne and proceeded to Rome. This left Titus in charge of the campaign against Judah, which had become a drag on Roman patience and resources. By February A.D. 70, Titus had advanced to the outskirts of Jerusalem, hoping for a quick victory. He was eager for an early return to Rome for the coronation celebration. He did not intend to destroy the city, but rather, to bring it to submission and restore peace to the volatile area. Titus had become enamored with Bernice, the beautiful and vivacious sister of Agrippa II (a descendant of Herod), which further inclined him to deal gently with the Jewish capital and its sacred shrines.

Just prior to this siege, masses of Jews had poured through the city gates from the outlying country to keep Passover and to help defend the city. According to Josephus, 2.7 million people were sealed up within its walls, including its 600,000 local citizens.[6] The terms of surrender offered by Titus were stubbornly refused. Convinced that God would come to their aid, as he did for the Maccabean faithful, the zealots felt certain their city and temple would survive the onslaught. The siege, however, lasted for nearly four months and brought only famine and pestilence. Many of the city's starving citizens resorted to cannibalism.

On the ninth of Ab (July–August), the Romans battered into the city and, in the melee, torched the temple. The city and its walls were broken and burned to the ground. "By a strange coincidence the second temple had fallen upon the anniversary of the destruction of the first temple" (in 586 B.C.).[7] The city was reduced to a pile of rubbish and charred corpses. Five hundred Jewish leaders were immediately crucified. Josephus exclaimed of the carnage: "The multitude of those that therein perished exceeded all the destruction that either men or God ever brought upon the world."[8] So thorough was the devastation that "there was left nothing to make those that came thither believe it had ever been inhabited. This was the end which Jerusalem came to by the madness of those that were for innovations; a city otherwise of great magnificence, and of mighty fame among all mankind."[9] Why would the Lord allow this monumental devastation of the Jewish "Holy City"? Jesus' comments some forty years before suggest it was not due merely to the fury of enraged Roman soldiers. It had a spiritual cause far more critical. The carnage was related to Daniel's prophecy of the city's destruction after the "cutting off" of Messiah.

The words of Daniel and Jesus could scarcely have been more literally fulfilled. Only the retaining wall that formed the platform on which the temple stood (part of what is today known as the "Wailing Wall" or "Western Wall") was left intact. Those who survived the carnage were sold into captivity. Jewish historian Heinrich Graetz describes how thousands of youths were taken to Egypt and the cities of Europe to be sold as slaves or fed to the beasts in arenas for royal entertainment.[10] He then notes the result:

> The Judean communities in Syria, Asia Minor, Alexandria, and Rome very nearly shared the fate of their brethren in Judea. For the war had aroused the hatred of the entire heathen world against the unfortunate children of Israel— a hatred which was fanatical in its intensity, its object being the entire destruction of the whole race.[11]

The Masada Holdouts
The last rebellious outpost to be taken was the desert fortress of Masada, captured three years later in the spring of 73. Here the Jerusalem debacle repeated itself on a smaller scale, as Eleazar the Sicarri zealot defied the Roman general Silva. Rather than submitting to be sold or slaughtered, 960 Jewish holdouts methodically took their own lives. This they appeared to do with flourish, except for two women and five children who hid and survived to tell the story.

Popular descriptions of this rebellion are often colored to highlight the valiance and commitment of the Jewish defenders. The only historical description we have, however, is by Josephus, who presents an entirely different perspective, portraying the Jews as anything but heroes. He described the Sicarri as totally given over to wickedness. "Vile wretches as they were," he says, they "cut the throats of the high-priests so that no part of a religious regard to God might be preserved. . . . They imitated every wicked work; nor, if their memory suggested any evil thing that had formerly been done, did they avoid zealously to pursue the same."[12]

Masada became a tragic footnote to the divine lesson taught at Jerusalem. There seemed to be no escaping the judgment, even at Herod's famous hideaway fort. The nation's failure to recognize God's visitation in the person of Messiah resulted in the destruction of nearly the whole population of Judea, leaving the nation in ruins.

Roman Persecution and Bar Kochba's Revolt (A.D. 135)

Following the war, anti-Jewish sentiment spread throughout the Roman Empire. Jews were seen as a menace. Because they had humiliated the power of Rome by defying its top troops for several years, Jews were made a spectacle to the world and a grim lesson of the consequences of rebellion. Vespasian, in fact, commissioned Josephus (after his surrender in Galilee) to accompany the Roman legions to Jerusalem to record that history.[13] Little mercy was shown the survivors.

During the reign of Hadrian (117–135), Jerusalem was rebuilt as a Roman city, Aelia Capitolina, and a temple to Jupiter was built on the temple site. The Jewish rite of circumcision was outlawed.[14] These continued oppressions so outraged the returned community that another revolt against Rome took place in A.D. 131. Many of the rabbis had concluded that the destruction of Jerusalem in A.D. 70 was a harbinger of the messianic age, commencing with the Lord shaking the heavens and the earth (Haggai 2:6).[15] They saw these cataclysms as necessary preludes to the messianic deliverance, and the persecutions led to renewed longings for a military "messiah."

So strong were these desires that in 132, Simon bar Kochba was proclaimed as Messiah. A mighty warrior with a gigantic physique, Simon bar Kochba's name meant "son of the Star," supposedly foretold by Balaam (Numbers 24:17).[16] He was a renowned military man and was promoted by one of the most honored and learned rabbis in Jewish history, Rabbi Akiba ben Joseph. This illustrious pair issued a call to arms against Rome in 132 and engaged them in a long standoff so successful it stunned the Romans. Hadrian sent his top general to the Levant (the region in the eastern end of the Mediterranean Sea) to quell the uprising. Even with their best troops, it took nearly three years to turn back the revolt. But the tactic he resorted to was devastating. He was forced to systematically "slaughter every living thing, combatant and noncombatant in his path—men, women, children, cattle. . . . After two years of grinding, ruthless, merciless butchery, the Jewish lines wavered as the populace was reduced to the vanishing point."[17]

This final insurrection so infuriated the Romans that they flushed every vestige of the Jews out of the land, selling into slavery all who hadn't been massacred. Even the land itself was renamed. The "land of the Jews" (Judea) became the "land of the Philistines" (Palestina).[18] Jerusalem became a pagan city, off limits to all Jews. No Jew dared approach it without risking the pain of death.[19] This was Jerusalem's second major revolt against Rome and, as if to memorialize it, the city was destroyed again on the ninth of Ab (August).[20]

Resulting Changes in Jewish Life

This destruction of Jerusalem brought several changes to the religious and social structure of the Jewish people. Without the temple, they had to halt their sacrificial system. They could no longer carry on the ritual offerings or feasts and therefore, they needed no priests or Levites. Interestingly, the New Testament book of Hebrews was written approximately A.D. 68 or 69, just prior to the temple's destruction. In it, the author stresses Christ's role as the final High Priest and the final offering—the only New Testament book to stress these priestly functions. As if to underscore that point, the destruction of the temple abruptly halted the old system of animal sacrifices for sin.

The temple's destruction also brought a change in Jewish leadership. Without priests, rabbis became the spiritual and social leaders of the people. The Pharisees became the dominant party of classical Judaism. Their work revolved around the synagogue and its activities. Here the rabbis studied and led the dispersed people to become a nation of students, delving into all aspects of community living in order to enable Jewish survival in a gentile world. At the destruction of Jerusalem, the rabbis moved first to Jabneh near the Mediterranean coast and later to Galilee, concentrating on the study of Torah and their oral traditions.

Jewish Treatment by the Church

During the first three centuries A.D., Jews and Christians alike suffered at the hands of the Romans. Both were regarded as "atheists," not serving idol gods and refusing to bow before Jupiter, the god of Rome. Without such gods, they were considered prime fodder for the games in the arenas, sent in to fight wild beasts and to otherwise entertain the Roman upper class.

Despite much persecution and martyrdom, the church grew over time to become a major power in the empire. The Roman leaders were well aware that Christians were emerging as a large minority, and this fact finally led to a breakthrough for both Jews and Christians. Constantine, known as the first "Christian" emperor, came to the throne in A.D. 312 and immediately declared religious toleration throughout the empire. In 325, he assembled the famous Nicean Church Council and made Christianity the state religion. While this was obviously a turning point in church-state relations, it also appeared to offer some hope to the Jews. Ever since the fall of Jerusalem, the people of Israel had watched and prayed for the defeat of Rome with its anti-Jewish policies.[21] As state persecution of religion was ending, it seemed their prayers were being answered and tolerance would be applied to all.

But this dream soon turned into a nightmare. As the church rose to prominence and power, it used its newfound might to further spread the gospel and convert the world. This good intention led to heresy hunting, with Judaism as one of its prime targets. The church had not forgotten the Jews' participation in Jesus' death. Because of this, many Christians and even church stalwarts came to regard the Jews as "assassins of God" and their religion the greatest of heresies. As Richard Gade notes, "During the period known as the Byzantine Empire [330–1000], the choices open to non-Christians were either conversion or oppression."[22] To those who refused to convert, the church showed little sympathy. Heinrich Graetz describes the Christian emperors who "entertained as passionate a hatred of Judaism and its adherents as of heathenism."[23] We will look further at this sad record later in the book.

Emergence of the Talmud and Rabbinic Judaism

The trials of the Jews in dispersion were useful in one respect: The people were forced to write down or codify their oral traditions. Prior to A.D. 200, rabbinic opinions were preserved only in the memories of scholars, being regarded as too sacred to write down.[24] These traditions gave practical interpretations of the Old Testament for common life or for new situations that arose. As oral traditions, they were rejected by the Sadducees but were highly revered and studied by the Pharisees. Their views reflected those of the liberal school of Hillel (40 B.C.) as later gathered by Rabbi Zakkai (A.D. 70), rather than the more conservative school of Shamai. Though not laws, as such, they were regarded as a "code of life" that many believed to have been handed down from Moses.[25] When the Jews found themselves scattered in dispersion, these oral traditions took on special significance because of their unifying force. They became almost like a Bible, as Max Dimont describes it—the "Bibliosclerosis of the Talmud."[26] In later times, they were "proclaimed to be God's holy words and were to be observed as religiously as the Sabbath itself."[27]

What began as various oral opinions of the rabbis eventually came to be organized and crystallized into a written code of life. This occurred in A.D. 199 when Rabbi Judah Hanasi broke with tradition and put them in writing. Seeing the need to preserve them for study by the scattered race, he compiled them into what is known as the *Mishnah* ("repetition"). This collection was a "code of laws arranged according to subject matter and divided into six sections."[28] Though the compilation was intended to close the "canon," or stop the multiplying of rabbinic interpretations, it was only the beginning. The coming centuries saw the addition of many more such elaborations. These were written in Aramaic and were called the *Gemara* (from a word meaning to "supplement" or to "complete").

The Hebrew *Mishnah* and the Aramaic *Gemara* were later put together and called the *Talmud* (from the Hebrew word for "learning"). Two Talmuds, in fact, were produced, the Palestinian (or Jerusalem) and the Babylonian. The first was designed for Jews living in the land and the latter for those in Babylon or dispersion. The Babylonian Talmud is by far the largest and the best recognized today.

To appreciate the range and complexity of these works, consider that the Mishnah began by codifying the Mosaic Law into 613 precepts. These were divided into 365 prohibitions and 248 commands.[29] Each of these might have hundreds of nuances or applications under different circumstances. Dimont remarks that much of this was trivia that made Jewish life "resemble a madhouse of obsessive rituals attributed to Moses and God."[30] The Talmud was an encyclopedic work of some thirty-five volumes, fifteen thousand pages, and 2.5 million words (sixty-three tractates). The work covered nearly every area of responsibility in life and has often been called the "educator of the Jewish nation." Not only did it provide a universal education for Jewish youths of ten to fifteen years' duration, it also "made them physicians, mathematicians, astronomers, grammarians, philosophers, poets, and businessmen."[31]

How were these rabbinic opinions regarded by Jesus and the apostles? On several occasions, the Lord referred to the "traditions of the elders" (Matthew 15:2-6; Mark 7:3-9, NASB). He warned the disciples that some of those "traditions" were being used to overturn God's Word. In particular, he mentioned their voiding of God's Law to honor one's parents by the slick trick of pronouncing *Corban* ("given to God") over their possessions (Mark 7:11). In his Sermon on the Mount, he contrasted what "the ancients were told" (not what "was written") with what he taught about the spiritual character of the Law. His quarrel was not with Moses, but with the distortions of certain rabbis. He recognized the danger of making human opinions divinely authoritative.

Not all Jews have venerated the Talmud. In the eighth century, there arose in Mesopotamia a group called the Karaites who rejected it. Anan ben David founded the movement about A.D. 770, after which it spread throughout the Middle East until the twelfth century.[32] The Karaites recognized only the Old Testament as authoritative, interpreting it literally, and rejected the rabbinic additions. Like Jesus, they also rejected many of the traditional practices of the Pharisees, such as dietary laws and wearing of phylacteries (small leather cases containing portions of the Torah that were worn on the left arm and forehead). They became a "threat to normative Judaism (the Rabbinites)."[33] The movement was a kind of Jewish reformation not unlike the Protestant Reformation, stressing the need to get back to the Scriptures and away from rabbinic traditions. In the eleventh and twelfth centuries they enjoyed a "golden age" with many scholars before being overwhelmed by a surge of Talmudism from Mesopotamia.[34] A small group of Karaites remains to this day in the Middle East and southern Russia.

Although the study of Talmud played an immense role in unifying and preserving the Jews in dispersion, it also tended to propound many views antagonistic to Christianity. In some ways, the Talmud was the Jewish counterpart to the Christian New Testament. It added rabbinic insights to Old Testament passages, often in contrast to those of Christ and the apostles. In so doing, the rabbis reinterpreted the Torah as a "dynamic and changing document," no longer regarding it as a fixed and stable code of laws. The later codification and indexing of the Talmud by Joseph Caro in 1565 made the formidable text accessible to every Jew.[35]

No Mere Accident

Israel's expulsion from the land of Judea in A.D. 70 was no mere happenstance in the crossfire of gentile fury. As Jesus and the prophets solemnly warned, it resulted from Jewish rejection of "God's visitation" in the person and ministry of Jesus. That is why the Jews would "be led captive into all the nations" (Daniel 9:26; Luke 21:24, NASB).

This assessment, of course, was unthinkable to the ancient rabbis. Yet it has been confirmed again and again in dramatic ways. It certainly does not absolve the Romans or the early Byzantine church for their persecutions, but it does show the prophetic relationship of events. It also speaks volumes in explaining the unmitigated sorrow of the Jews through church history and their relentless search for peace and fulfillment in a gentile jungle.

Few races have suffered so much at the hands of so many, yet persevered for so long. Anxiously groping for security in a hostile world, for centuries the Jews voiced their longings at Passover: "Next year in Jerusalem."

Jewish Migrations and Expulsions

THE LONGING for security took the Jewish people to distant shores and often made them targets of abuse. How did this recurring persecution affect the Jews as they sought peaceful coexistence among the nations? What new foes and unexpected friends lay before them? To understand their modern circumstances, we must walk with them through some of their circuitous journeys of the past.

ISLAM AND THE CRUSADES

Startling events in the early part of the seventh century forever changed the course of history. At that time, a man from the sun-bleached sands of Arabia began a religion that transformed much of the then-known world. His name, of course, was Muhammad, son of Abdullah.

At the age of forty, Muhammad felt called of God to give the Arab tribes their own religion. In so doing, he vitally affected the fortunes of the Jews and the medieval church. Deriving the concept of "one God" from the Hebrew *Shema* (Deuteronomy 6:4) and inspired by a series of supposed visions from the angel Gabriel, Muhammad set out to convert the Arabic tribes to a unified religion of "Allah" (from Hebrew *Eloah,* meaning "Almighty God"). His slogan was, "There is no God but Allah, and Muhammad is his prophet." Seeing himself as chosen by God to be the first prophet of true religion, he also considered himself the final prophet from God in the line of Moses and Jesus Christ. Most Muslims believe him to have been sinless.[36] The religion was named "Islam" (literally, "surrender"), from which comes the term *Muslim*.

Though rejected at first by the Arabs of his hometown of Mecca, he was welcomed by Christians in Ethiopia and a large Jewish population in Medina in A.D. 622. That year is called the *Hegira* ("flight") and became "year one" for the Islamic world.[37] Muhammad organized his followers and continued conveying his oracles, which were later collected into what became the Muslim holy book, the Qur'an. When the Jews of Medina refused to follow him, he killed or exiled them and confiscated their wealth and property. With this he built an army of ten thousand men that seized Mecca in 630. There he set up the Islamic shrine at the Ka'bah and moved on to conquer all Arabia before his death in 632.[38]

The Faith of Islam

The Qur'an is a book of 114 chapters (suras) of varying length. Muslims believe it was dictated to Muhammad by the angel Gabriel over a period of twenty-three years. In it, "God and his messenger [Muhammad]" are the absolute authority. The Qur'an relies heavily on the Old Testament and Gospels, especially stories of Abraham and Ishmael, Joseph, Moses, Jesus, and Mary. Abraham, it contends, was not really a Jew or a Christian, but a Muslim.[39] Numerous Old Testament stories are reinterpreted with an Arabic flavor. Abraham is usually foremost, and Jesus is but one among many righteous prophets. "Even so we recompense the good-doers—Zechariah and John, Jesus and Elias; each was of the righteous; Ishmael and Elisha, Jonah and Lot . . ."[40] The birth of Jesus by the Virgin Mary is depicted more in terms of Hagar's wilderness experience.[41] The Qur'an also denies that Jesus was crucified on the cross.[42] Muslim interpreters explain this in various ways, some believing that "God changed his [Jesus'] features into those of Judas, and those of Judas into the features of Jesus. So when the Jews came to take him they took Judas and crucified him by mistake, while God took Jesus up to heaven."[43]

The faith of Islam claims to be simple, uncomplicated, and universal. Five basic obligations are imposed on its adherents (often called the "Five Pillars of Islam"):

1. *the profession of faith* ("There is no God but Allah, and Muhammad is his prophet");
2. *the obligation to pray five times daily* (reduced from fifty after Muhammad's plea to Allah)[44];
3. *the giving of alms* (two and a half percent to the poor and to the house of Muhammad);

4. *the obligation to fast* (from dawn until sunset during Ramadan, the ninth lunar month); and
5. *the pilgrimage* (hajj) *to Mecca at least once in a lifetime.*

Some add a sixth pillar: the obligation to *jihad* ("holy war" or "struggle" for the faith).[45] Supplementing the "absolute and infallible" words of the Qur'an is the *Hadith,* a collection of how-tos explaining and applying the Qur'an to daily life. The two together are called the *Shari'a.*

Muhammad himself claimed direct descent from Abraham through Ishmael, whom he saw as the founders of Mecca.[46] Muslims believe the promise to Hagar and her son Ishmael of a "great nation" was fulfilled in the Arabian people unified by Muhammad.[47] The Qur'an argues this from the fact that the Jewish nation had been judged and destroyed by God.[48] Jerusalem is sacred to Muslims because of the Dome of the Rock, a shrine built in the seventh century over the temple ruins from which Muslims believe Muhammad sprang to heaven on an Arabian horse (Sura 17:1, "The Night Journey").[49]

Though the power center of Islam moved from Medina to Damascus to Baghdad, Mecca in Arabia still remained its religious center. Muslims gradually supplanted the fasts and feasts of the Hebrews with others relating to Abraham's sacrifice as well as Muhammad's birth and death. Friday is Islam's holy day.

The Power of Islam

The spread and conquest of Islam came like a whirlwind in the desert sands. The Arabic tribes gradually united under Muhammad and his successors, the caliphs. Though the founder was at times both passionate and compassionate, seeking peace and morality for his idolatrous people, the conquest he inaugurated moved by glint of steel. Strong discipline was essential to its reform around monotheism.[50] Struggling early with meager results, the movement adopted a strong militancy, and within a hundred years nearly the whole civilized world from India to Spain fell before it.

> In the sixth century the Arabs were desert nomads; in the seventh century they were conquerors on the march; in the eighth century they were masters of an empire that made the Mediterranean a Mohammadan lake; and in the ninth century they were the standard-bearers of a dazzling civilization, leaders in art, architecture, and science, while Western Europe was sinking deeper and deeper into a dark morass of its own making. One by one,

countries in the path of the Arabs fell before their onslaughts—Damascus in 635, Palestine in 638, Syria in 640, Egypt in 641.[51]

In less than a century, Muslims took the eastern half of the Byzantine Empire and all of North Africa and Spain before finally being stopped at Tours, France, by Charles Martel in 722. For the first time in history, a mighty international empire had been built with a religion of conquest. This militant religion brought a fearful counterforce to Christianity as it spread west.

In order to maintain a semblance of peace, the Muslim caliphs began to adopt a more tolerant attitude toward other religions. Following Muhammad's death in 632, hostility toward Jews greatly diminished. Though the Pact of Omar (637) enacted definite discriminations against non-Muslims, it was primarily directed at Christians. That pact barred Christians from displaying crosses, wearing distinctive dress, proselytizing anyone to Christianity, or preventing Christians from converting to Islam.

Islam also developed a rich cultural heritage, raising literature, science, medicine, art, and architecture to new heights and making immense contributions to the numerical system and astronomy.[52] During Europe's dark ages, Muslim philosophers and scientists were the thinkers and innovators of world culture. The empire of the Crescent and Sword (two of the symbols of Islam) continued to prosper until about A.D. 1000, when it fell prey to various barbaric assaults from the east and began a gradual decline.

Non-Muslims were forbidden to strike a Muslim, ride a horse, or to build houses taller than their Muslim neighbors'. They were to rise in deference to any Muslim in their assemblies. No disrespect was to be shown to the name of Muhammad. The Jews fared relatively well under Islamic rule, prospering in many ways. Though sporadic massacres against the Jews did take place, overall they enjoyed a kind of "Jewish golden age" under their Arab overlords from the seventh to the eleventh centuries.[53]

The Arabs' conquest of the Holy Land in A.D. 640 began a period of nearly thirteen centuries of Muslim rule in the Levant. The Arabs themselves, however, controlled Palestine only about five of those centuries. Arabic control ended when the Seljuk Turks took Jerusalem in 1071 (followed by the Fatimids shortly after that), bringing a period of slaughter of both Christians and Jews.[54]

The Turks' pillaging of the Church of the Holy Sepulcher (built in A.D. 326 by Helena, mother of Constantine) signaled increasing barbarities toward Christians and ignited the wrath of the European church. Thus ended a period of relative peace for Jews in Europe and Palestine and began the infamous era of the Christian crusades. During the next two centuries (1095–1292), nine crusades were assembled in Europe, each aimed at "purifying" the Holy Land. Under the "sign of the cross" (from whence comes the term *crusade*), the church determined to liberate the holy places of Palestine from Turkish "infidels."

Jewish Massacres during the Crusades

In spite of Jesus' many warnings, the Byzantine church adopted a militancy not unlike that of pagan Rome. The pious cheerfully took up the sword—for the "right reasons," of course (e.g., handling heretics and winning converts). The result was a crystallization of Jewish opposition to the gospel. Rather than convert or assimilate into the "Christian" cultures, the Jews chose to migrate. They became the "wandering Jews," staggering with knapsack "from sea to sea" (Amos 8:12).

The first Crusade was launched in 1095 by Pope Urban II after Peter the Hermit delivered a report from the Holy Land decrying the desperate conditions there for Christians. "To encourage enlistment, absolution was offered to any who would join this First Crusade, and an entrance into heaven was assured to all that fell in the struggle."[55] The offer attracted a motley crowd of social outcasts, misfits, and malcontents who journeyed from England, France, and Germany to the Levant with initial backing from the rich. When resources ran out, these renegades sacked and looted villages along the way.

Some of the Crusades did accomplish their objectives. Jerusalem and parts of the Holy Land were conquered for short periods, enabling the rebuilding of the sacred shrines. The rebuilt Church of the Holy Sepulcher dates to that time, as does St. Anne's Church. However, the Mamelukes from Egypt finally ousted the Crusaders from their last outpost at Acre in 1292.

For Jews in the empire, the Crusades constituted a two-century horror story. "Most of the Jewish communities in Palestine were destroyed by the Crusaders,"[56] notes Louis Finkelstein. "Massacre became the accompaniment of each Crusade."[57] This spirit of revenge was not limited to Palestine, but spread throughout Europe. "'Why go to the Holy Land to kill the enemies of God when there are Jews right here? Kill a Jew and save your soul. . . .' Thus hatred was stirred up in these mobs, and they mercilessly attacked and plundered community after community as they marched through Europe" en route to Palestine.[58] Historians further note that "from the time of the Crusades on, for more than 750 years, race hatred made them a hunted, persecuted people to whom life became something to endure, and tomorrow something to fear."[59]

In 1202, for instance, Pope Innocent III issued "an edict which required Jews to wear special clothing, or a red or yellow badge, on the front and back to distinguish them. . . . As a result, the Jews were constantly jeered, mocked, insulted, stoned, and pelted with mud. In seeking to escape these indignities they frequented back alleys and little traveled roads or came out only at night."[60]

The Crusades also prompted a social revolution throughout Europe. Volunteers recruited from local farms got a taste for and urge to travel. Many of the recruits were serfs and criminals who were offered freedom, pardon, and absolution. Though Jewish communities were attacked first, the ravenous mobs soon began to sack any village in their path. As the looting became general, Christians as well as Jews became victims. Dimont notes, "As the nature of the Crusades shifted from that of freeing the Holy Land from the infidel to that of pillaging the rich Byzantine Empire, the enemy became the Greek Orthodox Catholics instead of the Muhammedans. What had started out as desultory looting of Jews ended up as a bloodbath for Christians."[61] This brought a rift between the Catholic Sees of Rome and Constantinople. The two pontiffs, in fact, pronounced anathemas on each other. Byzantium is said to have been carved up like a cadaver and its towns looted. The "bestiality of the Crusaders shocked Pope, prince, and people, but their horror in no way stopped the slaughter."[62]

The taste for Jewish blood, however, was especially acute, being whetted early in the Crusades. This hunt spread throughout the empire, even into England. The notion became popular that "the blood of Christ should be avenged in the blood of the Jews."[63] In the coming centuries, no slaughter seemed sufficient to appease that thirst. For the Jews, it was a mercy that the Turkish Mamelukes took Palestine in 1292, though the invaders massacred the remaining Crusaders.[64]

Europe's "Black Death"

The passion of the first Crusades for Jewish blood continued in the following centuries. Cecil Roth writes: "There was barely any intermission in the constant sequence of massacres."[65] The Jews seemed to be at the mercy of every wave of prejudice, superstition, or dissatisfaction. Several decades after the last Crusade, the ultimate excuse for their destruction seemed to present itself. One of history's most devastating catastrophes hit Europe in 1348 and 1349 in what is known as the "Black Death." The epidemic (thought to be bubonic plague) swept from China to the Atlantic and wiped out more than a third of the population. Some estimate that as much as three-quarters of the population of Asia and Europe died in the disease's twenty-year rampage, spread to Europe in part by the returning Crusaders.[66] No natural explanation for this plague could be found. However, fingers soon pointed in a familiar direction.

The handiest scapegoats for such a calamity were the Jews, both for spiritual and racial reasons. First, they were thought to be under a divine curse for their rejection and killing of Christ. Second, they were suspected of using their intellectual talents to seek revenge against their oppressors. In the hysteria of the time, Jews were seen as the obvious villains. Accordingly, a rumor soon surfaced that Jews had compounded a poison, "a mixture of spiders, lizards, frogs, flesh, the hearts of Christians, mingled with the dough of the Host, which they reputedly scattered through the land."[67] With this devilish potion they were supposed to have poisoned the wells of their gentile overlords. As Heinrich Graetz noted, "In Europe the invisible death with its horrors turned the Christians into veritable destroying angels for the Jews. Those whom the epidemic had spared were handed over to torture, the sword, or the stake."[68]

Jewish villages were burned to the ground in Germany, Switzerland, France, and Spain. In the town in southern France where the plague first struck Europe, "the whole Jewish congregation, men, women, and children, together with their holy writings, were cast into the flames."[69] More than two hundred communities of Jews were exterminated in 1348 and 1349.[70] Half the Jewish population of Europe was massacred, according to William Hull.

Time and events have obscured the immensity of that atrocity, though it was a debacle of worldwide dimensions. By any assessment, the Black Death hysteria measured high on the persecution scale of Jewish history. The horror was the fact that the Roman church poured fuel on the flames by construing the Jews as instigators and conspirators with the devil. Religious bigotry fanned itself into racial bigotry, and the earth suffered one of its worst abominations ever.

JEWISH EXPULSIONS FROM EUROPE
The Spanish Inquisition and the Jews

Up to this point, Jews had had a long history of residence in Spain. Even under the Muslims, they enjoyed a period of relative tolerance and tranquility. That climate, however, gradually changed as the Moors were driven out and the church resumed control of the country. Even Thomas Aquinas saw the Jews as "condemned to perpetual servitude for the act of deicide."[71] As noted, the Fourth Lateran Council (1215) decreed that Jews were to wear a distinguishing mark on their clothes (the law of the patch), a move designed to further drive them into isolation. Church officials justified this as a necessary prod to bring Jews to conversion—conversion by coercion.

Though most Jews scorned and denounced this policy as religious bigotry and bondage, many did succumb for expediency. In fourteenth-century Spain, the Inquisition was instituted to bring many Jews to "conversion." All means were used to wring out confessions of faith. Some Spaniards called the Jewish converts *Marranos* (pigs) or crypto-Jews, but their superior learning allowed many of them to rise to positions of power, becoming nobles and even bishops and archbishops. They learned to fade into the environment—just to survive. As the Inquisition progressed, however, they were often suspected of hypocrisy. The result was a new Spanish Inquisition of the Jews in 1482.[72]

The arch villain of the Inquisition was Tomás de Torquemada, charged by the church to purge heresy from the realm. In his zeal, he persuaded Queen Isabella and King Ferdinand to sign an order expelling all Jews from Spain, arguing that the preservation of the church depended on it. For the Jews this was especially excruciating, since many dated their ancestry there back fifteen hundred years. Furthermore, Spain had become a great center of Jewish intellectual and social activity (from whence came Moses ben Maimonides). This decree was signed immediately after the capture of Grenada on March 30, 1492, and was to be carried out that summer. In the meanwhile, some fifty thousand Jews "surrendered" to baptism, while a hundred thousand remained resolute and chose exile. The edict was later extended to all Spanish dependencies, a policy that continued for more than three centuries. European Jewry thus lost one of its most solid moorings on the continent.

The actual expulsion occurred August 2, 1492, the same day Columbus left Spain for the new world.[73] (It was also the ninth of Ab, the anniversary of the destruction of Jerusalem.) Columbus's logbook incidentally lists several Jews among his crew, his interpreter being Luis de Torres who was brought along to greet the supposed Oriental natives in Hebrew or Aramaic. Many have noted that funding for Columbus's explorations also came from Jewish wealth confiscated in Spain. It was not the jewelry of Queen Isabella that financed his expeditions (as the popular story goes), but the Jewry from which it confiscated so much property. In his diary, Columbus notes that as his three ships set sail, other boats loaded with Jewish refugees were also leaving the harbor.[74] An ancient land was closing its gates to the Jews, but another was opening up beyond the western sea. Many of the hundred thousand deportees perished at sea in the Mediterranean, being refused harbor at other ports of call. But a large number did enter Turkey, where the Ottoman Turks received them. The Sultan welcomed them for their acknowledged professional skills and prowess, hoping to buoy up his depressed kingdom.

As in Spain, Jews were progressively expelled from most countries dominated by Rome. In 1290, they were ousted from England, after residing there for two centuries as "property" of the king. In 1394, they were expelled from France (many with only the clothes on their backs). Portugal banished them in 1497. Lithuania threw them out in 1495. "By the middle of the sixteenth century, Western Europe, which for one thousand years had been the center of European Jewry, had practically no Jewish population left."[75] These events forced the flow of Jews back toward the East, where they gradually shifted their center of gravity to eastern Europe, especially Poland.

The Protestant Reformation and the Jews

Other events of the sixteenth century contributed to the Jewish movement back toward eastern Europe. The Protestant Reformation was partially a by-product of the Renaissance. Great scholars such as Erasmus and Reuchlin spearheaded a return to the classics of Greek and Hebrew. In so doing, they emphasized the study of the biblical text, rather than Latin commentaries. This inspired people to think for themselves from original sources, even to the extent of questioning the established church.

When Martin Luther nailed his "Ninety-Five Theses" to the door of the Wittenberg Church in 1517, the questioning came to a head. It quickly spread throughout northern Europe, igniting a revolt that had been smoldering for more than a century. Joining Luther in this revolt were other notable Reformers such as John Calvin in France, Huldrych Zwingli in Switzerland, and John Knox in Scotland.

The Catholic church responded to the challenge by instituting a counter-reformation. This in-house struggle set the stage for a strange role for the Jews: The church rediscovered them as subjects of evangelism, and suddenly they became the mission field of both Catholics and Reformers.[76]

Such a turn of events might suggest a new day of tolerance. But the record shows otherwise. Though Luther was a friend of the Jews in his early ministry, roundly castigating the Roman church for its Jew-baiting, his charity did not last long. Luther had never been known for his patience with the obstinate. When the Jews refused his offer of salvation by faith alone, he lost patience with them and joined his enemy John Eck in vilifying the race. His tract, "Concerning the Jews and Their Lies" (1542), denounced them as a wicked, accursed race whose synagogues and sacred writings should be reduced to ashes. He advised Christians to "destroy the houses of the Jews," the clergy to "fill the minds of their hearers with hatred of Jews," and princes to expel them from the country.[77] Historian Heinrich Graetz gives a succinct summary: "As Jerome had infected the Catholic world with his openly avowed hatred of the Jews, so Luther poisoned the Protestant world for a long time to come with his Jew-hating testament. Protestants became even more bitter against Jews than Catholics had been."[78] This notion that Christianity could be force-fed down Jewish throats was a delusion afflicting both branches of the church.

Accordingly, Jewish intolerance only hardened.

Jewish Vicissitudes in Russia and Eastern Europe

The story of the Jews in Russia is also crucial in understanding their history in Europe, as many of their recent scholars and movers came from Eastern Europe. Their sojourn in Russia actually dates to the early centuries, but was highlighted in the Kingdom of Khazaria from A.D. 700 to A.D. 1016.

The Khazars (nomads) were a tribe of mixed Mongolian Turks who settled on the trade routes north of the Caspian and Black seas. Their language was Greek and their religion was a mixture of Islam, Christianity, and Judaism. Sandwiched between Muslims to the south and the Byzantine Empire to the southwest, they tried to show tolerance toward all religions. This policy was dictated by their trade and commerce up and down the Volga and Don rivers.[79]

In 740, King Bulan, the ruling prince of Khazaria, adopted Judaism and was followed by many of his people, especially the aristocracy[80]— a rare instance of Jewish "evangelism" on a large scale. Caught between militant Christians and militant Muslims, the Khazars found it expedient, both for politics and commerce, to settle for something in between. Judaism appeared to be neutral, inasmuch as all groups claimed Abraham as their father. It was also less threatening to adopt Judaism because it was not an aggressive religion, seeking territory and converts. Choosing either Christianity or Islam would be to invite invasion.

The Khazars' choice of Judaism brought many Jewish refugees into the kingdom. For the next two hundred years, Khazaria was considered Jewish. In the late tenth century, however, the Prince of Kiev to the north became strong and invaded the country. Historians describe how the Kingdom of Khazaria dissolved in 969 when it fell to Svyatoslav I, who took the Crimea. The Russian nation then adopted Christianity (Russian Orthodoxy) under Vladimir the Great in 989.[81] Though some Jewish settlers remained, especially in the Crimea, they mainly dispersed north and south. In 1240, the barbaric Tartars invaded Russia, after which the country was outside the bounds of civilized Europe for several centuries. Russian Khazaria was for two centuries a kind of blip in Jewish medieval history.[82]

Later Jewish Migrations to Eastern Europe

The large population of Jews in Russia actually came primarily from Europe through Poland. From the time of the Crusades, Poland opened its doors to Jewish refugees expelled from Western Europe. The Polish nobility was shrewd enough to recognize Jewish monetary and commercial abilities and welcomed their help to compete economically with the West. Therefore, Poland became the center for world Jewry for several centuries. At the beginning of the seventeenth century, no Jews refusing conversion were allowed to stay in Spain, Portugal, England, France, Scandinavia, Sicily, or Northern Italy. Nor were they allowed in most of Germany.[83] Thus, at the time of America's colonization, Holland, Turkey, and Poland were the three great centers of Jewish refuge. Most, by far, had fled east to Poland.

That all changed in 1648. A revolt by the Greek Orthodox Cossacks began an era of unprecedented brutality in Poland. The Polish nobility and the tax-collecting Jews were the special victims of the Cossacks. Within a decade, a hundred thousand Jews perished while the Poles themselves lost nearly a million[84]—abruptly ending the era of Jewish tranquility in the Polish hinterland. During the following century, Poland was invaded several times, and likewise partitioned three times—by Russia, Prussia, and Austria (1772, 1793, 1795).[85] The result was that Catherine the Great of Russia, who in 1762 had banished all Jews from her land, found herself with nearly a million of them after receiving her share of the partitioning of Poland in 1795. The harder Russia tried to expel the Jews, the more it acquired.

At the beginning of the nineteenth century, the Jewish population of Russia stood at about one million. As the Jews continued to grow in number and prosper, however, their presence struck fear in the Romanov czars. This fear is described by Arnold White:

> It is not from innate brutality that the Russian government herds the Jewish peddler, moneylender, and artisan into ghettos and restricts him from fishing, tillage, or market-gardening, but because the Russian government deems itself compelled both by policy and by duty to protect the majority of the Russian population from contact with the astute, temperate, industrious, and money-loving Jew. . . . Men with muscle and the sword will not voluntarily pay

tribute or come under the heel of the most intellectual race in the world if the physique of the latter is inferior to their own.[86]

The czars then took measures to isolate the Jews, one even banishing them to a large area of Western Russia called the "Pale of Settlement"—an enormous ghetto designed to restrict Jewish movement and contact with the Russians. Here they could govern themselves, but were not allowed to own or cultivate the soil. This kept them separated from 95 percent of the Russian population.[87] The confinement began in 1791 and was not legally abolished until March 1917.

The Jews of nineteenth century Russia experienced cycles of leniency and terror. Nevertheless, their numbers grew. From a population of one million in 1800, the Jews multiplied to nearly six million by 1900. Thus, at the close of that century the majority of world Jewry lived in Russia.

The Pogroms and "The Protocols of the Elders of Zion"

Growth of the Jewish population occurred despite Russian resistance. When the czars saw the Jews quadruple in the short span of forty years (1842–1882), they responded like the Pharaohs of Egypt. In fear, they instituted *pogroms,* officially sponsored uprisings against the Jews. These began in 1881 as a means to force either Jewish migration (hundreds of thousands escaped to the United States) or destruction. A maniacal Slavophile named Pobedonostsev spun out a formula for solving the "Jewish question" and aroused the depressed and starving masses to quench their thirst for revenge by attacking the Jews. In effect, he threw the Jews into the jaws of the working-class peasants.[88]

Many consider this state use of pogroms as the beginning of anti-Semitism. As the Age of Enlightenment de-emphasized religion, the case against the Jews also became secularized, degenerating into disdain for the Jewish race, rather than just their religion.[89] The word *anti-Semitism* was first used in 1879 in a pamphlet by Wilhelm Marr, a German agitator. Though the Jews make up only a small part of Semitic-speaking people, the term speaks exclusively of Jew-hatred. Anti-Semitism's charge against the Jews is their "crime" of being Jewish, apart from their religion. This left them without defense or appeal. They could not atone themselves of the charge through conversion or baptism, as the Spanish Inquisition allowed. It diagnosed Jewishness as a disease itself. Soon it became open season on all Jews, leading in the early twentieth century to the murderous racism that culminated in the Holocaust.

Anti-Semitism offered a "rationale" for anti-Judaism, making it a nationalistic and patriotic cause. Racists used it to gain a semblance of respectability. Hatred of the Jews became a bread-and-butter issue, appealing to the insecurities and anxieties of the working class. It gave focus to the search for a handy scapegoat. The Jews in Russia and Poland at the beginning of the twentieth century were ideal targets for this role. The virus of anti-Semitism gradually infected England, Germany, and Austria-Hungary. In France, it was a political centerpiece in the infamous Dreyfus Affair (1894). Several popular books promoting anti-Semitism were published in the wake of Friedrich Nietzsche's Aryan superman philosophy. Nietzsche was a nineteenth-century German philosopher who became one of the most influential of all modern thinkers. His philosophy was both anti-Christian and anti-Semitic; yet it swept through much of Northern Europe.[90] As the moral climate of the age continued to degenerate toward barbarism, it prepared the way for a new round of Jew-baiting and pillage.

Recall that Polish Russia in the late nineteenth century boasted the largest population of Jews in the world, a group that was making significant contributions to Russian society. But in that very society, the acknowledged virtues of the Jews became their ruin. Russians viewed their superior skill and intellect as a threat. That threat was magnified and politicized in an infamous document called "The Protocols of the Elders of Zion," a forgery devised to incite the working classes of Russia against the Jews. From whence did this diabolical fabrication originate?

Research points an accusing finger at two modern-day Hamans, Czar Nicholas II and a monk by the name of Sergei Nilus.[91] Using a French novel published in 1865 that satirized Napoleon, Nilus concocted a Jewish conspiracy aimed at taking over the world. "The Protocols," published in 1902 and translated into many European languages, circulated worldwide.

"The Protocols" soon found sympathizers outside of Russia. The forgery internationalized anti-Semitism, ultimately supplying a pious ground for genocide. It practically became the bible of anti-Semites in later years, and the lie persists even today. "Though 'The Protocols' had been definitively proven to be a forgery by the London *Times* in 1921, it continued to be utilized by anti-Semites, and was believed by millions of people."[92] Henry Ford, for example, elucidated the "threat" of "The Protocols" in many articles in the *Dearborn Independent* in 1921.[93] Ford circulated millions of copies in the United States.

The falsehoods of "The Protocols" were later incorporated into Hitler's doctrine of National Socialism as expressed in his book *Mein Kampf ("My Struggle")*. "During the 1960s 'The Protocols' was republished by President Gamal Abdel Nasser of Egypt, and also distributed by King Faisal of Saudi Arabia in the 1970s."[94] The vile document became one of the twentieth century's cruelest hoaxes, with far-reaching, worldwide consequences. Though "The Protocols" is widely acknowledged today as phony, its spirit is far from extinguished. Most recently it was broadcast as a fact-based television drama in Egypt. The program, entitled *The Horse without a Horseman*, was produced by Arab Radio and Television of Saudi Arabia and broadcast in Egypt in November 2002 during Ramadan.[95]

The Rise of Jewish Professionals and Capitalists

Many writers have noted the disproportionate numbers of Jews who have distinguished themselves by gravitating to the top. They often rise to prominence in business, the courts and legal professions, medicine and psychology, the media and journalism, Wall Street, theater and entertainment, tobacco and liquor industries, sports management, popular music and jazz, labor organizations, and politics.[96] Even under such a persecutor as Charlemagne, "Jews were the leading merchants and bankers in Europe."[97] They seemed indomitable. It is said that in the ghettos of Poland during the stagnant period of the sixteenth century, it was almost impossible to find an illiterate Jew.[98]

As Dimont has noted, though the Jews constitute less than a half percent of the world's population, "no less than 12 percent of all the Nobel prizes in physics, chemistry, and medicine have gone to Jews. The Jewish contribution to the world's list of great names in religion, science, literature, music, finance, and philosophy," he said, "is staggering."[99]

How is this intellectual prowess and business savvy to be explained? Is it some strange superman psyche bestowed upon them by virtue of their divine "chosenness"? Let's observe several logical reasons that contributed to this uncanny ability to succeed.

The first is the Jews' perennial position as underdog. In their difficult situation among unfriendly Gentiles, they were forced to more concentrated and disciplined effort. The constant threat of extinction honed their survival instincts. Rather than succumb to oppression, they became fierce competitors with strong loyalties to each other.[100]

The second is the churlish and greedy attitude with which their gentile antagonists sought to squelch them. This generated an ability to rise above circumstances and turn a disadvantage into a boon. An illustration of this might be noted in the way Jews became bankers in the Middle Ages.

> Why did not the Christians themselves go into banking?
> Why were the Jews so reviled for performing this essen-

tial service? The answer hinges on a definition. The Church called the lending of money not "banking," but "usury." To modern man the word "usury" means the lending of money at exorbitant rates; in medieval times it simply meant the lending of money for interest, no matter how low. Any Christian today who accepts 3 percent interest on his bank savings or government bonds would have been regarded as a blackhearted usurer by the medieval Church, for the simple reason that the Church viewed the lending of money at interest as a mortal sin. How then could it permit Christians to lend money if that meant their souls would go to hell? With the Jews it was another story. As the Jews were not Christians and headed for hell anyhow, one more sin—that is, moneylending—could not add much to the punishment they would receive in the Hereafter. [101]

The Talmud forbade the taking of excessive interest, but did allow lending at a permissible rate set by the rabbis (controlled in Europe by the pope or emperor). Thus Jews introduced credit buying and loan negotiating in the medieval centuries, Rabbi Maimonides even asserting that such equitable lending was necessary to business. In ingenious ways they developed a system of monetary exchange that served princes and nobles, especially learning the art of barter. Denied the right of producing from the soil, they were driven to moneylending for the upper class. In the process, they became the vanguard of modern capitalism in Europe as the feudal system gradually gave way to this new economic system.

A third factor contributing to Jewish success is their early and incessant study of Talmud. The educative process has always been at the core of Judaism.[102] In all the migrations and settlements, education was a consuming interest from the cradle to the grave. Whenever ten Jewish males lived within commuting distance, they would establish a religious community; where there were 120, they established a social community supporting education and charity for all. The Talmud was their "religious-legal code" which they relentlessly studied for almost fifteen hundred years.[103] This stimulated memories and nurtured inquiring minds. In the process, the Jewish people became scholars, physicians, financiers, legal experts, and practitioners in most of the professions and sciences. Refusing to let their minds stagnate, even in ghetto living, they built a heritage of study and inquiry.

These factors help to explain why so many Jews rose to positions of prominence and power. They were driven to succumb or succeed.

Their difficult circumstances developed in them a dogged instinct for survival in a world that afforded them neither national home nor personal writ of habeas corpus.

In what seemed like endless dispersion, the Jews somehow maintained a unity of mind and spirit. That dogged determination, however, did not improve their plight. After nineteen centuries of "cat and mouse" living, their future seemed no less bleak than at the beginning of their scattering. Nor was their longing for a homeland diminished. The plaintive cry of each new generation at Passover continued to be: "Next year in Jerusalem."

How that dream would be fulfilled in the following decades is a story full of unprecedented perils—even for the ghetto-wearied sons of Israel. A rash of new pharaohs and Hamans would arise to terrorize and destroy them, but new Moseses and Mordecais would also arise to plead their cause and point the way back home. That path, however, would be through another wilderness lurking with dangers that would challenge the stoutest hearts among them.

5

Zionism: Turning Dreams into Drama

THE EMERGENCE OF ZIONISM at the end of the nine-teenth century was a crucial turning point in Jewish history. That movement put feet to ancient hopes and dreams for a Jewish home-land. It repudiated once and for all the notion of assimilation, sum-moning world Jewry to a nationalism of its own. From the confining ghettos of Eastern Europe, prophets arose to stir the inertia-laden Di-aspora (a term referring to the dispersion of the Jewish people among the Gentiles, which began at the time of the Babylonian exile) with visions of the impossible. These modern-day Moseses energized the Jews for a new exodus to the Promised Land, challenging their broth-ers to reclaim the ancient homeland.

The movement quite early was styled "Zionism," meaning a return to Zion, the City of David. The title itself invigorated and quickened Jewish heartbeats. Though the concept lay embedded in every Jewish mind since the dispersion of A.D. 70, modern Zionism added a new fea-ture to the old dream—a more active militancy.[104] From the time of bar Kochba's revolt in A.D. 135 and Rome's vicious attack on all things Jewish, passive resistance had been their only weapon. The "sword of David" was kept sheathed as they patiently waited for a militant Mes-siah to take up their cause. In Zionism, however, that responsibility was shifted from Messiah to their own shoulders.[105] In many ways it replicated the ancient Maccabees who reluctantly took up the sword in

167 B.C. to reclaim their sacred shrine in Jerusalem. In Zionism, united and determined action supplanted passive resistance.

FACTORS IN THE AWAKENING OF ZIONISM

The social climate of both East and West played a part in the birth of Zionism. The French and American Revolutions in the eighteenth century had emphasized political independence and democracy. That spirit unleashed a torrent of discussion throughout Europe on the issue of political authority. Gradually, religious authority began to be supplanted by civil authority.

At the same time, there arose a new spirit of nationalism in many parts of Western Europe[106] that did not go unnoticed by the many communities of isolated Jews. In the spirit of the time, they longed to be part of the larger society by having a land they could call their own.

A grassroots youth movement also contributed to this Jewish awakening in Eastern Europe where the greatest concentration of Jews lived, especially in the Polish and Russian regions. Czarist policy aimed at restricting the Jews prompted "thousands of idealistic young Russian Jews" to organize themselves "into a political and cultural group called the 'Lovers of Zion.'"[107] These young people held their first convention in Constantinople in 1882, boldly issuing a manifesto declaring their need for a Jewish homeland and their God–given right to Zion, if only under the sultan's sovereignty. These spurts of restlessness presaged the awakening movement of Zionism in the nineteenth century.

Though many modern "Maccabees" might be listed as forerunners of Zionism, the movement may be surveyed by noting three prominent individuals—Theodor Herzl, Chaim Weizmann, and David Ben-Gurion. All three came from Eastern Europe, and each possessed a unique personality for the task to which he was called. Their work spanned the half century that gave birth to the new State of Israel (1896–1948).

THEODOR HERZL AND *DER JUDENSTAAT*

Theodor Herzl, a Hungarian Jew, is acknowledged as the first leader of Zionism. A quintessential leader, he has been called the most important Jewish personality of the nineteenth century. Born in Budapest in 1860 and educated for the bar, he became a journalist and playwright. This providentially led him to cover the infamous Dreyfus Affair in Paris, where an assimilated Jew on the French General Staff was wrongly accused of treason and imprisoned. The racial indignities of this trial in liberal France so fired up the Jewish blood and journalist's ire of young Herzl that he became a flaming evangel for Jewish liberation and independence.[108]

Two years later (1896) Herzl drew up and outlined a plan to solve the Jewish question in what became a benchmark book, *Der Judenstaat* (The Jewish State). He was not the first to put pen to the Zionist cause, for others, such as Leo Pinsker, a Russian physician, had also written brilliantly, calling for "Auto-Emancipation." The concern was widespread and generated by a grassroots undercurrent. Herzl's book, more than any other single factor, however, served to galvanize world Jewry and fire them with a dream that turned their eyes and hearts toward home. His solution called for individual Jews to immigrate to Palestine, buy up the land from the Turks, cultivate it into productivity, build a Jewish majority in the land, and thus reestablish the Jewish homeland. The next year (1897) he called the first Zionist Congress at Basle (the first united Jewish council in more than eighteen hundred years) to inspire Jewish communities throughout the Diaspora. Here he officially launched the Zionist movement with a specific statement of purpose: "The object of Zionism is to establish for the Jewish people a publicly and legally assured home in Palestine."[109]

So daring was this proposal that European Jews fiercely opposed it, fearing the reprisals it might bring. Both Orthodox and Reform rabbis branded it as visionary and impractical. Undaunted, Herzl pressed on and was cheered by gathering crowds of Jews. Funds were collected, and several thousand settlers began migrating to Israel to till the soil and set up colonies. Herzl's energies seemed boundless as he assumed the role of roving ambassador for the Jews in the highest echelons of government. No confrontation fazed him. He fearlessly challenged opulent financiers; held audiences with the German kaiser, the Turkish sultan, the king of Italy, and the pope; and approached leading officials of Russia and Great Britain. With his unique, polished demeanor he became a diplomat par excellence for the Zionist cause.

At the height of his career in 1904, however, Herzl died of a heart attack at the age of forty-four. This occurred shortly after the Sixth Zionist Congress in 1903, when a British offer of a Jewish homeland in Uganda had been considered. That offer brought division and bitter dissension to the congress, as well as to the whole Diaspora. Though the great leader was driven to consider it briefly, he again affirmed the futility of Zionism without Zion. The issue of settling for soil outside Palestine as a Jewish homeland was rarely considered again.

At his death, Herzl was revered as something of a martyr, never flagging in zeal for the impossible goals he set. Though often opposed by the rich or the assimilated and comfortably positioned Jews in Europe, Herzl became the voice for the poor and oppressed. His body was later transferred from Vienna to Jerusalem with great pomp and ceremony for burial on a high hill just west of Mt. Zion.[110] He was the first noted hero of Israel's "Second Exodus."

CHAIM WEIZMANN AND THE BALFOUR DECLARATION

The diplomatic effort begun by Herzl was soon taken up by several others such as Nahum Sokolow in Rome, London, and Paris, and Judge Louis Brandeis in the United States. The House of Rothschild, of course, had great influence in Britain from the time of Benjamin Disraeli, the man largely responsible for the British purchase and control of the Suez Canal.

But the new leader of Zionism was another Eastern Jew, Chaim Weizmann. Born in Poland in 1874, Weizmann trained in German and Swiss universities to become a chemist and began teaching in Manchester, England, in 1904. He sensed that England was the most fruitful arena to pursue the goals of Zionism. As Herzl's journalism had thrust him into the Zionist cause, so Weizmann's chemistry did the same for him, catapulting him into high diplomatic circles in Britain. Unlike Herzl, however, Weizmann gave no ground to the Ugandan scheme but tirelessly preached the gospel of a homeland in Palestine as the only solution to the Jewish question. This he saw as a political fact of life, not primarily a religious sentiment.

Having gained the friendship of some of Britain's leading statesmen, Weizmann early put himself in a position of great influence. He found himself at the right place at the right time in high diplomatic circles. The major result of his diplomacy was the Balfour Declaration, which gave the Jews a political "foot in the door" to Palestine. That document came to be a monumental breakthrough for the Zionist cause. It established the Jews' international right to a homeland in Palestine under the patronage of Great Britain. Though later revised and vigorously challenged, it became part of the British Mandate to govern the Middle East. The substance of the Declaration was given in a letter to Lord Rothschild by British Foreign Secretary Arthur Balfour on November 2, 1917.

> His Majesty's Government view with favour the establishment in Palestine of a national home for the Jewish people, and will use their best endeavours to facilitate the achievement of this object, it being clearly understood that nothing shall be done which may prejudice the civil

and religious rights of the existing non-Jewish communities in Palestine, or the rights and political status enjoyed by Jews in any other country. (See Appendix B.)

How did the Zionists acquire such a prize, especially after being rebuffed by so many other powers that could have helped? That strange reversal is part of the story of World War I. The end of that great conflagration saw enormous changes come to the world: The long rule of the czars in Russia was overthrown by the Bolsheviks under Lenin; Europe was recarved by the Allies at Versailles, especially the Eastern sector; the Turkish Ottoman Empire came to an end after ruling the East for half a millennium; and the Arabic peoples of the Middle East began their struggle for independence as modern states (see Map 1). These wrenching changes reshaped Europe and the Middle East.

For the Jews, however, those changes gave unexpected energy and direction to the Zionist cause. Besides the devastation that overtook many who found themselves caught between opposing armies, that war brought world Jewry blessings of inestimable value in the form of the Balfour Declaration. That document evolved primarily through two fortuitous events, one personal and the other international.

The first developed through a need in Britain that Weizmann was able to meet. The leading figures in England at that time were Prime Minister Lloyd George, First Lord of the Admiralty Winston Churchill, and Foreign Secretary Arthur Balfour, all officials to whom Weizmann had made appeals. When the Allies' supply of acetone to produce munitions (previously imported from Germany) began to run out, the British staff called on Weizmann to find some substitute. Following a two-year project, his team developed a superior synthetic that made a considerable contribution to the Allied war effort.[111] This success so elated the British cabinet that Lord Balfour exclaimed to Weizmann, "You know that after the war you may get your Jerusalem."[112]

A second providential event was the entrance of Turkey into the war on the side of Germany. This brought great initial terror to the Jews living in Palestine, but it also brought the British army, which drove out the long-entrenched Turks. The Allied conquest of the Ottoman Empire was not a surprise to the British and French, who had increasing interest in the Suez Canal and the Middle East.

The British and French even devised a plan, known as the Sykes-Picot Agreement, to carve up the Ottoman Empire (see Map 2). As the fortunes of war shifted back and forth in Europe, the British sent Sir Edmund Allenby to first secure the Suez and then to take Palestine. Following fierce encounters at Gaza and Beersheba, Allenby's forces moved up the Levant to drive the Turks beyond the Euphrates. So ended four hundred years of Turkish rule over Palestine and six hundred years of Muslim dominance in the area. The Palestine armistice was signed on October 31, 1918, just eleven days before the World War I Armistice was signed. This coincidence prompted Lord Balfour later to declare that "the founding of the Jewish National Home was the most significant outcome of the First World War."[113] Oscar Janowsky has summarized this relationship between Zionism and World War I:

> The first World War proved decisive in the history of Zionism. On November 2, 1917, the British government issued the Balfour Declaration, pledging to facilitate "the establishment in Palestine of a national home for the Jewish People." Soon thereafter the British conquered the country and, when the war was over, Palestine was administered as a Mandate under the League of Nations, with the United Kingdom as Mandatory or trustee. The Balfour pledge was incorporated in the terms of the Mandate, which recognized "the historical connection of the Jewish people with Palestine" and the right to reconstitute "their national home in that country." Britain was to encourage the immigration and close settlement of the Jews on the land; Hebrew (as well as English and Arabic) was to be an official language; and a "Jewish Agency" was to assist and cooperate with the British in the building of the Jewish National Home. [114]

This mandate was given international approval by the Council of the League of Nations on June 28, 1919. Before its final sanction on September 19, 1922, however, the homeland projected for the Jews had been whittled down to exclude Transjordan (literally, "beyond the Jordan"), which is the land east of the Jordan River. In the meantime, Great Britain had created the state of Transjordan under the kingship of Abdullah ibn Hussein.[115] Though the original intention of the Balfour Declaration had been to include Transjordan, this action made the Jordan River the probable eastern border of the Jewish homeland (see Map 3).

The Balfour Declaration became one of Zionism's grandest prizes, ranking with Herzl's *Der Judenstaat* in its importance to the homeward movement. The two came just twenty years apart. Together they helped galvanize the Diaspora to pursue Zionism's most cherished goal, the return of a dedicated enclave of Jews to establish a homeland in *Eretz Yishrael*. [116]

Map 1: Arab Nations after WWI

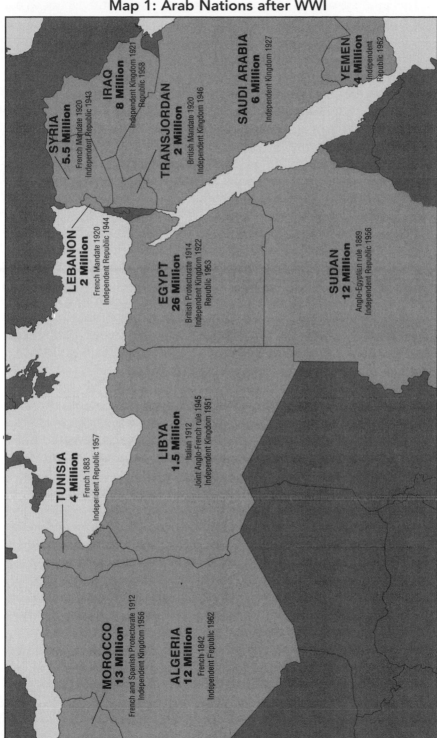

SYRIA
5.5 Million
French Mandate 1920
Independent Republic 1943

IRAQ
8 Million
Independent Kingdom 1921
Republic 1958

TRANSJORDAN
2 Million
British Mandate 1920
Independent Kingdom 1946

SAUDI ARABIA
6 Million
Independent Kingdom 1927

YEMEN
4 Million
Independent
Republic 1962

LEBANON
2 Million
French Mandate 1920
Independent Republic 1944

EGYPT
26 Million
British Protectorate 1914
Independent Kingdom 1922
Republic 1953

SUDAN
12 Million
Anglo-Egyptian rule 1889
Independent Republic 1956

LIBYA
1.5 Million
Italian 1912
Joint Anglo-French rule 1945
Independent Kingdom 1951

TUNISIA
4 Million
French 1883
Independent Republic 1957

MOROCCO
13 Million
French and Spanish Protectorate 1912
Independent Kingdom 1956

ALGERIA
12 Million
French 1842
Independent Republic 1962

This promise of help from mighty Britain, however, was not as cut-and-dried as many expected. A Jewish occupation of Palestine inevitably meant social changes for some of its Arab occupants. At first this was overlooked as the ancient cousins celebrated the routing of the Turks. Both sensed the coming of a new era of friendship and freedom. Weizmann, in fact, held a famous meeting in January 1919 with Emir Feisal, a leading Arab landowner from Arabia (the Hedjaz), at which time the Arab leader (who later became king of Iraq) welcomed the prospects of a new Jewish state in Palestine.[117] The odd couple even signed an agreement of cooperation. The honeymoon was short-lived, however. Feisal soon had a falling-out with the French (when he tried to assume the kingship of Syria) and renounced his agreement with Weizmann. This dashed the high hopes of many for a congenial Jewish-Arab cohabitation of Palestine.[118]

The hard reality is that the great majority of Arab leaders viewed the Zionists with keen distrust. They saw them as foreigners invading their sacred Arabic domain. Their formal clash really began with Arab absentee landowners who were exploiting the working peasants as vassals or sharecroppers.[119] The landowners feared that the higher standards of living and better pay of the Jewish pioneers would breed dissatisfaction and discontent among Arab peasants.

> In one area was the Jewish colony: green, tidy, and productive, with well-paid laborers who were educated, secure, and content. Adjacent to it was the miserable, squalid, dirty Arab village, where ignorance was the rule, discouragement the climate. Some romantic outsiders tried to sentimentalize a picturesque Arab life and lament the fact that Jewish immigration was eliminating the flavor and color of the storybook stereotype. But there was little of the picturesque in villages full of tuberculosis and amoebic dysentery, where food was scarce and shelter primitive, where cow dung was applied to wounds and camel's urine to diseases of the eye, where children slept almost completely covered by flies. The Arabs worked as hard as the Jews did, but they were paid practically nothing and were left with nothing. How long would it be before the dispossessed and disinherited, stirred by the example of Jewish standards, cried out for a decent way of life? [120]

Not a pleasant picture and perhaps overstated, but it points out the contrast in cultures and the problem this presented. The landlords felt it was in their best interest to stifle the influx of Jewish settlers, and

Map 2: Sykes-Picot Frontier Proposal

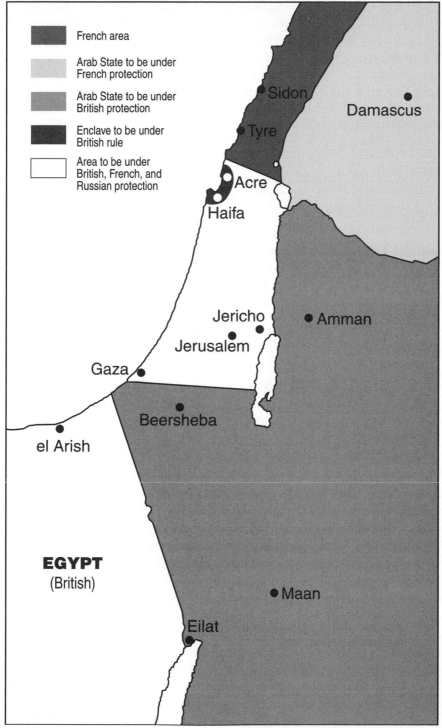

French area

Arab State to be under French protection

Arab State to be under British protection

Enclave to be under British rule

Area to be under British, French, and Russian protection

Sidon

Damascus

Tyre

Acre

Haifa

Jericho

Amman

Jerusalem

Gaza

Beersheba

el Arish

EGYPT
(British)

Maan

Eilat

they did so by convincing Arab peasants that Jews were trespassers bent on defrauding them and destroying their holy places. They hoped to show Jewish immigration as a racial conspiracy and threat to all Arabs. In 1920 and 1921, "the traditionally friendly relations between the Arabs and Jews gave way to Arab hatred and rioting in Jerusalem."[121] The Jewish and Arab leaders didn't hold another joint conference to negotiate their differences until Begin and Sadat in 1978.

DAVID BEN-GURION AND THE "YISHUV"

While Weizmann worked in diplomatic circles of the West, another spark plug for Zionism worked mainly among the *Yishuv* (people of Palestine). His name was David Ben-Gurion (formerly David Green). Born in Poland in 1886, he migrated to Palestine at age twenty and quickly became the most active Zionist in the land. Though keen of intellect, he was also a hands-on pragmatist. He worked and tilled farms, organized the Hebrew labor union *Histadrut,* and led the Jewish Legion against the Turks in World War I. His activism included a stint in the United States where he recruited Zionist volunteers, but his primary work was organizing Zionists in Palestine. He later became Israel's first prime minister, guiding the young nation for nearly fifteen years. His white-maned figure and presence became almost legendary among his people as he sought to give birth to what Herzl and Weizmann had conceived. As a shrewd thinker, organizer, practical diplomat, and courageous soldier, Ben-Gurion spearheaded and defended the home front of Zionism.

The decade following international approval of the Balfour Declaration was most crucial. Ben-Gurion recognized and stressed the futility of claiming the land without a significant number of Jews living there. During that period several waves of returnees came, especially from Russia and Eastern Europe. "They came and built roads, drained marshes, planted trees, and established large collective farms."[122] These Jewish refugees even purchased the vast malaria-ridden Valley of Esdraelon after much negotiation, draining and transforming it into a fertile fruit basket.

Great strides also were made in culture and education. By 1925 the Hebrew University was established on Mt. Scopus by Weizmann, with Lord Balfour giving the opening address. Ancient Hebrew became the common language, which all immigrants were required to learn. This revival of a "dead" language was a miracle in itself. One man, Ben-Yehuda, was largely responsible for it and is remembered as the creator of modern Hebrew. Though he migrated from Russia with tuberculosis in 1882, Ben-Yehuda devoted his life to rejuvenating the

Map 3: British Balfour Declaration Borders, 1917

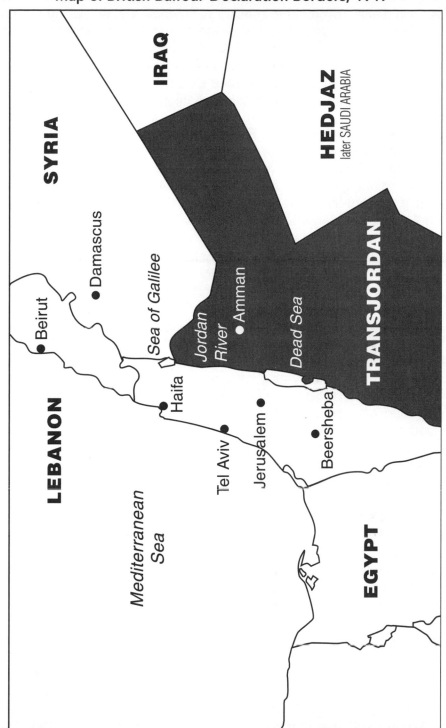

language for modern use, even producing a Hebrew dictionary. In spite of much ridicule, he and his wife "took a vow that no words would ever again pass their lips except in Hebrew, a vow that proved to be one of the turning points in the history of Palestine."[123] Few things have so contributed to the unifying of modern Israel as this renewal of the ancient tongue. With this, the Jewish return to Palestine became cultural and spiritual as well as physical.

Central to the movement was the Jews' continued immigration to Palestine. That was what the Balfour Declaration was all about. Vigorous immigration and time were needed for the nation to succeed. The pogroms of the previous century reminded the Jews of that need, and the uncertain open door before them made it urgent. Beginning at the turn of the century, the vast majority of European refugees had headed for America, making the New World the center of world Jewry. Up to this point, assimilation had been their general policy. Zionism, however, pointed in the other direction—to the native soil of Palestine. This insistence on open immigration to Palestine became nonnegotiable. The building of a political base for world Jewry depended on it.

It was this insistence that really seemed to stir up Arab antagonism, which eventually built into a countrywide revolt. The main source of agitation was the Grand Mufti of Jerusalem, Haj Amin al-Husseini. The British had sought to control the country through two leading families of Palestine with large land holdings, the Husseinis and the Nashashibis.[124] Haj Amin was appointed president of the Supreme Muslim Counsel in 1922, giving him immense political, economic, and religious clout.[125] His fierce opposition to both the Jews and British forced his exile on several occasions. During World War II he defected to the Nazis, moving to Rome and Berlin. In the twenties and thirties he missed no opportunity to stir antagonism and wage war against the Jewish families who were settling in Palestine.

Despite this Arab opposition, a flood of Jewish immigrants—one hundred fifty thousand—entered Palestine from 1931 to 1935. This influx of Jews and their possessions brought a time of relative prosperity to both Jews and Arabs, even while the rest of the world suffered the Great Depression. In April 1936, however, the Mufti instigated a massacre of Jews in Jaffa that spread carnage throughout the cities of Palestine. A general strike was called by the Arabs, inciting the Arab people to join the revolt against the British Mandate. Riots and sniping continued until World War II. During this time Europe was also smoldering with unrest and fear as Hitler feverishly armed and incited his Third Reich to pursue his anti-Semitic campaign. If the European Jews ever needed a refuge, it was during the climactic year of 1939.

When they needed it most, however, it was cut off. On May 17,

1939, British Prime Minister Neville Chamberlain issued a paper that shook the halls of Zion. That paper, infamously known as the "MacDonald White Paper" (after Malcolm MacDonald, the Colonial Secretary), cut the immigration of Jews to Palestine to almost nothing.[126] It seemed to be a virtual surrender to the demands of Arab terrorists. Yet even the Grand Mufti rejected this paper, demanding "the immediate setting up of an independent Arab state in Palestine and no further Jewish immigration."[127] The paper was bitterly denounced by Winston Churchill before Parliament for its repudiation of the Balfour Declaration. It also aroused a storm of protest from around the world.

What happened to the Balfour agreement? It fell victim to the Chamberlain government's policies of "appeasement," sacrificed to stroke the Mufti in Palestine. Even the British House of Commons sheepishly, but nonetheless overwhelmingly, concurred with this "prudent cowardice."

The fact is that British sympathies were shifting away from the Zionists and toward the Arabs who threatened the British control in the Levant. Discovery of oil in the Middle East and a nearly completed pipeline from Iraq to Haifa also fueled economic concern. A situation that called for backbone received only wishbone.

One year later Chamberlain was forced to resign as Germany threatened the British Isles. Nevertheless, the Chamberlain policy on immigration continued throughout the war. Although thousands did escape Hitler's clutches, they were halted as they approached Palestine. Many were turned back at gunpoint when coming ashore; many more died at sea.

Some say this restrictive British policy received an immediate frown from heaven. Four months after issuing this White Paper (May 1939), Britain was reluctantly drawn into World War II on September 1, 1939. One year later at Dunkirk, Britain's whole military operation in Europe was forced to flee the continent. For several years thereafter, Britain became the target of incessant bombing by the Luftwaffe. The Island Empire stood practically alone in Europe, threatened by the menacing tide of Hitler's Wehrmacht, the most destructive force ever assembled. A bleaker scene is hard to imagine.

In this dark hour of British history the aging Sir Winston Churchill was recalled into His Majesty's service (after ten years of writing about the dangers of Nazism). He eloquently summoned the beleaguered nation to a determined struggle for survival. He who had helped open Palestine for Jewish refugees after World War I was now called upon to preserve the British homeland in World War II. His greatest challenge lay ahead.

If that were true for Churchill, it was even more so for the anxious sons of Israel. The ship of Zion was indeed launched and commissioned with the Balfour Declaration, but its turbulent voyage was just beginning. Extremely troubled waters lay ahead. The cause of Zionism and its followers were now caught in the eye of another hurricane.

World War II and the Holocaust

AS WORLD WAR II ERUPTED, Jewish emigration to Palestine came to a virtual halt. Though more than half the Jews in Germany had managed to escape the clutches of Hitler's storm troopers, the rest found themselves trapped in double jeopardy. Visas from Europe were cut off by the Führer, and entrance into Palestine was shut off by the British. Thus when German tanks rolled into Poland on September 1, 1939, and the conflagration began, all escape hatches were slammed shut.

But though World War II burst upon the world suddenly, it did not develop in a vacuum. Many evil forces conspired to bring it forth, anti-Semitism not the least among them. The fact that such Jew-hatred developed in the heart of "civilized" and "Christian" Europe makes it imperative that we recognize some of those forces. How could such a fiend as Hitler arise in that soil?

THE DEVELOPMENT OF HITLER'S ANTI-SEMITISM

Adolf Hitler's great passion was to create a super Aryan race that would build a thousand-year empire. Germany's humiliating defeat in World War I drove him to maniacal dreams of a comeback. After the Peace Treaty of Versailles, Germany was made not only to groan, but to grovel. Two million German youths had been slain, and millions more were wounded. The staggering reparations Germany was forced to pay further shattered and demoralized the populace. "Inflation increased so rapidly in Germany that within a few months the price of bread ran into billions of marks for a single loaf. . . . At the height of the inflation, one U.S. dollar was worth 4.2 billion Reichmarks."[128] Depression was rampant.

The ravages of war and its aftermath drove Germany's embittered people to seek a scapegoat. Having suffered himself from shrapnel and gas in the four-year conflict, Hitler vowed revenge.[129]

Out of this venomous milieu grew the National Socialist Party, of which Hitler quickly became the head. A central plank of his party was the placing of blame for Germany's defeat on the Jews. The Nazis charged the "wily Jews" with betrayal on the economic level of supply and the psychological level of propaganda. They accused them of undermining the people's will to win by their control of German money and media.[130]

With a hateful mob of malcontents as his base, Hitler vowed to fulfill two passionate desires: to replace the new German Republic with a militant, aristocratic state comprised of a super Aryan people, and to eradicate the "parasitic" Jewish race. He considered all Jews either Marxists or "Social Democrats," inasmuch as Karl Marx and Ferdinand LaSalle, the founders of Marxism, came from Jewish stock.[131] Even Lenin was thought at that time to be part Jewish.

Stressing his own brand of totalitarianism, Hitler complained that "the Jewish doctrine of Marxism rejects the aristocratic principle in nature." After making a cursory study of Jewish history, he sarcastically wondered whether "inscrutable destiny, for reasons unknown to us poor mortals, had not unalterably decreed the final victory of this little race?"[132] Scorning the notion, he wrote, "the greatest change I was ever to experience took place in me. . . . I had turned into a fanatical anti-Semite." Further, he asserted that "if, with the help of the Marxian creed, the Jew conquers the nations of this world, his crown will become the funeral wreath of humanity, and once again this planet, empty of mankind, will move through the ether as it did thousands of years ago."[133] Believing that social democracy led to anarchy, he boasted, "By warding off the Jews, I am fighting for the Lord's work."[134]

What brought on such fierce hatred? Many researchers have pondered the question. Germany had been a breeding ground of Judeophobia in the late 1800s, especially through the writings of Englishman Houston Stewart Chamberlain.[135] In 1882 the first international Anti-Semitic Congress was convened in Dresden, leaving its mark on the whole nation and embarrassing many by its irrationality.

HITLER'S PERSONAL EGOTISM

It's clear that Hitler's malice was not only racial and national but also deeply personal and psychological. In his book *Mein*

Kampf, Hitler describes clashes with his stubborn father over his future profession and displays the beginnings of his paranoia. His father wanted him to be an "official" (politician), while he insisted on becoming an artist (architect, for which he failed to qualify).[136] In school his two favorite subjects were geography and history, an interest furthered by Germany's unrest.

Racial tensions were high among the "mishmash" (Hitler's term) of Prussians, Austrians, Bavarians, Hungarians, and other ethnic groups in Germany. With his fiery temperament, young Adolf was drawn into the fray, becoming "a fanatical 'German nationalist.' "[137] Community debates spurred the development of his oratorical gifts. Passionate and hysterical rhetoric soon came to be his sharpest political weapon, and fierce nationalism his theme. "He to whom passion is denied and whose mouth remains closed is not chosen by Heaven as the prophet of its will," wrote this self-appointed prophet.[138] He thus became the "politician" his father had insisted he become.

Hitler's nationalism soon put him on a collision course with Marxists, whose movement was sweeping Europe. Marx declared that "everything is material and that change takes place through 'the struggle of opposites' " (thesis, antithesis, and synthesis).[139] Class struggle, Marxists claimed, inevitably resulted in history progressing toward a final uniformity. This equalization of all by economics was intended to eliminate social classes, especially the self-employed, middle-class bourgeoisie. Communism sought to speed up the process by revolution.

HITLER'S BOUT WITH BOLSHEVISM

Though Hitler agreed with the Marxists' materialistic, this-world view of life, he despised their "social democratic" conception of government. Whereas democracy emphasizes individual responsibility or representation through parliamentary procedures, Hitler insisted on a militant leadership that manipulated society for its own good.[140] Aggressive aristocracy brings stability, he asserted; democracy is cumbersome and panders to the whims of the masses. The masses need not be heard, but herded.

Hitler's primary foe was "Bolshevistic Judaism," as he called it (*bolshe* meaning "majority"). Such was the main bogeymen of *Mein Kampf.* Though he wrote the book as a propaganda tool (begun while in Landsberg prison in 1924), Hitler's scorn for the Jews developed gradually. Early in his life in Vienna, he debated fiercely with some Jews over Marxist doctrine.[141] In these disputes he seemed to have met his match in haranguing. Their skill left him speechless and baffled. "I talked until my tongue was weary and till my throat was hoarse. . . . Often I was stunned. . . . I gradually began to hate them."[142]

Humiliated by their superior dialectics and cool rejoinders, Hitler braced for battle. To outflank them and to confirm his own racial biases, he began a cursory study of Judaism. He even used Jesus' condemnation of the Pharisees in his argument, appealing also to Luther's anti–Semitism. He began to detect sinister Jewry behind all of society's problems, pointing to them as the hidden jokers who had secretly orchestrated Germany's defeat by the Allies. To Hitler, their refusal to assimilate into gentile cultures smacked of an international conspiracy. He believed they were covertly infiltrating all countries in order to build a kind of superstate, an "International Jewry." He was sure that, if left alone, they would eventually control all nations through a web of international banking and by manipulating labor and industry. Hitler saw the Jews as an international demon out to terrorize the globe.

HITLER'S "BAD BLOOD" JUDEOPHOBIA

But in time, this madman came to see the Jews as worse than a demon; soon he began to think of them as a "disease." A demon can be exorcised, but a disease must be purged. He saw them as a bleeding ulcer in a society whose Marxism was paralyzing the national body.[143] "Bad blood" became one of his favorite terms for denouncing the Jews. Quack eugenics darkens the pages of much of his writings, especially in his chapter in *Mein Kampf* on "Nation and Race." The progress of mankind, he asserted, depends on the purity of races, especially the purity of the Aryan race. Borrowing from Nietzsche's notion of the "survival of the fittest," Hitler pronounced the need to purge the "less fit"—meaning Jews and blacks. Who the Aryans (true Germans) were he was not sure, but he constantly distinguished them from the Jews.[144]

The irony is that Hitler's own heritage was anything but thoroughbred. His father, Alois, was born out of wedlock, and the true identity of his father was unknown. One of Hitler's most reliable biographers, Dr. Oskar Jetzinger, maintains that Adolf's grandfather was a "nineteen-year-old Jewish lad in whose family home Maria Anna Schickelgruber [his mother] had lived before the birth of her child. Adolf Hitler would then have been one-quarter Jewish."[145]

Such was this self-appointed architect who was out to purify the race. Though touting himself as a pious vegetarian, nondrinker, nonsmoker, and nonsexist out to purify his homeland, his own heritage was hardly the "pure stock" he claimed would "germinate" a super German race.

THE NAZI GANG AND ITS STRATEGY
The "Purification" of Germany

Plotting with this megalomaniac were other misfits and war victims such as Hermann Goering, Rudolph Hess, Gregor Strasser, Heinrich Himmler, and propagandist Josef Goebbels. Alfred Rosenberg, a fierce "non-Jewish Jew" from Moscow, served as his philosopher and party strategist. With worldwide expansionist goals, the Nazis' passion to "purify" Deutschland was not limited to expunging the Jews, but included communists and Christians as well. At that time, Christians were as vulnerable as Jews, having their roots in Judaism. In fact, "Hitler's aim was to eradicate all religious organizations within the state and to foster a return to paganism."[146] Eventually many of his own people, and even those who helped organize the party, became his hapless victims.

Such a massive eradication of "misfits," however, required more manpower than what the Nazi party chiefs and their storm troopers could provide. It called for a unified effort by the whole nation. To acquire that cooperation required a conversion (or reversion) of the people's traditional ethics and morals. It demanded also a violation of the much-lauded principles of "The French Declaration of the Rights of Man and of the Citizen" of 1789. Human dignity itself was at stake.

Ultimately, the Nazis knew they had to repress and silence the human conscience itself. As German historian Friedrich Meinecke wrote, "One half of the German people today [under Hitler] are educated to insolence and the other half to cowardice."[147] While that statement does injustice to the few Bonhoeffers who heroically led resistance drives, it speaks volumes of the general attitude that allowed the Holocaust to take place.

How did these butchers so successfully suppress the nation's conscience and realign its morals? It required a thorough reeducation of the people. For this Hitler relied mainly on Dr. Josef Goebbels, his Propaganda Minister. His primary tools were mass advertising and continual repetition of racist themes.[148] All approved activities and goals centered on the German State and its future, a patriotic focus that appealed to ego-oppressed Deutschland. The youth movement and military service were stressed, and such words as "blood," "honor," "fighting and dying for the Fatherland," and "loyalty to the Führer" were used to challenge and inspire recruits.[149] Motherhood laws were changed, and by "1940 the Nazi state had turned from legalized sterilization to legalized euthanasia or mercy-killing."[150]

Reeducation of the populace was essential if Hitler was to succeed. In fact, "Hitler's deepest hatred of Christianity . . . was directed toward . . . the idea inherent in Christianity of an independent conscience answerable only to God; the command to obey God rather than man and . . . to obey laws other than those proclaimed by National Socialism."[151] Such devotion to God and his laws would torpedo the kind of state the Nazis had in mind. To combat this "nonsense," they made the State supreme over the individual conscience, enforcing its philosophy through political intrigue, terrorism, and propaganda that flooded the country. The brainwashing they pursued was not merely of the mind, but of the collective conscience. Hitler came to see himself as the god and savior of his people.[152]

Though the initial targets of this demagogue were communists and Christians, Hitler's deepest passion, as Dimont points out, was to exterminate the Jews. Therefore, *Judenrein* ("Jewish purge") became a central doctrine of the party.[153] Inflamed by the old delusion of a Jewish "mafia" seeking international power, the Nazis came to regard Jewish extermination as the only cure for Germany's ills. This they called "the final solution." The ultimate irony is that "the Third Reich, which Hitler boasted would endure for a thousand years, perished after twelve. The Jews, whom Hitler boasted he would eradicate, survived to create a new, independent Jewish State."[154]

The Extermination Plan of Hitler and Eichmann

Hitler's demonic program of genocide was first fueled by Goebbels's pen in an incessant barrage of anti-Semitic propaganda. The propaganda minister (with "a rodent's face as well as a rodent's mind," as the U.S. Ambassador's daughter described him) controlled the press.[155] In January 1933, Hitler forged his way to the chancellorship of Germany—the same month Franklin Roosevelt became president of the United States. (Both also died in the same month twelve years later in April 1945.) Hitler came to power in a time of worldwide stress and economic depression. Everywhere, national saviors were eagerly sought. At the death of President Paul von Hindenburg, this evil ex-corporal assumed command, itemizing the nation's problems and pointing to a solution. That solution, of course, was already outlined in *Mein Kampf:* the Jewish "disease" infecting the nation called for radical surgery.

In Hitler's twelve-year rampage as Führer, five progressive stages of that surgery can be observed.[156] The first stage, beginning immediately when he took office, was designed to destroy all Jewish businesses in Germany. Thugs provoked, looted, and boycotted long-held Jewish businesses, forcing them into bankruptcy. At the same time, Jews were progressively barred from all public offices, educational institutions, bar associations, and the medical profession. These severe restrictions began to reduce all Jews to a starvation diet, rich and poor alike.

The second stage came in 1935 when the Nuremburg laws were passed, depriving all Jews of citizenship. Extreme reprisals were given for any agitation; every offense by a Jew was an excuse for brutal retaliation. When a Jewish exile in Paris, for instance, went berserk and killed a German embassy officer, the storm troopers responded in Germany by burning all six hundred Jewish synagogues and sacking nearly all remaining businesses.[157] In November 1938, Jews were forbidden to patronize any theater or public amusement place, and Jewish children were barred from all German schools. A month later Heinrich Himmler, chief of the German police, revoked the driver's licenses of all German Jews, and forbade them to own any kind of motor vehicle.[158]

The third stage began with a mass arrest of Jews in September 1939 at the outbreak of war. Jews were required to wear the "Badge of Shame," a yellow Star of David, to distinguish them from non-Jews. For those still allowed to migrate, the ransom price was the surrender of all possessions. The spoils from this pillage were immense for the Reich. By 1939, only two hundred thousand of the five hundred thousand Jews living in Germany six years earlier still remained.

The fourth stage came in 1940 when all Jews were incarcerated in concentration camps. At the same time, Jews in Germany and Austria began to be deported to specially prepared ghettos in newly-conquered Poland. The doomed were robbed of all they had and herded into large corrals, where they joined two-and-a-half million Jews from Poland. Their lot was to be "annihilated by disease, starvation, execution, or suicide."[159] This roundup was later extended to all parts of German-occupied Europe. Nazis hauled Jews in from Austria, Czechoslovakia, Hungary, Poland, Romania, France, Holland, Switzerland, Belgium, Northern Italy, Yugoslavia, Denmark, and Norway, with only a few outstanding exceptions. To this point, Hitler's strategy was to deprive, segregate, and starve the Jews, not to commit systematized murder.

The chilling thing is that the populace of many of these countries willingly collaborated with the Germans; it would have been impossible without their cooperation. And why did the outside world protest so feebly? It's well documented that those abroad knew of what was happening to the Jews.[160] And to be sure, many heroic individuals in occupied countries carried out courageous underground rescues. These include individuals such as Dietrich Bonhoeffer, who was executed April 9, 1945; Corrie Ten Boom of *The Hiding Place* fame in Holland; and Oskar Schindler, whose exploits were documented in the award-winning film *Schindler's List*. Few, however, were willing to defy the Gestapo, whose furious reprisals were well known.

The "Final Solution"

The fifth and final stage of this madness was called the "final solution" and was initiated by Nazi leadership in 1942. The purpose of the concentration camps changed from detention to extermination, and murder became a full-time German occupation. Adolf Eichmann was in charge of the liquidation, engineering the entire operation and, on occasion, even bartering captive Jews for needed goods.[161] Though most victims were transported to concentration camps in Germany and Poland, millions were gunned down by special extermination squads. The *Einsatzgruppen* ("deployment groups") consisted of approximately three thousand men who traveled with the German armed forces as they advanced. Max Dimont describes their brutality:

> Their procedure for mass murder was as follows: Jews or Czechs, or Poles, or Russians were rounded up, marched to a deserted area, and forced to dig pits or trenches, after which they were forced to undress, lined up in front of the trenches, and machine-gunned. Those that fell along the edges, dead and wounded, were shoveled by soldiers or bulldozers into the pits, and dirt was thrown over all, the dead and the living, the adults, the children, and the infants. Altogether, the Einsatzgruppen were responsible for the murder of several million Christians and a million Jews.[162]

The murderers soon found this process of individual slaughter too slow and laborious. By chemical experimentation they developed a gas known as Zyklon-B that could kill thousands in minutes. The old concentration camps were modernized to make the operation more efficient and new train spurs and cars were constructed to transport masses of captive Jews from Eastern Europe directly to the "bakeries," as the death camps were called. Gas chambers were constructed as shower rooms so unsuspecting victims would not resist. James Korting explains the technique:

> Some of the condemned had been putting up too great a struggle before their death, and this wasted time, so far as the Nazis were concerned. In one refined technique, those who were to be killed were told to undress, were given a towel, and were led to what appeared to be a large shower room. Then the doors were sealed, making

the room airtight, and poison gas, not water, was sprayed into the chamber. After the victims were dead and the fumes had been drawn off, prison dentists were sent into the gas chambers to take out the gold fillings and to cut the long hair off the female corpses—the hair could be utilized for other purposes, and the gold fillings were too valuable to be put in the ovens where the corpses were disposed of. [163]

The main death camps were located in Germany, Poland, Austria, and Czechoslovakia. The memorial at Yad Vashem lists twenty-two of the largest camps, names known in infamy: Auschwitz, Buchenwald, Dachau, Mauthausen, and Treblinka. The largest was Auschwitz in Poland, where over three million were murdered.[164] Richard Gade describes the tragic scene that met Allied eyes when soldiers broke through to stop the butchery:

> The aftermath of the war found the victorious armies of the Allied Powers walking through a world that defied description. In the vaults of German banks lay gold smelted from human teeth; in her hotels, mattresses stuffed with human hair; in her shops, gloves fashioned from human skin. Mortar pink with the tint of human blood, trains laden with the dead and dying, corpses piled like lumber in the camps, vast graves of a once great and proud people overrun with rats—all of Germany was a vast slaughterhouse. [165]

So important was this carnage to Nazi leaders that it was given an even higher priority than that of the war effort itself.[166] Although the Nazi cause was clearly lost by early 1945, the gas chambers and furnaces were kept running full blast. As Finkelstein remarks, "The actual annihilation of the Jewish population was one of the main ideological and military objectives of the German Nazified war machine. And this objective was to a large extent achieved."[167]

No savagery in all recorded history remotely approaches that of this Nazi slaughter. Never before had the world witnessed an orgy so coldly calculated and wholesale, perpetrated on the innocent and helpless. All of Europe had been bludgeoned and charred by the Nazi machine. Dimont summarizes the enormity of the bloodbath:

> From that first day in power . . . the Germans exterminated with systematized murder twelve million men,

women, and children, in concentration camps, by firing squads, and in gas chambers—1.4 Christians for every Jew. But because the Nazis shouted, "Kill the Jews," the world blinded itself to the murder of Christians. . . . World War II represents the biggest killing spree in the history of man. . . . In six years of war, 17,000,000 able-bodied men of military age were killed in battle; 18,000,000 civilians were killed as a direct result of war; and an additional 12,000,000 people were murdered by the Nazis. The Germans, who in 1933 had jubilantly "heiled" their Führer, could now mournfully count their dead: 3,250,000 battle deaths; 3,350,000 civilian dead, and some 5,000,000 wounded. [168]

The scene defies comparison, seeming more reminiscent of pages from Dante or Milton than to our "civilized" world just yesterday. But lest its truth be denied and its lessons be lost, two world-famous trials were held in its aftermath to scrutinize, validate, and document the records. These were the International Tribunal of Nuremberg in 1946, and the Israeli trial of Adolf Eichmann in 1961 and 1962. Here the personal diaries of Himmler, Goebbels, Eichmann, and other participants in the tragedy grimly verified the facts.

Yad Vashem: Hall of Remembrance

As time passes, some have questioned whether the Holocaust really happened, insisting the stories are nothing more than wild propaganda designed to generate sympathy for the Jews.[169] Recognizing the inconceivable nature of those events, the Israeli Knesset in 1953 established a center in Jerusalem to commemorate the Holocaust. Located on Memorial Hill (next to Mt. Herzl, Israel's national military cemetary), this complex is called *Yad Vashem* (in Hebrew "a memorial and a name," taken from Isaiah 56:5). There in the Hall of Remembrance, as well as the museum and the library, is preserved incontestable documentation of that human tragedy. The display includes Nazi diaries, photographs of the death camps, scores of personal testimonies, and records of the Nuremburg and Eichmann trials. The statistical records of the Holocaust are also displayed, listing the before and after Jewish populations in the European countries where the slaughter took place.

Look at the following census figures on Jewish populations during the twentieth century. Compiled by *Judaica Encyclopedia*, these figures reflect Jewish casualties and migrations before and during the Holocaust:

World Redistribution of Jewish Population*

Country	1900	1939	1948	1967
Palestine	78,000	475,000	750,000	2,436,000
Europe:	8,690,000	9,480,000	3,780,000	4,070,000
Czechoslovakia	—	357,000	42,000	15,000
Germany	520,000	504,000	153,000	30,000
Hungary	—	445,000	174,000	80,000
Poland (Part of Russia)	—	3,351,000	88,000	21,000
Romania	267,000	850,000	380,000	100,000
Russia	5,190,000	3,100,000	2,200,000	2,650,000
Turkey	300,000	30,000	80,000	39,000
Africa	300,000	627,000	745,000	196,000
Americas:				
Argentina	30,000	275,000	360,000	500,000
Canada	16,000	155,700	180,000	280,000
U.S.	1,000,000	4,975,000	5,000,000	5,870,000

Distribution of Jewish Victims of Holocaust

Austria	65,000	Hungary	402,000
Belgium	24,000	Italy	7,500
Czechoslovakia	277,000	Luxembourg	700
France	83,000	Norway	760
Germany	125,000	Polish-Soviet	4,565,000
Greece	65,000	Romania	40,000
Holland	106,000	Yugoslavia	60,000

Total Jewish Victims   **5,820,000**

*Finkelstein, *The Jews, Their History,* 1534; cf. Sachar, *History of Israel,* 249.

The purpose of Yad Vashem is not to shame the perpetrators, but to memorialize for Israel's children and the world the price paid for Jewish freedom and the need for eternal vigilance to preserve it.

These cold statistics tell only part of the story. As the Allies closed in on Berlin in March 1945, the hysterical Führer ordered a scorched-earth policy for the destruction of Germany.[170] Though Albert Speer revoked the order after Hitler's suicide, much of the country was left in ruins.

To its credit, Germany responded to the shock of a second military defeat and the enforced repentance process by implementing a turn-around that led to sanity and spiritual recovery. The rule of law and order in accord with liberated human conscience was again established. And in a dramatic and climactic way, the world saw the rigor of God's law of inexorable justice enforced. The demonic tools of genocide were obliterated. Hitler ordered Goering and Himmler to be shot for treason, and Goebbels, his wife, and their six daughters took their lives with poison the same night.[171] Their bodies were burned in the courtyard—a fitting climax to Hitler's bizarre and nightmarish rule of twelve years. Hitler and his new bride, Eva Braun, committed suicide as well, she with poison and he with a shot in the mouth. Adolf Hitler and his Nazi stooges became their own executioners in a fit of maniacal hysteria.[172]

New Centers of Jewish Population

The Holocaust did more than snuff out the lives of millions of Jews; it also rearranged the centers of Jewish population throughout the world toward the West. Whereas Eastern Europe, especially Poland, had been the most populous center of Jewish life for nearly seven centuries, that population center moved to America, where the majority of Jews now live.

In the "melting pot" of America, Jews have tended to assimilate into the gentile culture. In this sense, they have become casualties to the Zionist cause, whose purpose is to arouse a nucleus of Jews worldwide to return to Israel and revive the Hebrew culture, faith, and nation.

While the Holocaust nearly crushed that purpose, it also gave Zionism an unprecedented stimulus. But was it enough to bring about the long awaited return to the land? Very quickly those Jews who survived were to discover that even the world's horror over the genocide of the Holocaust did not guarantee them a homestead in their Promised Land.

CHAPTER 7

The Tattered Remnant and the New State of Israel

IN THE AFTERMATH of the Holocaust, reason might suppose that a welcome mat would be out for the tattered Jewish remnant. Nearly a half million Jews waited in refugee camps, seeking a place of settlement. To return to their homes and neighborhoods in Europe was the last thing they wanted to do. Many, in fact, felt safer cooped up behind barbed wire in the camps than exposed to the defeated Germans.[173] Thousands desired to settle in Palestine, the land of their forbearers—to forget the past and start life anew. Some chose to emigrate to the United States only "if that means I shall reach Palestine sooner."[174]

When international teams of investigators confirmed the horrors of the Holocaust, most of the Western world agreed that immediate measures should be taken to open the door to Palestine. Even the British Labour Party agreed. With "regard to the unspeakable horrors that have been perpetrated upon the Jews in Germany and other occupied countries in Europe," it said, "it is morally wrong and politically indefensible to impose obstacles to the entry into Palestine now of Jews who desire to go there. . . ."[175] It furthermore proposed that the American, Soviet, and British governments should "see whether we cannot get that common support for a policy which will give us a happy, free, and a prosperous State in Palestine."[176]

This almost universal outburst of sympathy, however, was not matched with effective action. As Finkelstein notes, "The European refugees who fervently dreamed of escaping the Vale of Tears, of leaving the unholy earth saturated with Jewish blood, faced closed gates in the countries richest in land. . . . The gates of the historic homeland, the object of Jewish dreams for two thousand years, were barred even tighter in the very years of greatest despair."[177]

How can such a contradiction be explained? What happened in the postwar world to make the heart and hand of world sympathy contradict each other?

CHANGES IN POST-WORLD WAR II POLITICS

Even before the war ended, a significant shift occurred through the British elections of July 1945. At this time, Britain still had the League of Nations' Mandate to control Palestine. During the war Prime Minister Churchill had been strongly supportive of Zionism and gave Weizmann his word that after the war a State of Israel would be set up in Palestine with three to four million Jews.[178] That was the view of both the Labour and Tory parties in their electioneering campaigns.

But in 1945 Churchill's coalition was voted out of office in a landslide.[179] This ouster was produced as a result of Britain's severe economic setbacks during the war and its shrinking world empire. The Labour party of Clement Atlee took over with high expectations from everyone—including the Zionists.

Despite candidate Atlee's pro-Zionist stance, however, his new administration soon reversed itself on the Palestine issue. Ernest Bevin was made Foreign Secretary and thus became czar of the Middle East and its problems. Though a sharp statesman who was keenly perceptive of growing Soviet power, he did not share the pro-Zionist sympathies of his colleagues and the former administration. "Bevin repudiated all the pledges that had been made officially and unofficially by Labour speakers for the last ten years, some of which may have helped the Party win the election."[180]

Several changes made this reversal of policy the politically prudent course for the new foreign secretary. The Arab world was gaining prestige and becoming a factor to be reckoned with. It had just added several independent states to its number, and its oil power was claiming international respect. In juggling interests in the Middle East, Bevin tended to favor the Arabs and downplay the rights of Jews. He did this partly in reaction to Zionist pressure stemming from the needs created by the Holocaust.[181] Worldwide sympathy was with the Jews, especially in the United States, which strongly urged international redress for the victims.[182] This irked Bevin, who was engrossed in settling the squabbles of the Mideast and the growing turmoil in India. Thus the key agent in Britain for dealing with Palestine gradually came to fiercely oppose the creation of a Jewish state in the troubled area.

Another factor contributing to this problem was the continuing repercussions of the MacDonald "White Paper" of 1939, an anti-Jewish document that continued to be in effect throughout the war. Designed to mollify the Arabs, this paper had, in fact, reduced Jewish immigration to Palestine to a trickle and intended to cut it off entirely. Had the White Paper been fully carried out, the hard-won advantages guaranteed the Jews in the Balfour Declaration would have been nullified.

Arabs responded to this British reversal by increasing their opposition to Jewish immigration. They saw Weizmann and his Zionist agents as exploiting the Holocaust to establish a Jewish state in Palestine through homesteading. Encouraged by Bevin, they boldly demanded that all Jewish immigration be stopped and a new Arab State be set up in Palestine.[183]

The irony is that many Arab leaders had failed to support the Allies in World War II. They remained carefully neutral until the final months when Allied victory was assured. The Palestinian leader (ex-Mufti Haj Amin al-Husseini), in fact, defected to Iraq before the war and later joined Hitler and Eichmann in Germany in their butchery of Jews.[184] Many Arabs saw their fortunes with the Axis powers: Italy, Germany, and Japan. Thus they hardly deserved to join the victors in dividing the spoils. Yet the Arab states were shown amazing respect by the Allied powers in the postwar era; in fact, seven seats were given them in the United Nations Assembly. The Jews, of course, received none, having no nation at the time.

The political changes in Britain after the war left the Zionist cause in jeopardy. The new caretakers of the Mandate seemed to summarily dismiss the advantages gained in two world wars. At a time when their help was most needed, Zionism's British patrons were put out of office.

THE ZEAL OF PRESIDENT HARRY TRUMAN

Half a world away, however, another change in Zionist fortunes was taking place. On April 12, 1945, United States President Franklin D. Roosevelt died in office, three months after his fourth inauguration and less than a month before the Axis powers surrendered in Europe. Zionists had made many appeals to this long-term president but found him lukewarm. He followed a policy of action "which did not fully commit him to either side in the dispute."[185] As David Niles, the president's assistant, remarked, "There is serious doubt in my mind that Israel would have come into being if Roosevelt had lived."[186]

Succeeding him as president was the little-known vice president, Harry Truman, a total novice in foreign affairs. Truman was known as a "poker-playing Southern Baptist from Missouri," plucked from the backwoods to serve in the nation's highest offices. In sharp contrast to his sophisticated, Harvard-trained predecessor, the new president was largely self-educated and Bible-trained with respect to Jewish claims in Palestine.[187] Fiercely independent, Truman developed a sharp distaste for the "striped-pants" officials of the State Department, but was greatly influenced by Clark Clifford, his special counsel on Palestine.[188] As he grew in the office and was forced at critical times to make quick decisions that often had to be retracted, the Washington papers cynically punned, "To err is Truman."

On many issues, however, this hayseed president was right on target. Endowed with strong moral convictions concerning the oppressed and mistreated, and determined to expedite justice, Truman moved decisively to get action on the Jewish refugee question at the Potsdam Conference in July 1945.[189] To both Churchill and Atlee he emphasized the urgent need to get quick relief to the victims. More specifically, he put pressure on Britain to immediately admit one hundred thousand refugees into Palestine, promising U.S. aid to finance the operation.[190] This the Atlee government summarily refused.

Truman's action, however, served notice to the world of a new source of Zionist support. The land discovered by Columbus with Jewish help (when Spain expelled its Jews in 1492), had now become the center of world Jewry and the postwar power center of the world. If Zionism's support in Britain was slipping, it was gaining another champion in an impetuous son of Missouri who suddenly found himself leader of the Free World. In taking a Zionist position, Truman had the strong support of Congress and the American people.[191]

Though the question of Jewish statehood in Palestine was not in the forefront of Truman's mind as he endorsed immigration, it was the primary Zionist aim. The president's intentions were basically humanitarian. In fact, he resented the politicking of the British and Zionists because it tended to complicate the movement of refugees. His concern was for those crowded into filthy camps in Europe, for "by the end of 1946, more than a quarter of a million Jews were packed into the displaced persons' camps of Western Germany."[192] Instead of the hundred thousand refugees he asked the British to allow into Palestine, only fifteen hundred a month were permitted—just what the MacDonald "White Paper" had stipulated. Several committees were formed to resolve the issue, but none were able to reach an agreement. In the process, the Atlee-Bevin government of Britain became more and more adamant in rejecting the Zionists' demand for immigration.

THE JEWISH RESISTANCE MOVEMENT

This British foot-dragging led to one of the darkest periods of the postwar era. Many Zionists began to recognize that a political solution was not forthcoming, and they saw the need for military action. They concluded that if the British were impressed "on the assumption of Arab strength, then Britain must be equally impressed by Jewish strength."[193] Thus, with the help of the worldwide Jewish Agency, the *Haganah* (an underground Jewish paramilitary group) began serious covert operations. It started using every means, legal or illegal, to promote immigration to Palestine.

The Haganah set up its European headquarters in France, where it received much help from the populace. The French were piqued at the British after the war, having been maneuvered out of the Levant and treated as a lesser ally. Thus "frontier crossings were arranged, transit stations established, housing, food, and clothing secured, ships purchased and repaired in French Riviera ports."[194] Out of resentment of British occupation forces, the Italian government, too, showed sympathy to this underground operation. With such help, an ongoing battle of wits began to be continually waged between Jewish agents and British intelligence. Zionists sought to filter displaced persons through various ports in Europe. Many obsolete ships were repaired and secretly loaded with refugees from French and Italian ports, setting sail for the shores of Palestine.

Some of these efforts were successful, but most were not. The British put a tight naval blockade along the coast of Palestine and sent eighty thousand troops to patrol the country. Those who were caught were either sent back to Europe or put in barbed-wire internment camps on the Island of Cyprus. Of the sixty-three refugee ships that started out, only five actually slipped through the blockade; some were even fired on while landing. One Haganah ship, the *Exodus 1947*, was rammed by the British, forcing forty-three hundred survivors of Hitler's inferno to board other ships and return to France. They were finally sent back to Germany. In the end, the affair turned into a fiasco for Britain, incurring the wrath of the world media.[195] None of this conniving actually did much for Jewish immigration, but it did turn world opinion against the merciless policies of Bevin.

Meanwhile, the *Yishuv* in Palestine stepped up their operations against the British. Although Weizmann and Ben-Gurion denounced terrorism, Zionist leadership often gave tacit approval where extreme acts were not involved. The main Jewish terrorist groups were the *Irgun* and the *Stern Group*.[196] These groups focused on promoting illegal immigration and on terrorizing the British who denounced it.

A key leader of the Irgun was Menachem Begin. Another Polish Jew, Begin had escaped a Siberian labor camp in 1943 and made his way to Palestine to join the Irgun. The Irgun could be ruthless, and they engaged in much conspiracy and marauding to sabotage the British and dramatize Jewish resistance. Though strongly reprimanded by Ben-Gurion, they intensified their attacks on military transports, destroyed vehicles, paralyzed railroad traffic, and even killed British personnel.[197]

By early 1947, the combined terrorism of Arab and Jewish extremists made order and security in Palestine almost impossible. The British sent in a force of nearly one hundred thousand troops and local police, a huge expense when British coffers were going empty. Tense conditions transformed the land almost into another war zone. Nonmilitary personnel were evacuated or sealed off in security zones.

It was becoming more and more evident that Britain's anti-Zionist policy was bankrupt and that a new approach was needed. The fault lay primarily with "Bevin's agonized intransigence on the immigration issue, provoking maximal Zionist demands for Jewish statehood." This "ignited the terrorism, launched the illegal refugee traffic to Palestine, undermined Britain's economy, eroded its international reputation, and finally doomed the Palestine Mandate itself."[198] The Atlee–Bevin government came to see how impossible it was to carry out the British Mandate with conflicting policies. Bevin finally used the British withdrawal from India to ease the humiliation of his nation's exit from the Levant because it appeared to fit with the new policy of consolidation by the British Empire.[199]

THE PARTITIONING OF PALESTINE
The United Nations' Decision

Acknowledging a deadlock on the issue, the British cabinet announced on April 2, 1947, that it was referring the Palestine problem to the United Nations General Assembly. This body set up an eleven-nation investigative board (UNSCOP) to devise a plan of action. Its recommendation after several months of review was to endorse the principle of independence for both sides, but it was divided as to whom should control what. The majority voted for "partitioning" Palestine, advocating three divisions, an Arab state, a Jewish state, and an internationalized zone in the Jerusalem area (see Map 4).[200]

Map 4: UN Partition of Palestine, 1947

Jerusalem to be under international control

Jewish State
Arab State

Though this wasn't quite what the Zionists had hoped for, they saw it as a way to get a solid foot in the door to Jewish statehood. Independent statehood, of course, was their ultimate goal. Achieving that would allow for unlimited immigration and provide the political base necessary to pursue their other goals. Therefore, the Jews gave cautious support to the UNSCOP recommendation of partitioning.

The Arabs unequivocally rejected it, perceiving it as another step toward Zionist expansionism. To maintain good relations with the Arab League, Britain also rejected the plan. Joining them, the United States State Department under Secretary of State George Marshall cautioned against the plan. Marshall feared it would be unworkable, leading to bloody clashes in the area.

Events in the coming months seemed to turn things around. In May 1947, the Soviet delegation surprised everyone by endorsing partitioning. Then in October, as the Arab League began a troop buildup in Palestine, President Truman—under pressure from American Zionists—chose to part company with Marshall on the issue. He accused his State Department of having an Arabic mentality. "Like most of the British diplomats," he quipped, "some of our diplomats also thought that the Arabs, on account of their numbers and because of the fact that they controlled such immense oil resources, should be appeased. I am sorry to say that there were some among them who were inclined to be anti-Semitic."[201] He then instructed the State Department to support the United Nations plan of partitioning Palestine.[202]

Thus, despite last-minute jockeying and Arab threats of war and reprisals, the General Assembly of the United Nations voted on November 29, 1947, to support partitioning. The vote was thirty-three to thirteen—mainly the Western bloc against the Muslim and Asian blocs. Eleven nations abstained, including Britain. The partitioning was to be implemented at the termination of the British Mandate on May 14, 1948.

The plan was to partition the land into three sections: forty-five hundred square miles to the Arab state, fifty-five hundred to the Jewish state, and Jerusalem set off as an internationalized island in the midst of the Arab portion. Many Palestinians, of course, were already in Transjordan. The Jews would have the eastern Galilee region with the Sea of Galilee, the coastal plain from Acre and Haifa to south of Tel Aviv, and the southern Negev. The Arab state would have the large central section of Samaria and Judea, northwestern Galilee, and the Gaza Strip.[203] This division would put a majority of Jews and Arabs in their respective states and allow for a large immigration of displaced Jews from Europe.

The United Nations expected Britain and the two new states to cooperate in making the transition, but those hopes were quickly dashed. The British, in fact, refused to allow the United Nations commission even to visit Palestine before May 1, 1948, fearing that pending negotiations with Egypt might be affected. They also reasoned that a quick military triumph by the Arab League was inevitable, making it more prudent to curry the Arabs' good will. Britain's top generals argued that the armies of the Arab League "would have no difficulty in taking over the whole country."[204] The British made no attempt to disguise their partiality toward the Arab cause in Palestine.

The Arab Response

Arabs responded to the Partition Resolution by carrying out their oft-repeated threats. Jewish homes and synagogues in the major cities were immediately attacked while the British stood by. Calls went out for all available forces from the Arab States to mobilize for war. Arabs saw the British withdrawal as an opportunity to drive out the Jews and settle the immigration question once and for all.

However, internal squabbles seemed to complicate things within the Arab community. The Grand Mufti moved from Cairo to Lebanon to take charge of the Palestinian operation. This move angered King Abdullah of Transjordan and other Arab members, who saw the Mufti as incompetent, though useful.[205] That rivalry became more noticeable as the Arabs prepared for combat. Syrian general Sir Ismail Pasha was appointed commander in chief of the "Arab Liberation Army," with headquarters near Damascus. His field commander was ex-Nazi Fawzi al-Qawukji, headquartered at Tiberias. But the Mufti disliked Qawukji and sought control of the Arab forces himself, putting his nephew in charge of central Palestine.[206] On May 14, King Abdullah appointed himself commander in chief by virtue of his legion's superior power.[207]

This disunity heightened as the deadline of the Mandate approached. While King Farouk of Egypt insisted that a separate Arab country be established in the area between the Jordan River and the Mediterranean Sea, Abdullah "retorted that Palestine and Transjordan were one, for 'Palestine was the coastland and Transjordan the hinterland of the same country.' They served notice on the league that Abdullah regarded Palestine as his domain."[208]

"To me," said Abdullah, "has fallen the honour to save Palestine." He had long expressed his hope of extending his kingdom to include Syria as well as Transjordan, and this withdrawal of the British presented him a golden opportunity.

When Abdullah did assume the role of supreme commander of the invasion forces, he found himself inundated with ego problems among his peers. At a famous meeting with future Israeli Prime Minister Golda Meir in November 1947, the two "agreed that the Mufti was their common enemy."[209] When she later disguised herself as an Arab to cross enemy lines and meet him on May 10, 1948, she found Abdullah depressed, fearing defeat, and on the verge of a nervous breakdown.[210] With this lack of leadership, Arab coordination was virtually nonexistent.

Despite this disorganization, however, Arab attacks on Jewish posts continued unabated. Even as their organization was obviously in disarray, the Arab League was itchy and anxious for battle.

The Jewish Response

The Haganah also responded feverishly, preparing for a life-and-death struggle. Unlike the Arabs, the Jews' great advantage was unity. Most significant, however, was their determination to seize this one opportunity to create the State of Israel as a haven for the Jewish people. Having gained experience in many local skirmishes, the Haganah had learned to take the initiative, first by quick mobilization and then by sharp reprisals. Armored cars were organized to escort convoys and to maintain communications, and the whole community was put on emergency alert.

Though guerrilla forces of roving Arab bands cut the route to Jerusalem, the Jews soon reopened it at the cost of more than one hundred lives. Tension mounted as the time for the British withdrawal approached. The Haganah's early military successes in countering Arab offenses built high morale as it prepared with meager forces to take on the vaunted Arab Legion. In the words of Golda Meir, "We have always said that in our war with the Arabs we had a secret weapon—no alternative."[211]

The Birth of a Nation, May 14, 1948

In the late afternoon of May 14, 1948 (the Jewish year 5708), the British kept their word and hauled down the Union Jack, leaving the warring cousins to fight out their differences. With the failure of all avenues of diplomacy, the outcome was left to mutual bloodletting.

Abandoned to this, Israel that afternoon proclaimed its independence and raised its newly designed flag featuring the Star of David. The gauntlet had been thrown. If this was an invitation to another round of genocide, so be it.

The proclamation was made by David Ben-Gurion, who was soon to be elected Israel's first prime minister. Beside him at that Tel Aviv ceremony stood Chaim Weizmann, who would also shortly be elected first president of the new republic. Both were immigrants from Polish Russia (as were many of the succeeding presidents and prime ministers).[212]

Within minutes, President Truman issued a statement extending *de facto* recognition to Israel as a sovereign state. The action did not come easily, being vigorously opposed by Secretary of State Marshall until the last minute. Marshall worried about "the oil in the area, our relationship with the Arabs, our ability to keep peace."[213] Truman's special counsel, Clark Clifford, however, had convinced both Bob Lovett and the secretary the day before, enabling the president to extend recognition with the full blessing of the State Department. This paved the way for Israel's international recognition by the world. Guatemala, Soviet Russia, and many other nations—even Britain—quickly followed the lead of Truman.

Many commentators believe this courageous action by Truman received the smile of heaven. That fall, Truman ran for reelection against the highly favored Republican governor of New York, Tom Dewey. Contrary to all expectation, the doughty "Missouri mule" astounded the country and world by his victory. Truman later referred to himself as "Cyrus," the biblical Gentile who in Persian times had assisted the postexilic remnant in returning from dispersion.[214] He thoroughly enjoyed fulfilling such a role for modern Israel. In turn, the grateful nation practically adopted Harry Truman as one of its own, naming forests and monuments after him.

Israel's War of Independence

The day of Israel's rebirth brought jubilation to Jews worldwide. It was, in fact, a Sabbath eve, symbolic of a coming Sabbath rest. In New York, London, Rome, Paris, and many other cities, the new flag of Israel was unfurled by those rejoicing that the "wandering Jews" at last had regained their homeland.

In Israel itself, however, there was little time for Sabbath rest or celebration. Before the day ended, Egyptian planes were already bombing Tel Aviv. Most of the Arab states sent men and matériel to the attack, including Syria, Transjordan, Lebanon, Egypt, Yemen, Iraq, and Saudi Arabia. Additional forces came from North African states.[215] Long before the British left, the armed forces and artillery of the Arabs had been moved into strategic positions. Jerusalem was again completely surrounded, threatened with isolation from the west. The Arab attack came from all sides. Their leaders were confident that their sheer numbers and superior armament would quickly overwhelm the ill-equipped Jews.[216] Their plan was to take Palestine's key cities within a few weeks and then quickly "drive the Jews into the sea."

That expectation of a smashing victory was shared by nearly the whole world. From a statistical standpoint, an easy triumph was practically a given: the Arabs' overwhelming power came from seven nations with a combined population of more than 140 million people; the Jewish remnant they opposed totaled only 650,000 in all Palestine, with no promise of backing from other nations; the Arab Legion of Transjordan was "financed and officered by the British";[217] the West had placed an embargo on all sales of arms to the area in a pretense of neutrality. The only question the world had to ponder was how long it would take to sweep the tattered Holocaust survivors into the sea.

The mistake the world made, however, was to underestimate the Jewish will to win. Imbued with a sense of divine destiny and Maccabean courage, they fought like David taking on Goliath. And against overwhelming odds, they persevered. Short of everything, the Jews' greatest shortage was in arms and ammunition; in the early stages, troops often shared one rifle to two men.[218] Under Ben-Gurion's leadership, the Jewish operation was commanded by Yigael Yadin, a thirty-year-old student of archaeology in civilian life who was also a brilliant military strategist. His total force, as the battle began on May 15, was thirty thousand men and women.[219]

Multiple detachments of Arabs on four fronts were arrayed against Israel. Transjordan's Arab Legion concentrated on Jerusalem, its corridor to the west, and the Haifa region in the northwest; Syria and Lebanon moved into Galilee in the north; the Iraqi army and other Syrian units struck at the Jordan Valley; and Egypt attacked the Sinai and Gaza Strip in the south with two brigades.

At the first Arab onslaught, the Jewish defenders fell back on nearly all fronts. But they soon dug in and solidified their positions, gained their equilibrium, and countered with improvised weapons. In the agonizing weeks that followed, ground was recovered and the tables began to turn. The world watched in unbelief as this ragtag army stopped its attackers on most fronts and gradually took the offensive against superior mechanized forces. The fiercest battles took place at Jerusalem and Tel Aviv, where casualties were heavy. Some strongholds of kibbutzim and villages changed hands several times. The Jewish command capitalized on bluff and surprise to demoralize the invaders. Tel Aviv was effectively blockaded against the Egyptians, and the west section of Jerusalem was defended against the intense artillery and mortar attacks of Transjordan.

Calls for a Truce
On June 11, with both sides exhausted, a truce was called for through United Nations mediator Count Folke Bernadotte of Sweden. It was

Map 5: Israel's Borders Following War of Independence, 1948

intended to last one month. Though the Arab military counsel was inclined to call it quits right then, as was Egypt, the Arab League Political Committee vowed to continue the battle to save face. Both sides used the break to bring in new recruits and equipment, despite the ban imposed by the United Nations on additional weapons. During this breather Israel was greatly strengthened with incoming quantities of European and American equipment, which bolstered and transformed its army into a "modern fighting force."[220]

Before the truce ended, however, Egypt renewed its assault, followed quickly by allies. Israel responded with several sledgehammer blows, launching its new air force not only to defend the cities, but also to bomb Cairo, Damascus, and Amman. Colonel Moshe Dayan's forces routed the Egyptians attacking the Lydda airport with newly acquired mechanized equipment. On all fronts Israeli troops went on the offensive, gaining ground both in the north and south. "Nazareth in the north was captured, and ultimately all Galilee was in Jewish hands. The Arabs were on the run, and only the quick intervention of the British delegates in the Security Council, which brought about a second truce, saved the Arabs. A few more days and not only would the old city of Jerusalem have been captured, but the Legion would almost certainly have been driven right back across the Jordan."[221] This second truce was called by the Security Council on July 18.

Fighting broke out again in October, at which time Israel captured Beersheba. By December, the "battle-seasoned Israelis, supported by armor and fighter planes, were driving into Egypt, to the very gates of al-Arish, cutting the last exit routes of the Egyptian expeditionary force. Reeling from these blows, meanwhile, Cairo undertook feverish diplomatic activity to seek military assistance from other Arab states. It was a doomed effort. The Syrians and Iraqis were exhausted. Abdullah considered the war over for his kingdom."[222]

The threat of Israel taking the war into Egypt brought a warning from Britain, prompting Jewish troops to withdraw to the Negev. The Egyptians then sued for peace through the new United Nations mediator, Ralph Bunche, refusing direct negotiations with Israel except through the Security Council. On February 24, 1949, an armistice was signed with Egypt. Each of the other aggressors followed suit in the next few months, with the exception of Iraq. In May of the following year, the new nation of Israel was accepted into the United Nations, recognized as an independent, sovereign nation.

Counting the Cost of Independence
Though this war was costly and wreaked havoc on the young nation, it also brought many benefits. Not only did it establish Israel's sover-

eignty, it also demonstrated its ability to defend itself against all aggressors and asserted its presence in the Middle East. It allowed Israel to enlarge its territory considerably beyond what had already been received in the partitioning (see Map 5). The UN plan had assigned Israel 5,500 square miles, but the spoils of war added additional territory, which gave Israel a total of 8,050 of the total 10,400 square miles in Palestine.[223]

On the Arab side of the ledger, the only one to gain by the war was King Abdullah of Transjordan. He acquired 2,350 square miles in the West Bank, plus some 750,000Palestinians.[224] That, however, was small consolation for a king who had hoped to take Haifa harbor as his trade outlet and the undivided city of Jerusalem as his religious prize. The Palestinian state that the United Nations had projected alongside Israel never came into existence. And the coveted prize Abdullah received was the problems of the Palestinian refugees of the West Bank. Farouk and the Egyptians gained the problems of the Gaza Strip.

Having vowed to shove Israel into the sea, the Arabs wound up shoving themselves into a corner, humiliated by a people they despised. For the Arab psyche it was an intolerable blow—one that demanded redress.

Israel, however, was not gloating, for the victory came at great cost. With six thousand dead and many more wounded, with scorched fields and a gutted economy, it would be a long time before it could celebrate wholeheartedly.[225] The real miracle was that it had survived the ordeal and was able to proceed with the business of national elections and organizing a government, which it did in January 1949.

Overhead waved the flag featuring the Star of David, giving mute testimony to the past and future. Just four years before, Jews had worn that six-pointed star, earmarking them for extinction in Hitler's gas chambers. Now it proudly heralded their freedom and independence as a sovereign nation in the homeland of their forefathers.

CHAPTER 8

Israel's Defense and Expansion

ISRAEL'S TRIUMPH in the 1948 War of Independence did not guarantee its security. The armistice agreements were never intended to be permanent, but were merely to provide a short interlude for the development of more permanent treaties. In the coming years Israel's mettle was tested many times, proving that the first victory was for real and not just a fluke. On three more occasions in the next twenty-five years the nation was forced to mobilize its troops to defend its borders. Each of these was a traumatic episode in itself, but each also resulted in further gains that fortified its position in the land.

THE SINAI CAMPAIGN OF 1956—"OPERATION KADESH"

The nation's early years of independence were only grudgingly conceded by Israel's neighbors. Still smarting from defeat, Egyptian General Gamal Abdel Nasser led a coup to dethrone King Farouk in 1952, and was elected president in 1956. Until his death in 1970, the Arab world was dominated by the charismatic personality of Nasser. After several years of endeavoring to unite the Arab League and cozying up to the Soviets (Nasser was pro-Nazi during World War II), he began sending trained commandos *(fedeyeen)* across Israel's borders to harass the outlying villages.

Finally, on October 29, 1956, Israel was forced into a military confrontation with Egypt involving the Gaza Strip and its shipping lanes in the Gulf of Aqaba. In 1948 Egypt had closed the Suez Canal to Israeli ships. Then in 1955 it began a blockade of the Gulf of Aqaba, cutting off Israel's access to the Red Sea and Indian Ocean. The general's audacity stemmed, in large part, from a massive infusion of Soviet military equipment and an alliance with Jordan and Syria to destroy the Jewish state. Responding to this challenge, Israel again mobilized its citizen army in October 1956, striking at Egypt through the rugged Sinai wasteland.

That desert campaign became known as "Operation Kadesh." "In three days the Israeli Army outmaneuvered and outflanked the Egyptians, slashed its way into the Sinai Peninsula, seized stockpiles of military supplies, and stood poised at the Suez ready to invade Cairo."[226] Help from the French Air Force assisted Israel in this coordinated surprise attack. Having reopened its sea lanes (and having been warned by an ultimatum from the United Nations), Israel withdrew to its own borders.

This action, however, served as a warning to Israel's neighbors that it would not allow aggression to go unchallenged. It demanded respect as a sovereign nation. Besides opening its sea lanes in the Red Sea and bringing peace to its southern borders, this campaign also brought military respect from the world's power brokers.

THE SIX-DAY WAR OF JUNE 1967

Given its startling success in two crucial military confrontations, it might be thought Israel's days of harassment would be over. That presumption soon proved grievously wrong. Those early altercations only presaged two further attempts by the Arab League to obliterate Israel.

During the following decade a mood of optimism surged in Israel. The young nation enjoyed almost uninterrupted economic and political growth. The people came to feel relatively secure, and Jews worldwide shared their cautious optimism.

In the Arab capitals, however, old hatreds and new hostilities were simmering. From the hour of Arab surrender in 1956, the chastened leaders prepared for revenge. Nasser again assumed leadership of the Arab League, vowing to bring about a "cancellation of the humiliation they had undergone in the past and the annihilation (no less) of the State of Israel, whose existence they still refused to recognize and whose obliteration from the map was one of their main ambitions."[227] For them there was no turning back.

Finally, in the spring of 1967, following a vast military buildup of Russian equipment, Nasser again closed the Gulf of Aqaba to Israeli shipping and demanded that UN observers withdraw from the demilitarized zone in the Sinai. Calculating that world conditions were ripe, he attempted again to seize control of the Middle East. Meanwhile, Syrians in the north began raiding Israeli border towns, bombarding its villages from the Golan Heights. Jewish farmers were forced to plow with armored tractors. Of course, Israel retaliated. Summoning the Arab League to action, Syrian President Nureddin al-Atassi called for "a policy of scorched earth for Palestine."[228]

With the blessing of Moscow, Syria and Egypt began massing armored divisions on Israel's border. By May 17, soldiers from seven Arab nations had mobilized armor on three fronts, broadcasting their intentions to destroy the Jewish state. Hopes in Israel that these threats were only bluff soon vanished. The Israeli Prime Minister along with Israel's UN ambassador, Abba Eban, desperately sought for intervention by Washington, London, and Paris, but their calls were in vain. These nations replied that Israel should work through the diplomatic channels of the UN.

With its back to the wall, Israel again sounded the call to all citizens for total mobilization. The situation looked desperate. Nasser called for a *jihad* (holy war) of all Arabs against Israel, one in which none of the enemy would survive. Even the more cautious King Hussein of Jordan was persuaded to join the fray, collaborating with Iraqi troops. "The little Hashemite monarch clearly dared not abstain from an undertaking that was sweeping the entire Arab world into its vortex, one that seemed likely at last to annihilate the Zionist enemy."[229] The Arabs massed 547,000 troops, 2,504 tanks, and 957 combat aircraft. Israel mustered 264,000 troops, 800 tanks, and 300 combat airplanes.

Israeli generals Yitzhak Rabin and Moshe Dayan decided that surprise was their only hope. Though their forces were small, their officers, pilots, and ground crews were considered equal to any in the world. At the height of the Arab propaganda blitz, Dayan sent his armada into the air in the early morning of June 5 with every enemy target pinpointed. Takeoffs were scheduled to allow all planes to arrive over their targets at the same time, at 7:45 A.M. Israel unleashed all its might in one coordinated sweep.

The preemptive strike was decisive. "In 170 minutes Israel's pilots had smashed Egypt's best-equipped air bases and had turned three hundred of Nasser's combat planes into flaming wrecks. . . . The Egyptian air force, the largest in the Middle East, was in ruins."[230] The same scenario was replayed in Syria, Jordan, and Iraq. "By nightfall of June 6, Israel had destroyed 416 planes, 393 on the ground. It had lost twenty-six planes during that time, all to anti-aircraft."[231] This annihilation of Arab airpower left Israeli pilots free to confront the formidable force of enemy tanks and artillery.

In two days the Egyptian army in the Sinai was virtually wiped out, leaving Israel to occupy the Gaza Strip and Sinai Peninsula. Even Cairo itself became vulnerable to Jewish seizure. To the north, after a desperate and costly tank battle, the Syrians were routed and the strategic Golan Heights was taken. Thus ended the long nightmare of Syrian bombardment of Galilean villages. Israel was now secure on its northern border.[232]

But it was in the eastern battle with Jordan that the Israelis reaped their most provocative and unexpected benefit. King Hussein refused Prime Minister Levi Eshkol's conciliation efforts—being deluded by a Cairo report that Israel's air force had been destroyed—and joined the battle against Israel. Israel responded by attacking the Jordanian forces and driving them east to the Jordan River. The West Bank and the old city of Jerusalem fell into Israeli hands. Though the Israelis suffered many casualties in this battle for the West Bank and Jerusalem, they found themselves in control of many sites with great biblical and historical value. The ancient towns of Bethlehem, Hebron, Jericho, and Nablus (Shechem) were theirs, as was the city of Jerusalem—and the Temple Mount. For the first time in nineteen hundred years, the Jews had control of the old city of Jerusalem. A newly composed ballad, "Jerusalem the Golden," became Israel's popular anthem in the aftermath of the Six-Day War.

Historian Cecil Roth has described the Six-Day War as "perhaps the most brilliant campaign in military history, even outdoing the Sinai campaign of 1957; the Israeli army had shown itself the best fighting force in the world—and the more so since it was a citizen army, intent not on conquest but on self-protection."[233] Reflecting the lopsidedness of this victory were the casualty figures: "The Arabs suffered fifteen thousand casualties; Israel's losses were 777 killed, 2,186 wounded."[234]

For better or worse, Israel also occupied a vast territory previously claimed by Egypt, Syria, and Jordan (see Map 6). To its previous eighty-five hundred square miles it added twenty-eight thousand square miles in the Sinai, Golan Heights, and West Bank.[235] Though this acquisition represented a great triumph for the little nation, it later proved to be a millstone about its neck—a monstrous weight that Israel's adversaries would use against it. The disputed territories became the ideal bone of contention for the Arabs, leading to further conflicts that would dwarf even the monumental battles of Israel's first twenty years of nationhood.

THE YOM KIPPUR WAR OF 1973

Though Israel surprised its adversaries in 1967 with a preemptive strike, it was the Arabs who held the surprise party in 1973.

Map 6: Israel's Borders after the Six-Day War, 1967

LEBANON

SYRIA

• Damascus

• Quneitra

Golan Heights

Nazareth •

Jenin

Tulkarm •

Nablus

West Bank

Tel Aviv •

Jericho • Amman

Gaza Strip

Jerusalem

Bethlehem

Gaza •

Hebron

el Arish •

Beersheba

EGYPT

JORDAN

Suez •

Sinai Peninsula
(Returned to Egypt in 1979)

Eilat •

• Aqaba

SAUDI
ARABIA

St. Catherine's
Monastery

Sharm el-Sheikh

The Jews grossly underestimated Arab determination and ingenuity for retaliation and inexplicably discounted the huge Arab military buildup of that summer. Given Israel's track record, one wonders how such a fiasco could have happened.

Several things contributed to this costly complacency. Following the Six-Day War of 1967, Israel basked in the glory of yet another victory against overwhelming odds. Jews worldwide rejoiced in this turn of events. International diplomats were sure this victory would increase the prospects of peace in the Middle East.[236] As Israel's economy grew and stocks rose in international markets, unemployment plunged. Many politicians unveiled grandiose plans to make the West Bank into a modern Jewish Samaria. The temptation was strong to grind swords into plowshares—and refrigerators.

The early seventies also saw several changes in Egypt that distracted Israel's military vigilance. In September 1970, Nasser died of a heart attack, and the Egyptian helm fell to the little known Anwar Sadat (who had helped Nasser dethrone Farouk). A more congenial, moderate, and domestic-oriented ruler than the flamboyant Nasser, Sadat seemed to give promise of more peaceful relations with Israel. But as the general gained confidence, that hope was dashed. In early 1972, Sadat called for a showdown with Israel, declaring he was prepared to "sacrifice a million men" in the struggle.[237] To further confuse the scenario, that summer he ordered Soviet advisers out of Egypt. Sadat's wild and unpredictable fluctuations encouraged Israel to see him as mostly bluff—and that naïveté almost proved fatal.

Underestimating Arab Desire for Revenge

Israel had vastly underrated the revenge factor among its enemies. Arab pride had been grievously wounded by repeated defeat. Nasser of Egypt, in particular, suffered his greatest humiliation and refused even to talk of a peace agreement. "We shall never surrender and shall not accept any peace that means surrender," he said.[238] Moreover, when Israel captured the Suez Canal, Nasser sank all his ships in the lucrative waterway—a blunder that effectively closed the shipping lane for the next six years, costing Egypt more than 30 million dollars a month in lost revenue.

Several changes in the international scene also worsened Israel's relations with the Arabs following the 1967 war. In 1968 and 1970, coups d'état in both Syria and Iraq put into power implacable and bloodthirsty regimes. The Syrian takeover by General Hafez al-Assad triggered a sharp increase in guerrilla activity among the Palestinians. The Fatah leader, Yasser Arafat al-Qud al-Husseini, took charge of the Palestine Liberation Organization and launched new uprisings in the occupied territory. That guerrilla movement, though suppressed at first, was to become a monumental force in later Arabic strategies. The slower rise to prominence of Saddam Hussein in Iraq would later grab world attention.

The Soviets, too, became active and aggressive in the Mideast following the 1967 war. The pulverizing defeat of their Russian-equipped protégés humiliated them deeply. "Within two weeks, over two hundred crated MiG fighter planes were airlifted to Egypt and Syria, and throughout the rest of the summer and autumn between two and three ships a week docked at Alexandria harbor carrying replacement weapons."[239] The number of Soviet advisers in Egypt rose to nearly fourteen thousand, and Soviet pilots began flying reconnaissance missions from Egyptian bases. Sensing a possible Soviet invasion of the Mideast, United States President Richard Nixon sent large shipments of military supplies to Israel and moved the United States Sixth Fleet into the area.[240] Thus the superpowers risked one of their most ominous confrontations over the prized Middle East.

Tensions were at a peak in the fall of 1973. The Kremlin launched five satellites to help spy out Israel's defenses. Sadat and Assad this time were determined to seize the advantage of surprise. The day they chose for attack was October 6—Yom Kippur, the Jewish Day of Atonement, when many of Israel's military were home on leave.

The Arabs' Surprise Attack

At 2:00 P.M. on that holy day the Arab League set aside all bluff and launched a well-planned offensive. The initial attack was called an "earthquake of an assault," striking against Israel from both north and south. With 750,000 troops, 3,200 Soviet tanks, 860 planes, and the latest Soviet missiles, the Arab armies struck Israel's reservists stationed on the front lines at the Suez Canal and on the Golan Heights.[241]

Recoiling at the surprise attack, Prime Minister Golda Meir and Defense Minister Dayan called the nation from its Yom Kippur rituals. They knew they had two strikes against them in a game of hardball; their manpower was approximately one-third of the enemies' and their weaponry less than half. Having resolved not to initiate a second preemptive strike, the Israelis were caught off guard and threatened with another Holocaust in their own backyard.

In the first grim hours at the Suez Canal, Israeli reservists were obliterated. Their token defenses consisted of "precisely 436 Israeli soldiers in a series of bunkers seven to ten miles apart, together with three tanks and seven artillery batteries."[242] Their main armored division was twenty miles to the rear. Coming at them "were five

Egyptian infantry divisions, three mixed infantry and tank divisions, and twenty-two independent infantry, commando, and paratroop brigades. With the air force, the enemy constituted not less than 600,000 men, 2,000 tanks, 2,300 artillery pieces, 160 SAM missile batteries, and 550 combat planes."[243] The Egyptians quickly smashed the shallow defense and crossed the Canal, penetrating deep into the Sinai.

Even more grim was the Israeli debacle in the north. With eight hundred infrared-equipped tanks, the Syrians moved to retake the Golan Heights and head for the Jordan River. Israeli intelligence had failed to uncover Syria's plan to attack, and the Jewish outposts were caught flat-footed. Within forty-eight hours the Seventh Armored Brigade was virtually wiped out, along with most of its personnel. Though Israel had destroyed much of the Syrian tank force in the process, fresh waves of Soviet replacements kept rolling in to devastate the exhausted Jewish forces.[244]

Meanwhile, in diplomatic circles far from the battlefield, the two superpowers watched nervously. Each had a vital stake in the area, both economically and politically; the Suez Canal was a key to international commerce. The Soviets backed the Arabs; the United States supported the Israelis. Both claimed they were helping to maintain a balance of power in the Middle East. On October 9 the Soviets launched a massive airlift of replacement equipment. By October 12, eighteen planes an hour were landing in Cairo. President Nixon countered (at the urging of Secretary of State Henry Kissinger) with an emergency airlift to Israel. Within the next thirty days, United States pilots flew 566 cargo loads of ordnance to the beleaguered Israeli troops.[245]

The operation cost the Soviets $3.5 billion in aid to Egypt and Syria, while the United States supplied Israel with $2.2 billion.[246] Neither side, of course, was doing this for charity, for both had ulterior motives. Rather than striking swords with each other, the two world giants fought a war by proxy, supplying the two belligerents with the latest military hardware. The battle was hardly a minor skirmish between scrapping Semites; it had international ramifications.

Turning the Tide

Back on the battlefield, a strange turn of events on the third and fourth days of battle began to give Israel the advantage. By concentrating their attack on the Golan Heights, the Israelis were able to cut Syrian supply lines and reinforce their own, thus gaining a crucial advantage. The United States airlift also began to take effect. "By early afternoon, precisely four days after the Syrians had launched their avalanche against Israel, not a single one of their tanks in fighting condition remained. . . . Strewn along the route of the Israeli advance were 867 destroyed enemy tanks, over three thousand personnel carriers, hundreds of antitank guns, and vast piles of other military equipment . . . the pride of their army lay smoking and ruined on the Golan."[247] By October 18, panic struck Syria as Israeli troops headed toward Damascus.

In the battle for the Suez, a similar miracle began to unfold. By a freak turn of events, the reprovisioned Israeli tank force found itself driving a wedge between the Second and Third Egyptian Armies as it forged a bridgehead across the Suez Canal. Having lured the main Egyptian tank force into the Sinai desert and away from its missile cover, Israeli tanks were able to form a pincers movement on the Egyptian side, cutting off the Egyptian supply lines. While President Sadat entertained visiting Soviet leader Aleksey Kosygin—who had gone to Cairo to view a swift Egyptian victory—the war was taking an unexpected turn. Israeli forces quickly exploited their advantage by plunging north and south on the Cairo side of the Suez, extending their control over the whole west bank of the canal. "By then [October 23] the Egyptian Third Army was indeed hopelessly trapped, and Israeli forces were solidly emplaced on the Gulf of Suez."[248] As with Damascus in the north, Cairo itself was now vulnerable to the relentless Israeli charge.

By now Cairo and Moscow were panic-stricken. They demanded that the United Nations Security Council require Israel to pull back to its pre-1967 borders. Scorning such a demand, Prime Minister Golda Meir remarked that the Egyptians needed to taste the "full flavor of defeat." They were hardly in a posture to dictate peace terms with much of their army still trapped and at the mercy of the Israelis. In the end the UN instituted a general cease-fire, which resulted in a long-protracted diplomatic stalemate. Though it produced no real peace agreement, it brought the Yom Kippur hostilities to an end.

This fourth challenge to Israel's presence in the land exacted an awesome price. The total cost for Israel soared to seven billion dollars. In terms of casualties, "the nation had lost 2,552 dead and over 3,000 wounded in the eighteen days of fighting, with a high proportion of officers among the casualties."[249] But the defeated Arabs fared even worse. "The Egyptians had suffered 7,700 combat dead, the Syrians 3,500. The Israelis held 9,000 POWs, of whom over 8,000 were Egyptians. The combined Arab forces had lost some 2,000 tanks and over 500 planes, compared with Israel's loss of 804 tanks and 100 planes."[250] The war had no real winners except in the sense of mutual survival.

THE AFTERMATH OF FOUR WARS

By surviving four strikes at the jugular, Israel might be thought to have earned lasting world respect. The nation had taken the best punches its menacing neighbors could throw and yet had prevailed. But it was not meant to be. Third World countries especially came to view Israel's military successes as imperialistic. The military aggressiveness in the Six-Day War looked more and more to hem like expansionism. In their view, Israel should have been chari - table enough to return the occupied lands that the Arabs had used as a military staging ground against it. The United Nations, in fact, demanded this withdrawal from the West Bank and Gaza Strip in Resolution 242. When Israel refused to comply, the council nearly voted the nation out of the United Nations in the summer of 1975.[251]

The increasing importance of oil in world markets added to Israel's diminishing support and respect in the Middle East. To combat Israel and the West, Arab petroleum ministers met during the Yom Kippur War (October 17, 1973) and decided to cut oil production and exports. "It was under the facade of the war crisis . . . that the Arabs seized the opportunity to launch a drastic escalation of oil prices. Libya announced on October 18 that the cost of its oil would go up 28 percent—irrespective of the war and Israel's misdeeds. Iraq thereupon declared a 70 percent price rise. Kuwait matched this figure."[252]

This use of oil as a weapon threatened to create chaos in world markets, especially the oil-dependent nations of Europe. Members of the European Common Market took immediate measures to placate Arab demands, issuing new calls for Israel to give up the occupied territories. Though the Arabs suffered a devastating loss in the Yom Kippur War, they discovered a powerful new weapon and found themselves in the driver's seat of the world economy. By a simple turn of oil valves they could further their goals in Palestine.

In the ensuing years, however, the Palestinians themselves developed a new form of Arab militarism. A clandestine army of women and children arose to frustrate and infuriate their Jewish overlords, almost outpacing Arafat's guerrillas in effectiveness. Using primitive tactics to shake the land, this indigenous army would also make a strong appeal to the sympathies of world opinion. To appreciate the continuing dilemma in the Holy Land today, we need to briefly recount this ongoing story of anguish—anguish on both sides of the green line of occupation.

9

Convulsions from Within: *Intifada*

FOLLOWING THE YOM KIPPUR WAR OF 1973, some significant changes began to occur on both sides of the racial conflict. Israeli politics made an about-face, and Arab military tactics also took a strange turn. Both resulted from the anguish of that war, which seemed to gain nothing for either side.

THE ISRAELI POLITICAL SHIFT

It's important to recall that the early Zionists had divided into two groups on the issue of partitioning Palestine. The Labor Party of Ben-Gurion, the Socialist Zionists, accepted the idea of partitioning in order to obtain statehood. Another group, under the leadership of Ze'ev Jabotinsky, rejected any such notion. It insisted on Jewish sovereignty over all Palestine, including Transjordan.[253] This group came to be known as the Revisionist Party.

For the first twenty-five years of Jewish statehood the Labor Party of Ben-Gurion held sway. Following the 1973 war, the party took a nosedive in the polls, and Prime Minister Golda Meir, staunchly loyal to Ben-Gurion, became one of its casualties.[254] Her administration had served during prosperous times between the two recent wars; but in the aftermath of the Yom Kippur War, Meir was almost forced to resign. The high cost of the war soured the populace on moderation toward the Arabs (or any ceding of lands). This in turn diminished the ranks of the Labor bloc of parties who had championed those policies. Though the Labor Party won a hard-fought victory in the battlefield, it lost the confidence of the electorate at home.

THE RISE OF MENACHEM BEGIN

The election of Menachem Begin in May 1977 capped the shift from the left-wing socialism of the Labor Party to the no-nonsense conservatism of the Likud Party. Begin was strictly right wing. He was the supreme hawk, with a long history of belligerence toward both the British and Arabs.[255] He had served as a zealous, militant leader in the Irgun and became the leader of Jabotinsky's revisionist brand of Zionism in 1944. Violent terrorist attacks were part and parcel of the Irgun tactics in the early days under Begin. He never wavered in his Jabotinsky maximalism. For him the West Bank was Judea and Samaria, and he said, "We shall never yield our natural and eternal right."[256]

Though condemned for decades as a demagogue, he nonetheless ran doggedly in every election before finally being elected in 1977. His election stunned the nation and puzzled the rest of the world.[257] Politically, it represented a shift of power from those who were willing to divide the land into two states—one Jewish and one Palestinian—to those who viewed all the land as *Eretz Yishrael,* the "land of Israel." Part of this can be accounted for by the increasing influence of the Sephardim (Oriental Jews, originally from Spain, who came from the Muslim countries of northern Africa and the Middle East) over the Ashkenazim (European and American Jews). The poorer immigrants from Asia and Africa had been gaining political clout and by that time constituted 60 percent of the electorate.

Begin also found supporters in the religious Orthodox parties, "donning a skullcap at the drop of a biblical quotation."[258] Though politically motivated, he found biblical claims made to order for his rhetoric. Thus the Likud bloc curiously became the populist party, reflecting the mood of the time, while Labor became the establishment party.[259] These Likud Revisionists were generally anti-Arab and strongly uncompromising on the issue of occupied land.

The revisionists capitalized on new concerns for Israeli security raised by the Yom Kippur War. The buffer zones of the Sinai, West Bank, and Golan Heights came to be seen as essential to Israel's safety.

Despite Begin's hard line on the "territories," the prime minister soon found himself negotiating a "land for peace" deal with Egypt in the fall of 1977, just six months after his Likud party came to power.

Peace overtures began flying between Cairo and Jerusalem that summer. To the amazement of the world, the odd couple of sedate Sadat and blustering Begin embraced that November at a red carpet ceremony at Ben-Gurion Airport.[260]

This surprise compromise set a precedent in Arab-Israeli relations. For Sadat it was revolutionary and incurred the wrath of other Arab leaders. But it also seemed, at least initially, to be out of character for Begin. However, the prime minister explained his action by noting that the Sinai was not part of ancient Israel. Convinced of that by his pragmatic foreign minister, Moshe Dayan, Begin saw it as a useful bargaining chip. It served not only to secure Israel's southern borders but also relieved some of the huge military expense involved. Both he and Sadat needed this border settlement for economic reasons, as well as to show their peaceful intentions to the world.

As a result of this landmark agreement, both also saw their popularities soar at home.[261] One year later, shortly after the Camp David Accord of September 1978, both leaders received the Nobel Peace Prize for this surprising turnaround.

THE SHARON BLUNDER IN LEBANON

With its southern border secured, Israel focused attention on border conflicts to the north. Having been forced out of Jordan in 1971, the PLO had shifted its operations to Lebanon. From its head-quarters in Beirut the PLO engaged in terror attacks against Israel. Convinced by his defense minister, Ariel Sharon, that a decisive military engagement against the PLO would eliminate the border clashes, Begin launched a military campaign in Lebanon to clean up the area. As Yehoshafat Harkabi notes in his book *Israel's Fateful Hour*, "This war was to lead to a peace agreement with Lebanon and end missile attacks on Kiryat Shmona in northern Galilee; it would also destroy the PLO and defeat the Syrians, thus changing the political structure of the Middle East; it finally would erase the trauma of the Yom Kippur War."[262] Laudable goals indeed, for both Begin's hard-line adminis-tration and world Jewry.

Things didn't quite turn out that way. Though Sharon's Israeli defense force did win a striking victory in Lebanon, raising military eyebrows around the world, the force came to be seen as overly aggressive. Its viciousness gave it a reputation for overkill due to the many civilians who were caught in the cross fire. When Israel's Leba-nese Christian allies massacred hundreds of civilians in two refugee camps, Israel received international condemnation. "Israel's image throughout the world, a painfully achieved amalgam of heroism and humanism, had been grievously, if not irretrievably, disfigured among well-meaning Christians and Jews alike."[263] An official Israeli inquiry acquitted Ariel Sharon of direct responsibility for the attack though it condemned him for negligence in the matter. As a result, Sharon was forced to resign as defense minister.

The campaign turned out to be counterproductive. Though Israel effectively flushed the PLO out of Lebanon, the vacuum was soon filled by the Syrians and, most recently, the Iranian-backed Hizbullah fighters, who proved to be an even more formidable enemy. Caught between the Christian Lebanese, the Hizbullah, and the Syrians, the Israeli troops found themselves mired in a protracted war of attrition against guerrilla forces, which grew increasingly unpopular as the cost in lives and financial resources escalated. Though the campaign was designed as a quick cleanup, it became a quagmire for both Israel and the United Nations' peacekeeping force. The campaign finally ended in 2000 when Israel unilaterally withdrew its troops from Lebanon.

Moreover, the operation only further inflamed the Arab desire for revenge. In this way it did change the political structure of the Middle East, but not in the way Begin and Sharon had envisioned. Perhaps more than any other event, the Sharon-conceived war in Lebanon fired an international disgust toward Israel that soured its image worldwide. It also began an agonizing deterioration of morale at home.

Before discussing the ensuing struggle that culminated in the *Intifada* (a spontaneous uprising by the Palestinian people that began in 1987), another side of the painful story needs to be briefly reviewed. The plight of the refugees and Palestinians is a heart-wrenching aspect of the Middle East dilemma, but its complexity can only be appreciated through a historical perspective.

THE ARAB MILITARY SHIFT

The misfortune of the Palestinian people resulted not only from their conflict with Israel but also from their mistreatment at the hands of the surrounding Arab states, who used them as pawns to further their own political goals. Both sides exploited them. As Harkabi notes, their "nationalism developed not only as a reaction to Zionism but as a reaction to the Arab states' attempts to make the Palestinians subservient to their interests."[264] When their problem with Israel began, most of the Arab states were newly formed, their leaders jockeying for leadership of the "Arab nation." The Palestinians, being the "odd man out" without statehood, became the darling of all—and a political football as well. The Arab states all identified with them as cousins, but few were willing to harbor their refugees.

THE TROUBLED HERITAGE OF THE PALESTINIANS

This game of tug-of-war goes back to the early 1920s when the territory of the Levant was up for grabs following the ouster of the Turks. In the resulting skirmish, the British and French allowed the gradual formation of seven independent Arabic states in the region—Egypt, Syria, Lebanon, Transjordan, Iraq, Saudi Arabia, and Yemen—followed later by ten others. The British had planned independent statehood for Palestine (called Southern Syria), but erred in promising it to two different claimants, the Jews and the Arabs.

The Balfour Declaration was drawn up to guarantee the Jews a homeland in Palestine, which then included both sides of the Jordan. But the Arabs had also been promised "an independent pan-Arab state following the war—a state that would take in the Ottoman provinces of Syria [including Palestine and Transjordan], Mesopotamia [Iraq], and the entire Arabian peninsula."[265] That this was later qualified was conveniently forgotten. (See Appendix B.)

Both of these promises were obviously too flamboyant and ill defined, but both parties took them literally. Though the Balfour Declaration became a part of the Versailles Peace Treaty, the promise to the Arabs was mainly informal. These promises were later modified by Winston Churchill when he gave the area of Transjordan to Abdullah of Arabia. This he did to mollify the Arab leader for the help his father, the sharif of Mecca, had given the British in diverting the Turks in Arabia in 1917.[266] This gift of East Jordan (Transjordan) to Abdullah constituted three-quarters of the area known as Palestine.

TWO COMPETING FAMILIES OF PALESTINE RULE

The Arabs west of the Jordan River also wanted an independent state and had candidates vying for rulership. For many years, two leading families, the al-Husseinis and Nashashibis, had alternated in filling the position of Grand Mufti of Jerusalem.[267] Though a religious position, it carried strong political clout throughout Palestine. Both families claimed descent from the Grand Sharif of Mecca, who in turn claimed to have descended from Muhammad himself. These two clans exerted much influence in mayoral offices in the region, but were constantly at loggerheads. From the Nashashibis came King Abdullah, who was given Transjordan, and his brother Feisal. Feisal was first given Syria (until the French took it over) and was later made King of Iraq. At the assassination of Abdullah in 1951, Hussein, his grandson (not of the al-Husseini line), became king of Jordan. This family was known as the Hashemites.[268]

The al-Husseini family in Jerusalem was represented by Haj

Amin al-Husseini, who was appointed Grand Mufti by the British in 1921 when only twenty-one. Amin al-Husseini was a Muslim extremist who violently opposed Zionism. Insisting on Palestine becoming an Arab state, he used every influence to halt Jewish immigration. On August 23, 1929, he instigated a massacre of Jews praying at the Wailing Wall. Prior to that, "Haj Amin had instituted a plan to restore the mosques in order to reestablish the primacy of Islam over all of Palestine and to counter the increasingly vocal religious claims of the Zionists to a portion of Jerusalem."[269] The ensuing violence of the riot in Jerusalem spread throughout the country and gave their clashes with Jews a religious flavor as a jihad. It also gave Haj Amin the stature of a pan-Arabic hero. To the British and Zionists in Jerusalem, however, he was an enemy. Soon he began organizing guerrilla units throughout the area.[270] That year (1920) officially marked the beginning of armed conflict between the Jews and Arabs in Palestine.

While Haj Amin fought the British and Zionists in the early 1920s and 1930s, he was the dominant Arab voice in Palestine. When World War II erupted, however, he was forced to flee, first to Iraq and then to Germany, where he was welcomed by Hitler and Himmler. His purpose there was to lobby for Arab independence in the Middle East, believing that Hitler's conquest of Palestine was inevitable.[271] The Mufti never lived down that mistake.

These two families, the Hashemites and the al-Husseinis, came to represent the moderate and extreme factions of Palestinian Arabs.[272] Their special bitterness toward each other stemmed from Britain's bestowal of kingdoms on the Hashemites, which the al-Husseinis viewed as a sellout to the enemy. They considered this acceptance of separate kingdoms in lieu of the whole a virtual acknowledgment of the Zionist state. For this, Haj Amin and his followers came to regard both the Jews and the Jordanian Hashemites as bitter enemies.[273] The Mufti thus alienated himself from both friends and foes, forcing his exile several times, the final one in Beirut. An Arab leadership vacuum then developed in Palestine, leaving the stateless Palestinians dependent on other Arab states. First Nasser and later Sadat used them as pawns in pursuing leadership of the Arab world.

FORMATION OF THE PLO

The chief architect of the Palestine Liberation Organization was Egypt's Gamal Abdel Nasser. The idea was conceived and given impetus at the first Arab summit conference, which Nasser called in Cairo for January 1964. The occasion was the meeting of thirteen

Arab leaders to devise some way to respond to Israel's water diversion plan, the Jordan Valley Project.[274] Israel was just completing a water distribution system that would siphon water from Lake Galilee in the north and pump it the length of the land to various dry areas. Its ultimate target was the Negev desert in the south, the culmination of a long-held dream to open up the land for production and livability. The massive system would supply water to an estimated five million people.[275]

Failing to prevent that, Nasser sought to promote an underground forum for the Palestinian people. This was first called the Palestine Liberation Army and later the Palestinian Liberation Organization (the PLO). Ahmad Shuqairi, a puppet of Nasser, was chosen to lead the forum and set up headquarters in Cairo. The express purpose of this organization was to allow the Palestinian people "to play a role in the liberation of their country and their self-determination."[276] The Arab leaders who set it up, however, had other designs for the organization. They intended to make it an instrument of guerrilla warfare against Israel under their control. They had no intention of creating an independent Palestinian movement.[277]

Such an independent Palestinian organization, however, was already in operation. Following the 1956 Sinai War, an organization called the Fatah had been formed in Syria. The major figures were two young dyed-in-the-wool guerrilla operators, Yasser Arafat and Abu Jihad.[278] Both were from the militant Muslim community of Gaza. Arafat was born in Cairo in 1929 and grew up in the Gaza Strip during the tumultuous Jewish-Arab conflicts of the 1930s and 1940s. Arafat was related to Haj Amin al-Husseini, the Grand Mufti of Jerusalem, through his mother. That lineage supposedly traced back to Husayn ibn Ali, son of Fatima, the daughter of Muhammad.[279]

Though Arafat had a photographic memory and received a civil engineer's degree from King Fahd University in Cairo, he had little interest in school. As an engineer in Kuwait for some years, he became wealthy through real estate deals, helping to finance his operations. From his earliest years he was engrossed in liberation tactics, devising terrorist activities against the Israelis, whom he saw as invaders. As he and his compatriots began the Fatah, they saw themselves as the "generation of revenge"—seeking vengeance for the loss of Palestine.[280] Though just as terrorist-minded as Haj Amin al-Husseini, they blamed the Mufti's blundering for losing the land—first to the British and then to the Jews. They also came to regard the Arab regimes as ineffective in their fight against Israel, unable to win by political rhetoric and unwilling to win by military sacrifices.

ARAFAT'S FALLOUT WITH THE ARAB STATES

Arab regimes considered the goals of Arafat and the Fatah arrogant and nearsighted and regarded him as a nuisance. His fall from favor may be traced in several stages. To begin with, Arafat had little respect for Jordan's King Hussein. Hussein's father, Abdullah, had annexed the West Bank in 1950 and appointed his relative, Raghib Nashashibi, military governor of the area. This, however, was considered the political turf of the Grand Mufti, Haj Amin, a relative of Arafat. One year later the Mufti dispatched his agents to assassinate King Abdullah at the Jerusalem Mosque. This assassination further inflamed the bad blood between their ancient families and affected all their relations.[281] Arafat and Hussein became inveterate enemies despite all their smiles. Furthermore, Hussein had come to fear Israel's policy of quick, devastating reprisal for guerrilla attacks. Therefore, the king had no time for the underground tactics of Arafat and the Fatah. On several occasions, Hussein's generals even tried to assassinate Arafat.[282]

Arafat's relations with Egyptian leaders were likewise anything but warm. The very establishment of the PLO by Nasser in 1964 was intended to rebuff Arafat and his Fatah. Incensed by Arafat's deriding him in his paper, *Our Palestine,* Nasser "ordered his intelligence service to see to Arafat's liquidation."[283] Like Hussein, Nasser's main fear of Arafat was that his guerrilla attacks on Israel would drag Egypt into another disastrous war. In fact, that was precisely what Arafat wanted, for two reasons: It would shatter the egotistical ambitions of Nasser, and it would allow Arafat to take over the PLO. Nasser's fears were well-founded, for this is just what happened in the Six-Day War of 1967. That disaster catapulted Arafat to the leadership of the PLO in 1969 and nearly destroyed Nasser.[284]

Prior to 1968, Palestinians had looked to the pan-Arab nations to liberate their land. In the wake of the 1967 war, they gave up on the promises of the Arab League and determined that they would have to go it alone if they were to "restore their land." The further routing of Arab powers in 1973 underscored this fact and rocketed Arafat into the limelight as the leader of the Palestinian movement. The next Arab Summit Conference reflected this fact when the PLO was officially declared to be the "only legitimate representative" of the Palestinian people and Arafat to be its leader.[285]

Capitalizing on his newfound authority, Arafat secured an invitation to address the United Nations General Assembly the following year on the question of Palestine. To this body, which included many nations newly-born out of terrorism and guerrilla warfare, Arafat struck a sympathetic note. He had shaken off his benefactors and become his own man, projecting a colorful image in the Arab world, which he hoped could unite them for conquest.

Arafat's relations with Syria were even more tenuous than those with Hussein or Nasser. When Hafez al-Assad usurped the presidency of Syria in 1970, he also harbored dreams of ruling the Arabs. But to effectively challenge Nasser for this position, Assad had to be two-faced about the Palestinian issue. He had to convince the Palestinians that he was serious about another confrontation with Israel even while assuring his battered nation that his regime would avoid another conventional war with Israel—a war that would most certainly spell disaster for Damascus.

Thus, Assad was forced to do a careful balancing act. His formula was to promote guerrilla activity, but not enough to goad Israel into war.[286] To do this he needed a guerrilla leader he could control. That, of course, was not Arafat, and both men knew it. His choice was the radical Ahmad Jabril, who became his puppet in promoting terrorist activity even while Assad himself solemnly denounced it. Though Arafat trained his Fatah in Syria, he maintained control of the group, gingerly avoiding the heavy hand of the Syrian radicals. The PLO chairman early recognized that President Assad was interested only in his own personal agenda. Both were extremely wary of each other, Arafat being the target also of Syria's assassination squads.

THE MODUS OPERANDI OF THE PLO

How could such an ill-defined organization as the PLO, without political base or real support, hope to succeed? On what secret agenda or powers did it rely? What were its basic principles of operation?

It's important to recall that the PLO was really the product of anger and frustration—a frustration not just with Israel, but also with the Arab powers. When Arafat took over the PLO, the organization reverted to cell groups developed by its Fatah members in Syria. Though these contained both moderate and radical elements, the unified group had some common purposes and an underlying mode of operation. First, it was basically a guerrilla organization that worked underground apart from national armies or agencies. Its single purpose was to evict the Israelis from the land and set up an independent Palestinian state, not one in tandem with Jordan or any other Arab state.

Second, it intended to achieve its goals by armed conflict, using infiltration and terror to drive out the occupiers of the West Bank and Gaza Strip.[287] Its battle was not with armies, but with peoples. "It seeks an impact on attitudes, and so it must be spectacular. It relies on drama, it thrives on attention, it carries within the seeds of contagion."[288] What Arab regimes and armies could not achieve by politics and military operations, it sought to accomplish by intimidation and terrorism.

To express their determination its members called themselves the *fedeyeen,* meaning "to sacrifice oneself for the cause."[289] They dedicated themselves to make any sacrifice to reclaim the land. Their deep-seated hatred of Israel had both a religious and political base. Since the Jews were the original rejecters of Muhammad, Judaism was regarded as an infidel religion and the object of Islamic scorn. Arafat himself had been named after "the sacred mountain near Mecca where Muhammad had been transformed into the final messenger of God"; he had been regarded from birth as chosen of Allah for a special mission in life.[290] He believed that mission was to clear the land of its Muhammad rejecters, and the killing of Jews was a necessary act of religious revenge rather than murder. Even Palestinian school manuals justify such acts by approving *jihad.*[291]

In pursuing its political goals, the PLO had been schooled to work through a network of cells and cadres. This intricate intelligence and underground communication system was essential to its operation. Some of this it learned from "General [Vo Nguyen] Giap, who masterminded Vietnam's victory over first the French and then the Americans."[292] Arafat developed links and contacts with Palestinian operatives in every Arab country, as well as in Europe and America. This worldwide base of Palestinian support took on greater importance as the indifference of the Arab states became evident. Recalling how Israel gained support from the world community by highlighting its plight in World War II, the PLO began its own media blitz. Its use of revolutionary rhetoric, symbolism, and slogans rapidly won ideological support, especially from leftist groups in Europe, America, and the Third World. Perhaps its stroke of genius was its linking of Israel and world Zionism with "imperialism," "colonialism," and "reactionism." This allowed the PLO to snatch the same underdog image that Israel had utilized so well.[293]

Such a psychological strategy, however, required time—and fortunately, patience was a proverbial Arab strength. It seemed that media favor had begun to turn toward the Palestinians by the late 1960s.

At the same time, Palestinian demographics were beginning to change. With a majority of Christians, Lebanon had long been considered by Israel a nonbelligerent buffer state in the north. By 1970, however, its "population explosion was such that the Muslims were on their way to becoming the majority, and it was obvious that a day was coming when that Muslim majority would insist on having most of the political power—according to their numbers and the democratic principle."[294] Unfortunately, it was the radicals who exploited that demographic principle and moved in to devastate the nation. Assad's fellow radicals watched with glee as Arafat and his PLO took the blame for the situation and were driven out in 1982.

That was not the end of things, however. Arafat and his compatriots eventually discovered that this demographic principle, coupled with time, could become their ally. The Palestinians could win the battle in their bedrooms. It was only a matter of time before the Jews in the occupied territories would be outnumbered by Arabs.

The Israelis were well aware of the mounting urgency of the situation, recognizing its potential to undo all their military successes. They realized that they were being forced into the role of the pharaohs of Egypt—with Arafat, of all people, snatching the role of Moses! The dilemma they faced was how to maintain the democratic principle of equal rights while ensuring that demographics would not undercut the Jewish state. Failure to do so could even put the Knesset up for grabs. This time bomb demanded some kind of action.

THE FIRST *INTIFADA:*
A BATTLE OF BRICKS AND BULLDOZERS

With both sides at a standoff in the West Bank and Gaza Strip, Palestinian resentments lay smoldering. A single spark might ignite them. That spark was provided in December 1987 when Palestinian patience ran out and long pent-up feelings were suddenly unleashed with stones and homemade bombs. The racial struggle erupted from within.

Several versions of how it started exist, but the following incidents appear to have been involved. On December 6, 1987, an Israeli businessman, Shlomo Sakal, was fatally stabbed in Gaza City. Two days later, an Israeli truck driver was involved in a traffic accident in which four Palestinians were killed. Taking this as intentional and retaliatory, local Palestinian youngsters surrounded an Israeli patrol, attacking it with rocks and Molotov cocktails. Israeli troops opened fire, killing a seventeen-year-old and wounding sixteen others.[295] Racial tensions then exploded into the urban and rural neighborhoods, and the battle was dubbed the *intifada* or "uprising."

Frustrated women often led the demonstrations while their children bombarded Jewish troops with stones and other objects. Since Palestinian men are more subject to imprisonment and harsh penalties, including separation from their families, they purposely remained in the background. In this way the first *intifada* took the form of a "children's crusade"—the weak and vulnerable taking to the streets. Their weapons of revenge were rocks or homemade missiles.

Though it ignited spontaneously, even surprising the PLO, the *intifada* quickly spread through the Gaza Strip and the West Bank. The cities of Nablus, Hebron, and Jerusalem in the West Bank soon became centers of agitation. It became a war of "children and grandmothers" fighting Israeli patrols, who were charged with keeping the peace. In the first twenty-six months, seven hundred Palestinians were killed by Israeli soldiers and another 182 by fellow Palestinians who suspected their countrymen of collaborating with Israel. In addition, some thirty-seven thousand were wounded and forty thousand arrested.[296] Israeli casualties amounted to approximately fifty.

A WINDING PATH TOWARD PEACE

The first *intifada* ran out of steam and eventually collapsed following the Gulf War. Yasser Arafat's support for Saddam Hussein had angered those oil-producing countries that had been financing the PLO, and they withdrew their support. Sensing an opportunity to achieve a breakthrough in the Middle East, the United States convened an Arab-Israeli peace conference in Madrid in October 1991. Unfortunately, the talks between the Palestinians and the Likud government of Yitzhak Shamir quickly stalled.

The Oslo Accords

National elections in 1992 brought Yitzhak Rabin and the Labor Party back into power in Israel. Almost immediately, his government began secret negotiations with the PLO in Oslo, Norway. Arafat seemed willing to accept the idea of reaching a peace treaty with Israel in exchange for Palestinian autonomy. In September 1993 Israel and the PLO signed the Declaration of Principles on Palestinian Self-Rule, the first agreement between the two sides that became known as the Oslo Accords. The declaration was signed on the White House lawn in September 1993 with President Clinton looking on as Rabin shook Arafat's hand.

The Oslo Accords were actually a series of agreements (see Map 7). The second, also known as the Cairo Agreement on the Gaza Strip and Jericho, was signed in May 1994. This agreement implemented the provisions of the original declaration. It included provisions for a five-year interim self-rule for the Palestinians to be put into effect in two stages. Final status talks were to begin after three years, with a two-year deadline for reaching agreement on final borders, the issue of refugees, and the status of Jerusalem and all Jewish settlements.

Map 7: Agreements and Land Transfers (1994–99)

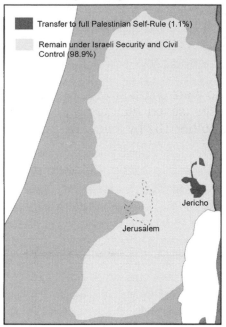

Cairo Agreement, 1994

Transfer to full Palestinian Self-Rule (1.1%)

Remain under Israeli Security and Civil Control (98.9%)

Jericho

Jerusalem

Taba Agreement, 1995

Transfer to full Palestinian Self-Rule (2.0%) (Cairo Agreement, 1994)

Additional transfer to full or partial Palestinian Self-Rule (26.0%)

Remain under Israeli Security and Civil Control (72.0%)

Nablus
Kalkilya
Ramallah
Jerusalem
Jericho
Bethlehem
Hebron

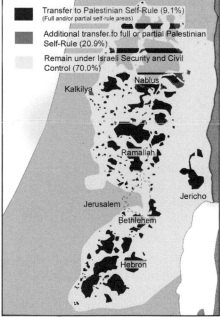

Wye Agreement, 1998

Transfer to Palestinian Self-Rule (9.1%) (Full and/or partial self-rule areas)

Additional transfer to full or partial Palestinian Self-Rule (20.9%)

Remain under Israeli Security and Civil Control (70.0%)

Nablus
Kalkilya
Ramallah
Jericho
Jerusalem
Bethlehem
Hebron

Sharm el-Sheikh Agreement, 1999

Transfer to Palestinian Self-Rule (17.2%) (Full and/or partial self-rule areas)

Additional transfer to full or partial Palestinian Self-Rule (23.8%)

Remain under Israeli Security and Civil Control (59.0%)

Nablus
Kalkilya
Ramallah
Jericho
Jerusalem
Bethlehem
Hebron

Adapted from a map developed by Jan de Jong for the Foundation for Middle East Peace and used with their permission.

Oslo II

In September 1995 Rabin and Arafat returned to the White House to sign the Interim Agreement on the West Bank and Gaza Strip, often called Oslo II. This agreement established a schedule for Israeli withdrawals from the Palestinian population centers and divided the occupied territories into three zones: Area A, which was fully controlled by the Palestinian Authority; Area B, under Palestinian civil authority but Israeli military control; and Area C, under full Israeli control. Over time further Israeli deployments were to move more land from Area C into Area B and Area A.

The agreement was not universally accepted by the Jews or the Palestinians. Two months after the White House ceremony, Yitzhak Rabin was assassinated in Tel Aviv by a Jewish religious fanatic. Islamic fundamentalists also launched a series of suicide attacks against Israeli civilians. These developments created a sense of anger and betrayal.

New elections in May 1996 brought Binyamin Netanyahu and the Likud Party back into power in Israel. Netanyahu had been a vocal critic of the Oslo Accords and campaigned on the promise to be tougher on Arafat. His refusal to meet with Arafat for four months created further friction.

The opening of a new exit for an archaeological tunnel that extended along the western side of the Temple Mount in September 1996 brought the simmering tensions to a boil. The Palestinians claimed that the tunnel was a threat to the Dome of the Rock, and bloody riots ensued that included gun battles between Palestinian policemen and Israeli soldiers. At an emergency White House summit, Netanyahu shook Arafat's hand and pledged to negotiate an agreement on the West Bank city of Hebron. That agreement was concluded in January 1997.

The construction of a new Jewish neighborhood (called *Har Homa*) on the southern outskirts of Jerusalem brought a new round of Arab protests. Arafat released suspected terrorists from Palestinian jails and suspended all security cooperation with Israel. The peace process was quickly breaking down.

The Wye River Memorandum

The escalating conflict between Israel and the Palestinians led the United States to intervene once again. Both sides met with President Bill Clinton in Maryland in October 1998, and crafted the Wye River Memorandum. The agreement reaffirmed some of the earlier promises, but it also linked phased Israeli withdrawals to corresponding

Palestinian actions. In addition, the agreement increased the role of the United States in monitoring the compliance of both parties.

The Camp David Summit

New Israeli elections in 1999 returned the Labor Party to power under the leadership of Ehud Barak, who campaigned on the promise of a renewed drive for peace. After several futile overtures to Syria, Barak focused on seeking a comprehensive peace treaty with the Palestinians. This was a last-ditch effort to find a way to cobble together an agreement between two groups who were quickly losing patience with each other. But events were already spiraling out of control.

THE SECOND *INTIFADA:* A BATTLE OF BULLETS AND BOMBS

The fuse for the second *intifada* was lit when the Camp David Summit in July 2000 ended without reaching an agreement. The Israelis and Palestinians each blamed the other's intransigence for the failure. "Ask Barak, and he might volunteer that there was no Israeli offer and, besides, Arafat rejected it. Ask Arafat, and the response you might hear is that there was no offer; besides, it was unacceptable; that said, it had better remain on the table."[297]

The building tension ignited in September when the head of Israel's Likud Party, Ariel Sharon, visited the Temple Mount. Less than two weeks earlier the Palestinians had announced that they would accept no deal with Israel that didn't include all of the territory in the West Bank and all of East Jerusalem, including control of the *Haram es Sharif* (the Temple Mount). They saw Ariel Sharon's walk as Israel's rejection of their demands—and their reaction was swift and violent. The al Aqsa *intifada* had begun.

Rioting erupted throughout the West Bank and Gaza Strip. Before any efforts to restore peace could take effect, two events happened that doomed those efforts. Cameras recorded the death of a twelve-year-old Palestinian boy caught in the cross fire between Israeli soldiers and Palestinian gunmen. The image was repeatedly broadcast on Palestinian television, inciting the people to greater acts of violence to avenge the young boy's life. Then two Israeli soldiers were lynched by a mob in the West Bank. Images of their brutal deaths—along with Palestinians lifting blood-soaked hands in triumph—also made the evening news.

The Palestinians became convinced that Israel had been insincere in their offers of peace and would respond only to threats of continued violence. Israel became convinced that Arafat was cynically orchestrating the violence to force additional concessions and could never be trusted as a partner in peace. Even when Arafat called for a cease-fire, as he did at the end of 2002, Israelis doubted his sincerity. Raanan Gissin, an adviser to Israeli Prime Minister Ariel Sharon, succinctly expressed the view of most Israelis when he responded to Arafat's call by saying, "Arafat has constructed throughout the years an empire of terror and a kingdom of lies. He promised us the peace of the brave and gave us the peace of the grave."[298]

Though Palestinians in general have little love for Arafat and his corrupt cronies in the Palestinian Authority, they continued to back his leadership in their struggles against Israel. But in the meantime, Islamic fundamentalism has emerged as a new threat to Arafat. It offers an alternative to the corruption of the PLO and Palestinian Authority. Hamas and Islamic Jihad have arisen as the more dynamic leaders of the al Aqsa *intifada.* Their suicide bombings against Israeli civilians have pushed Arafat into an awkward political corner. He has been forced to condemn the attacks to satisfy the Western governments who still support him but who find such terrorist actions to be abhorrent. But he refuses to act against the Islamic fundamentalists causing the attacks for fear of causing civil war among the competing Palestinian groups.

Arafat's inability to stop the terrorism has greatly diminished his ability to lead the Palestinian Authority. Following the terrorist attacks against the World Trade Center and the Pentagon on September 11, 2001, the United States and other major nations became far less tolerant of terrorism in any form.

Israel took advantage of this new political reality by aggressively attacking the terrorist infrastructure throughout the West Bank and Gaza Strip. Thousands of suspected terrorists were arrested and scores of terrorists were killed through targeted assassinations. Israel also has reoccupied much of the land that had been under Palestinian control, effectively rolling back the clock on many of the gains made by the Palestinians over the previous decade. The prospects for peace between Israel and the Palestinians that once seemed so promising now appear to be nothing more than fading shadows at twilight.

COUNTING THE COST AND SEEKING SOLUTIONS

Is there any hope for peace, or is the Holy Land doomed to perpetual hatred and strife? It's hard to tell.

Palestinian Agitations

Any solution to this dilemma will come only by recognizing the main points of friction. First, Palestinian morale has suffered a devastating blow. The Palestinians' deep cultural aspirations for a land of their own have been both promoted and continually frustrated, leading to a breakdown in morals. Seeking liberation, the people have succumbed to a new kind of slavery in the form of corrupted morality and behavior.

This breakdown has been carefully portrayed by David Shipler, a reporter who lived among the Palestinians for five years.[299] He describes how their history and schooling under the PLO have woven terrorism into the very fabric of their national psyche. To deny terrorism—both toward innocent civilians and the military—is to deny their racial heritage. Terrorism is justified in the same way one might justify fending off an intruder in your home. Having no other recourse, they feel driven to use terrorism in any form—although they do not call it that. The PLO has redefined "terrorism," declaring that "attacks against Israelis are not terrorism."[300] Violent action in the disputed territories is not considered terrorism, but part of the "nationalist struggle."[301] Thus their deterioration in morale has brought an inevitable deterioration in morals.

Another point of friction is the charge that Israel, a democracy, treats Palestinians as less than human. Palestinians in the West Bank and Gaza Strip cannot become citizens of Israel, and they do not have access to the basic rights granted to citizens. This inequity has been especially noticeable during the two *intifadas* as Israel has allowed little or no appeal to judgments against Arab suspects.[302] When appeals are granted, they are often long delayed. Suspects can be held indefinitely without trial.

Perhaps the most blatant provocation of the Palestinians is the Israeli settlement of Jewish communities in the West Bank and Gaza Strip. This has received almost continuous coverage by the press since 1977 when Menachem Begin began encouraging the program.[303] There are various reasons for this colonization. Some Jews settled there for religious reasons, searching for their biblical heritage. Others simply sought a place of residence from which to commute to the big cities of Tel Aviv and Jerusalem.[304] Many Soviet Jews who immigrated to Israel to escape a rising wave of anti-Semitism in Russia created a market for housing that these new settlements helped satisfy. Though most of the settlements are on barren areas not previously occupied, their existence alarms the resident Arabs. They believe the settlements are a way of conquering the land without the sword.

The Palestinians have therefore looked to the media to dramatize their plight.[305] In the words of Mona Charen, a Washington D.C.-based political writer, "trashing Israel" is a media mania and "what the television news does every night" in the United States.[306] Public

Broadcasting channels have shown a number of films such as *Arafat* and *Days of Rage: The Young Palestinians,* which highlight the Arab cause. Palestinians view the Jews settling in the West Bank as "criminals" and racists, defining racism as "when you don't see another person as human."[307] In their frustration they exaggerate their hardship, "inflating it into a parallel with Jewish suffering at the hands of the Nazis."[308]

Israeli Reactions

Israel's response to the *intifada* was measured and patient at first, but soon accelerated into fierce reprisals. Trained to smash powerful armies with sophisticated weaponry, Israel's Defense Force seemed less prepared to deal with this type of conflict. Officials first tried closing schools and colleges. Later they began demolishing the homes of terrorists and suicide bombers. Then they bombed Palestinian Authority buildings and leveled most of Yasser Arafat's compound in Ramallah, imprisoning Arafat within the few rooms left standing.

Israel justified its actions by basing them on a 1945 military regulation that said: "A military commander may issue an order confiscating . . . any house, building, or land, if there is reason to believe that any firearm was illegally fired from it, or from which were illegally thrown, detonated, exploded, or shot in any other way a bomb, hand grenade, or any other explosive or inflammable device. . . . With the confiscation . . . the commander may destroy the house."[309] Unable to punish rock- and bomb-throwing kids, the Israelis resorted to bulldozing the houses of their parents. This same punishment is now being used against the families of suicide bombers.

From the Palestinians' perspective, the legal principle here seems patently lopsided, like "an eye for a scratch," or "a home destroyed for a suspicion of terrorism." "The injustice . . . turns normal people into criminals."[310]

The most extreme reaction in Israel was that of a radical minority that adopted the views of the late Rabbi Meir Kahane, who advocated the expulsion of Arabs from the land. The rabbi especially warned Jewish girls against dating Arabs at Hebrew University and other colleges, noting that this was another Arabic scheme to seduce younger Israelis to the Palestinian viewpoint. He claimed that "the sexually aggressive Arab is so overpowering that young Jewish women are often advised against going into Arab neighborhoods and villages."[311] So popular was his approach that the radical rabbi was elected to a seat in the Knesset in 1985 and won a 42.1 percent approval rating in a poll of young people.[312] The Knesset, however, strongly denounced Kahane's bigotry and racism.

Effects of the Intifadas

Harshness of life has been a boon to the Palestinians in one way—it has molded them into a closer-knit people. Their struggle has instilled in them a "gang instinct," a unity of the depressed, making sacrifice and even death preferable to submission. Many observers in the West Bank and Gaza have noted this effect. They report an indifference to squalor and order as Palestinians wait for their radical goals to be achieved.

The uprising has also underscored several other facts. First, racism inevitably degenerates morals and deteriorates the quality of living. This is true in both intellectual and domestic pursuits, at the universities as well as in the towns and villages. Even college studies are pursued with vengeance in view.[313] In this adversarial atmosphere the real goals of both peoples have been sidetracked or suppressed. Morality itself has degenerated, as acknowledged by both sides. Golda Meir said it bluntly in a previous struggle: She "could forgive the Arabs for what they had done to the Jews, but she could never forgive them for what they had made Jews do to Arabs."[314]

Second, the conflict and the poverty it has produced have also led to the rise of Islamic fundamentalism. Those passages in the Qur'an that call for the death of the Jews are now used to justify the hate crimes against innocent civilians. Hamas and Islamic Jihad find the squalid slums of Gaza, Nablus, or Jenin to be fertile ground for recruiting suicide bombers seeking immediate entrance into Paradise.

The racial struggle of the *intifada* has put real life on hold in many ways for both sides and has put personal fulfillment largely on ice for the duration.

The Need for Mutual Compromise

The *intifada* has also forced Israel to rethink its policies of annexation. Though some within the Likud Party have insisted on retaining all of biblical Judea and Samaria for secure borders, the need for compromise is becoming more and more apparent. There are, of course, strong elements in both camps that still insist the whole land belongs to them. They refuse to consider compromise. But most Israelis recognize that the basic aspirations of the Palestinians must find a degree of fulfillment. The crucial question is the extent of such a compromise. The idea that this might also mean a degree of independent governance for the Palestinians under Israel is gaining in acceptance. That idea and the guarantee of safe and secure borders for Israel are the essential features that any solution must embrace.

Arafat himself, however, continues to defend his position as the rightful leader and voice of the Palestinians. Israel views him as unacceptable because he broke his promise to renounce violence and secretly used the Palestinian Authority to promote terrorism against Israel. Both sides have hardened their positions since July 2000, and the voices crying for peace have almost grown silent. Any agreement between Israel and the Palestinians is looking less like a peace treaty and more like a settlement in a bitter divorce.

The Continuing Paralysis

In many ways the *intifada* is symptomatic of the quagmire in which Israel finds itself. Though the nation has successfully pursued many of its Zionist goals, its lofty ideals are far from fulfilled. Many are simply in a state of flux.

Though Israel has returned to occupy a good part of its ancient real estate, a tug-of-war yet exists with Palestinians who likewise claim the land. Ironically, the main turf in dispute, Judea and Samaria, is occupied by Arabs. And the coastal plain, once called "the land of the Philistines," is where most of Israel lives (except for the Gaza Strip). That's not a bad bargain, of course, in terms of agriculture, shipping, and material prosperity. Yet such prosperity falls far short of the traditional goals of Zionism.

The same is true for Jerusalem, Israel's long-cherished Holy City. Though the nation moved its capital there from Tel Aviv, Jews are largely restricted to the newer West side. The Old City (except for the Jewish Quarter) and East Jerusalem are occupied by two hundred thousand Palestinians. There stands the Temple Mount, once the religious and social center of the Jewish nation but now the site of one of Islam's international shrines. The Dome of the Rock occupies an elevated place of prominence adjacent to the al-Aqsa Mosque. Though most conquerors of Jerusalem through history had no qualms about renovating the Mount to enshrine their own religious relics, Israel refrained from doing so in 1967. It left intact all the religious shrines.[315]

Arab entrenchment on the Mount today is practically an article of faith for Islam. It's considered the third holiest site in all Islam, just behind Mecca and Medina. Yet that same hallowed spot represents the heart of Israel's religious and social system, the hub around which traditions revolve. Without it, the ancient ritual system and feasts remain but a fond memory.

In the present climate of belligerence, the issues that separate Jews and Arabs appear awesome indeed. Some fear the conflict will continue to escalate, threatening ultimately to engulf the rest of the world, unless the deadlock is soon broken. The area could easily become the breeding ground of endless strife and racial hatred, producing still more generations of terrorists.

This intractable dilemma in the land of the Bible challenges believers to ponder the question of birthright. To whom does the "Holy Land" really belong? Though the question is political, Bible believers do have a responsibility to discern the moral and biblical issues involved. Jesus bluntly rebuked the people of his generation for failing to discern the spiritual meaning of events. We are no less responsible today as God again moves empires to bring Israel to the fore of world affairs.

Having reviewed the political and social forces creating this deadlock, an evaluation of the opposing claims is in order. How do you unscramble scrambled eggs?

To Whom Does the Land Really Belong?

TO WHOM does the Holy Land really belong? The question is arguably one of the most explosive of our time. There is no easy answer, unless it is that the land belongs to the Lord. He laid claim to it long ago, reserving it for his special purposes.

The quiz gets a little stickier, however, when we press the issue and ask why he has allowed the land to be overrun for centuries and now permits it to be made an arena of worldwide strife. And since both Jews and Arabs make forceful claims to the land, what are the crucial factors that should decide a just settlement?

Since God is the architect of all history, overruling in the most precarious of international affairs, we can rest assured that the present conflict in the Holy Land is no mere accident. The Lord has allowed this confrontation between Jews and Arabs to deal with both clans. He will yet be glorified in it.

The current dilemma is by no means limited to Jews and Arabs living in the land; it affects the entire world. Every action of the *intifada* is instantly broadcast in gruesome detail by the world press. Events in one part of the region reverberate into every Jewish kibbutz and Arab village in the Middle East. Jews remember all too vividly the recurring anti-Semitism that periodically seems to sprout worldwide. And Arabs have been aroused to a fresh desire for Muslim world conquest, energized by vastly enlarged treasuries fueled by the sale of oil to the world. These pressing realities move both groups to intense concern over the land.

Evangelical Christians also have a vested interest in the affairs of the land. Besides a historical regard for its past and a moral concern for its present, they have a theological interest in its future. Many see Israel's return to the land as an integral part of Bible prophecy and consider its place on the world scene an essential part of the end times. This prophetic aspect was also one of the basic motivations of the Zionist movement itself. Jewish resurgence in the reborn State of Israel has a twofold significance: It confirms the accuracy of the Scriptures, and it dramatically alerts the church to the sovereign activity of the Lord as he works in international affairs to fulfill his program.

Before investigating that prophetic significance, however, let's briefly grapple with the perplexing issues of moral and international rights to the land. Both corners of the ring constantly charge the other with gross violations of those rights. And frankly, both seem justified in their claims. To whom does the land really belong?

THE PALESTINIAN CLAIMS TO THE LAND

The claims of both Jews and Palestinians are based on several factors, historical and religious. The religious factors must be included since both sides appeal to them as foundational to their historical and international rights to the land. The Palestinian claims may be summarized in five basic propositions, three historical and two religious.

1. *Their long residency in the land.* Palestine was conquered by the Muslim Caliph Omar in A.D. 638, and Arab groups have lived there ever since. When the British wrested the land from the Turks in 1917, Arabs made up the overwhelming majority of the population. The Wilsonian doctrine of "self-determination" ("consent of the governed") was generally accepted by the British as the basis of any post-World War I settlement. This long residency constitutes the main plank in the Palestinians' claim to the land.

2. *The British McMahon-Hussein agreement.* During World War I the British government assured various Arab leaders (mainly the Sharifians of the Hedjaz through Sir Henry McMahon and Winston Churchill) that the entire Levant would become a pan-Arab state. Though these were mainly personal notes, "shrouded in ambiguity, vagueness, and deliberate obscurity," they were taken by the Arabs as Britain's word that the whole of Palestine

would be under Arab rule.[316] This provided them with a claim to the land as part of the spoils of World War I. (See Appendix B.)

3. *Their claim to mini-holocaust reparation.* Many Palestinians who left their homes during the war of 1948 believe they have suffered a holocaust of their own in the refugee camps. Hundreds of thousands of them have "been living in a miserable state as if in jail," having lost their homeland.[317] "The Palestinians, as is well known, are making use of the ancient Jewish strategy of exile," demanding relief from their "krakows" in the refugee ghettos.[318] They maintain that more than fifty years of devastation at the hands of the Jews, without support from their Arab cousins, neutralizes any Jewish cries for Holocaust sympathy. They are convinced that the Jewish "theft and rape" of their country requires reparation and restoration of their people to the homeland.

Some, however, believe their deplorable living conditions were dictated by Arab policy.[319] When the Arab nations could not achieve their political goals through military might, they tried another tack. Palestinians fleeing Israel were refused residence in Arab lands (except in the cramped refugee camps). Nor were they allowed to travel or migrate. Rather than allow refugees to settle in Arab territories, these regimes held the Palestinians hostage in refugee ghettos as "Exhibit A" of Israeli injustice. In sixty-one camps in the West Bank, Gaza, Jordan, Syria, and Lebanon, the Arabs encouraged the Palestinians to become martyrs, "soldiers of pathos."[320] Israel's offer to alleviate these concentration camp conditions was rejected outright by Arab leaders. Proposals to build modern housing outside the camps were scorned. Instead, the Palestinians were left in continued squalor to heighten the wretchedness of their plight.

4. *Their appeal to Abrahamic ancestry.* The Arabs bolster their claim to Palestine by a religious argument derived from the Qur'an. They claim descent from Ishmael, the firstborn of Abraham, to whom the Lord promised the land of Canaan. Though this relation to Ishmael is generally accepted by both Jews and Arabs, "there is nothing in the Bible to indicate that Ishmael was the forefather of the Arabs, nor was this a belief held by the ancient Arabs."[321] This heritage, however, was claimed by Muhammad and is assumed in the Qur'an. "Abraham in truth was not a Jew, neither a Christian; but he was a Muslim."[322] "And We made covenant with Abraham and Ishmael: 'Purify My House for those that shall go about it and those that cleave to it, to those

who bow and prostrate themselves.'"[323] Ishmael is portrayed as a purifier and an elect, righteous leader.[324]

To further validate this, Arab commentators assert that though the Jews were a chosen people, they "forfeited their rights to the land by having broken the covenant with God."[325] This is seen also in Jordanian junior high school texts, which teach that the Jews "lost religion and this world as well . . . at the hands of the righteous Muslims."[326] This Qur'anic reconstruction gives their claim to the land a strong religious base and explains their call for *jihad.*

5. *Arab claims to Jerusalem as al-Quds, "the Holy."* The city of Jerusalem is regarded by Arabs as one of Islam's three Holy Cities (third after Mecca and Medina). This derives from the Hadith tradition that Muhammad ascended to heaven on a horse from the Temple Mount in Jerusalem. So sacred is the Arabic shrine of the Dome of the Rock, built over the ruins of Israel's ancient temple, that it is venerated by Muslims internationally. Prior to 1967, "several hundreds of thousands of Muslim pilgrims came here" every year.[327] Though the Qur'an does not mention Jerusalem by name, and Muhammad never actually visited the city, he at first directed his followers to pray toward Jerusalem and only later toward Mecca. Because of this the Arabs have named the city of Jerusalem *al-Quds,* "the Holy." No issue is so volatile or central to their claims in Palestine as the maintaining of Jerusalem as a Holy City of Islam.

THE JEWISH CLAIMS TO THE LAND

The basic Jewish claims to *Eretz Yishrael,* the land of Israel, can be summarized also in five propositions, both historical and religious. Though these are related, they can be noted separately.

1. *Their ancient and continuous residency in the land.* The land of Canaan was conquered by Joshua (as commanded by God) some two thousand years before the Arabs took it. During that time Israel occupied the region for nearly fifteen centuries. Though many aliens conquered parts of the land and killed or evicted many of the Jews living there, a small remnant continuously remained as caretakers. This continued until modern times. When the British conquered the area in 1917, it was ruled by the Ottoman Turks, not the Arabs. The land had been under Turkish control for about four hundred years. Nevertheless, the Jews always counted Palestine as their native land and never

relinquished their claim throughout their dispersion. Always they longed for restoration to the homeland from which they had been evicted.

2. *The Balfour Declaration.* An essential part of the Versailles Peace Treaty ending World War I was the Balfour Declaration, guaranteeing the Jewish people a national home in Palestine. It gave the League of Nations approval to establish this Jewish haven under the Mandate of Great Britain, which developed the plan partly as a tribute to Chaim Weizmann for his contribution to the war effort.[328] The failure of the British to fulfill this part of the Mandate is regarded by many as a significant factor in the spawning of World War II.

3. *Their need for a haven from the Holocaust.* The Holocaust became an ominous reminder to the world of its need to provide a homeland for world Jewry. Without a land of their own, the Jews were at the mercy of every genocidal madman and had no national government to which to appeal for justice.[329] While the Arabs were promised and received seven national homes carved out of the fallen Ottoman Empire, the Jews were denied a single place to establish a homeland until 1948. Their coming to Palestine was no bit of whimsy; they had no homeland or kindred nations to which they could turn.

4. *Their appeal to the Abrahamic covenant.* Like the Arabs, the Jews have a strong religious attachment and claim to the land. The land of Canaan was promised to Abraham and his seed forever (Genesis 12:7; 13:15). This covenant is the bedrock of Israel's claim to the land, both religiously and historically. Though Ishmael was promised certain divine blessings, it was Isaac whom the Lord named to be heir to the covenant promises (Genesis 17:19-21). This he also confirmed later to Isaac, Jacob, and the children of Israel (Genesis 12:7; 13:15; 15:18; 26:3; 28:13; Deuteronomy 1:8).

Though the privilege of occupying the land was conditioned on Jewish obedience, the ultimate fulfillment of that promise was irrevocable (cf. Deuteronomy 28–30). It was guaranteed by the Lord's sovereign oath, not by Israel's behavior. The land was called a "land that the LORD has given to you and your fathers forever and ever" (Jeremiah 25:5, NKJV; cf. Amos 9:15). This covenant formed the religious basis of the Jews' right to the land in the Old Testament and is also affirmed in the New Testament (Luke 1:32-33, 72-74; Romans 11).

5. *The Jews' religious attachment to Jerusalem.* Like the Arabs, the Jews make a nonnegotiable claim to the city of Jerusalem. This

mountainous citadel is a city "thrice holy," being sacred to three world religions—Judaism, Christianity, and Islam. For the Jews, however, it is central to all their historical and religious traditions. For this reason the new State of Israel quickly moved its government to Jerusalem, declaring the city to be its capital on January 23, 1950.

The destruction of Jerusalem in A.D. 70 traumatized the nation in two ways. It brought an end to Israel's political life and suspended the practice of most of its religious life. Without the temple, sacrifices and offerings ceased. For a nation whose life-blood traditionally flowed through its religious ritual system, the loss of Jerusalem and its temple were catastrophic. No substitute was permitted for these hallowed spots in the God-given system. Thus the plaintive cry of the Jewish people during their centuries of dispersion had been, "Next year in Jerusalem." The "City of Zion" is essential to the Zionist movement and always has been central to the nation. Jerusalem and the Jewish people are indispensable to each other.

EVALUATING THE CLAIMS TO THE LAND

Having read the claims, it's time to return to the question of rightful ownership. To whom does the land really belong? Both Jews and Arabs make convincing claims with compelling arguments. Both come from backgrounds of depression and deprivation that would warrant claims to a homeland. Each appears to deserve the prize, if only as a consolation for past abuses. The pity is that both seek to occupy the same small piece of land.

In evaluating the claims, some key considerations might suggest a path of compromise. Let's review the major claims of each, first the historical and then the religious.

Long Residency

This point has long been argued by both sides. The argument for ancient residency clearly goes to the Jewish side, however, for Canaan had long been their native soil. They antedated the Arabs by nearly two millennia. Long before the Romans called it "Palestine," it was known as "the Land of Israel."

On the other hand, the argument of more recent residency plainly goes to the Arabs who lived there for much of the last thirteen centuries. They conquered the land during Israel's national dispersion. Even so, during much of this time the Arabs did not rule Palestine, for there never was a politically organized State of Palestine. The land was ruled by the Ottoman Turks from 1516 to 1917 and was loosely governed as the lower part of Syria. Most of the land was owned by a small aristocracy of landed gentry, many living in Syria, who farmed out the land to peasants or *fellahin*. In 1922 there were also one hundred thousand Bedouin desert nomads who roamed the area.[330] Though the Arabs predominated in population during this time, they were under the rule of foreigners.

The question then arises as to how long a people may be absent from their land before that land may be appropriated by others. "Is there a statute of limitations that gives a thief the right to his plunder?"[331] Modern courts would doubtless rule that there is, especially when long centuries intervene. The world today is a product of yesterday, but it can hardly be held accountable for the deeds of its forefathers. Thus, although the residency issue seems to favor the Palestinians, it says little about political rule. They lived under the Turks for four hundred years. Accepting local autonomy under the State of Israel would not be atypical to their recent past.

British Mandate Guarantees

British promises to both Jews and Arabs were far too grand and unrealistic. The interpretations of each inevitably set the two peoples on a collision course. Both pressed their claims too widely. The Jews took the promise of a "homeland in Palestine" to mean a Jewish State over all of ancient Judea, Samaria, Galilee, and Transjordan. The Arabs assumed they would establish a state over the whole eastern Levant.

Events subsequent to World War I quickly disillusioned the Jews when the British gave Transjordan (three-quarters of the whole) to Abdullah as a consolation prize for his loss of Syria. The Arabs continued to dream of a pan-Arab state over the whole Levant. This was contrary to what the British Royal Commission of 1927 had said. "If King Hussein and Emir Feisal secured their big Arab State . . . they would concede little Palestine to the Jews."[332] When the territory was later carved up and seven Arab states were assigned, however, the Arabs insisted on a state in Palestine as well.

It's often noted that the Balfour Declaration not only guaranteed "the establishment in Palestine of a national home for the Jewish people," but also that "nothing shall be done which may prejudice the civil and religious rights of existing non-Jewish communities in Palestine."[333] The charter insisted that the civil and property rights of Palestinians would be carefully protected or compensated for. This responsibility was reinforced by the UN General Assembly, which passed a further resolution on December 11, 1948. It said that "refugees wishing to return to their homes and live at peace with their neighbors" should be allowed to do so, and that "compensation should be paid for the property which . . . should be made good by the Governments or authorities responsible."[334] Because of this, many have charged that the chief violators of the Mandate were the Jews who failed to protect the local Palestinians or to return the refugees to their homes in Israel after the war.

That charge levels a serious indictment against Israel and is frankly inescapable. The estimate is that "more than 60 percent of Israel's total land area consisted of tracts abandoned by former Arab proprietors or squatters," though much of this was wasteland.[335] "In 1954 more than a third of Israel's Jewish population lived on absentee property" of the Arabs.[336] This expropriation of Arab property was to be only temporary, but the Knesset legalized it in 1951.

To most observers this confiscation appears to be wholesale thievery. This, of course, has been the basic grievance of the Palestinians and the most potent moral charge by the Arab community against Israel.

There is, however, another side to the story. When the United Nations partitioned the land in 1947 and both sides prepared for war, many Arabs fled their homes in Israel due both to Jewish pressure and to warnings by Arab leaders. The expulsion was indeed a dark chapter in Israel's history, aggravated by the climate of war and Arab threats.[337] The first to leave were the two warring families, the Husseinis and the Nashashibis.

When the UN General Assembly called for peace negotiations after the war, the issue of repatriations got hung up on the requirement of peaceful relations. "The Arabs insisted that . . . the refugee question be fully resolved before they would so much as consider peace negotiations."[338] The Ben-Gurion cabinet, on the other hand, "took the position that return of the refugees was dependent upon the establishment of a formal peace; otherwise the repatriated Arabs would pose a threat to Israel's security."[339] One demanded repatriation first; the other required assurances of peace. Thus the process was deadlocked, and the refugees were padlocked.

Many of these homeless families were forced to remain in the squalor of the camps by their Arab leaders. A mere thirty-five thousand did return, but the rest became pawns in a game of Near East brinkmanship. This greatly complicated the repatriation provisions of the Balfour Declaration, making them almost impossible to fulfill. The terms of peace had to grow out of negotiations, but Arab leaders refused to negotiate.

Another part of the Balfour agreement has often been overlooked. Though Israel failed to repatriate the Palestinians who fled the land, Arabs also failed to fulfill their end of the bargain. The Balfour Declaration concludes: "Nothing shall be done which may prejudice . . . the rights and political status enjoyed by the Jews in any other country."[340] That provision was flagrantly violated. The fact is that most Jews in Arab countries were quickly deported, many with only the clothes on their backs. While nearly eight hundred thousand Arabs fled Israel in 1948, an equal number of Jews fled from Muslim countries (see Map 8). Without recourse, all Jews in East Jerusalem and the West Bank fled to Israel. Many were "stripped by the Arab governments of most of their belongings, and reduced to complete dependency upon the Jewish welfare organizations in Israel."[341] These Jewish refugees were accepted and integrated into Israel, while most of the Arab refugees from Israel were refused residency in Arab lands. The "Arab governments were to refuse to accept as equal citizens the kinsmen whose plight had been the direct result of their policies. . . . They threw full responsibility for their maintenance on the shoulders of other nations."[342]

These failures on both sides throw light on the modern refugee problem. Whereas Jewish refugees from Arab countries were quickly integrated into the life and workforce of Israel, Arab refugees outside Israel were abandoned, left to fester in isolated camps. While British intentions for the area were no doubt noble, they resulted in chaos.

The state of both Jewish and Arab refugees from that debacle can only be regarded as a fait accompli at this point. The documents that created it can be regarded as little more than dead letters today.

Religious Claims to the Land

Both parties to the conflict are unabashedly religious, basing their claims partly on religious grounds (though only 10 percent in Israel regard themselves as strictly religious). Both live in nations in which state and religion are closely related. Leaders of Israel's Knesset, for instance, are often forced to acquiesce to certain orthodox groups on key issues in order to stay in power. The aggressive settlements on the West Bank were spawned largely by such zealots. That is also true in the Arabic states where Islamic fundamentalism continues as a powerful, driving force.[343]

This accounts for some of the sharp differences between Jews and Arabs in the land. Religious separatism is a racial trait and almost a matter of patriotism. The two groups refused for more than forty years even to sit down to negotiate a peace treaty. When Israel and the Palestinians finally did try to negotiate a settlement, it collapsed over the issues of refugees, the status of Jerusalem, and control over the Temple Mount area. They are simply not on speaking terms today. The disturbing fact is that much of this contempt stems from each side's religious background. Each is on a mission that joins civil and religious ideals, demonstrated in their claims to the land itself. They both possess a passion for the land as their divine heritage.

The further significance of this religious claim will be elaborated under the fifth claim concerning the appeal to Abraham.

Claims to Jerusalem

Central to the affections and ambitions of both groups is the city of Jerusalem. Throughout history both have engaged in a passionate love affair with this mountainous metropolis. Though venerated as a royal city, it is supremely revered as a religious and holy place. The shrines on Mt. Moriah go back to the earliest times for both groups. Those shrines, of course, are located on the same spot, one built over the ruins of the other.[344] The Islamic shrines of the Dome of the Rock and the al-Aqsa Mosque now stand on the Temple Mount, the site of the Jewish temples of Solomon, Zerubbabel, and Herod.

In examining the histories of these shrines and the reasons they were built, some striking distinctions appear. The Jewish temple was ordered by the Lord and became the heart of Israel's ritual system. It was hallowed by many divine visitations and sanctified by the Lord's presence in many miraculous events. The temple was not just one revered shrine among several, but Israel's one and only God-given place of worship, the one specific spot ordained by God himself (Deuteronomy 12:4–14). Deprived of this ancient temple, Israel remains a political state but lacks the religious system that once held the state together.

For the Muslim world, on the other hand, Jerusalem's shrines are secondary and almost incidental. Jerusalem ranks third in importance after Mecca and Medina. Muhammad never even visited the city, only venerating it as a point toward which Muslims were to pray while he sought Jewish support in Medina. That all changed after he conquered Mecca.[345] The notion that he ascended to heaven on a winged horse is a later fabrication. Yet Muslims have assiduously sought to cover up or supplant Judaism and its religious relics in Jerusalem. They early bricked up the Eastern Gate through which Messiah was to come, and constructed the two great Muslim shrines over the Temple Mount, which they call *Haram es Sharif* (literally, "Noble Sanctuary").[346] Islam has always endeavored to supplant Judaism and Christianity, for it sees Muhammad as the final prophet, upstaging both Moses and Jesus.

These facts indicate that the various appeals to religious shrines in Jerusalem are more political than religious. So politically sensitive is the Muslim world to Jerusalem's shrines that it promises an Islamic

Map 8: Return of Jews to Israel since 1948

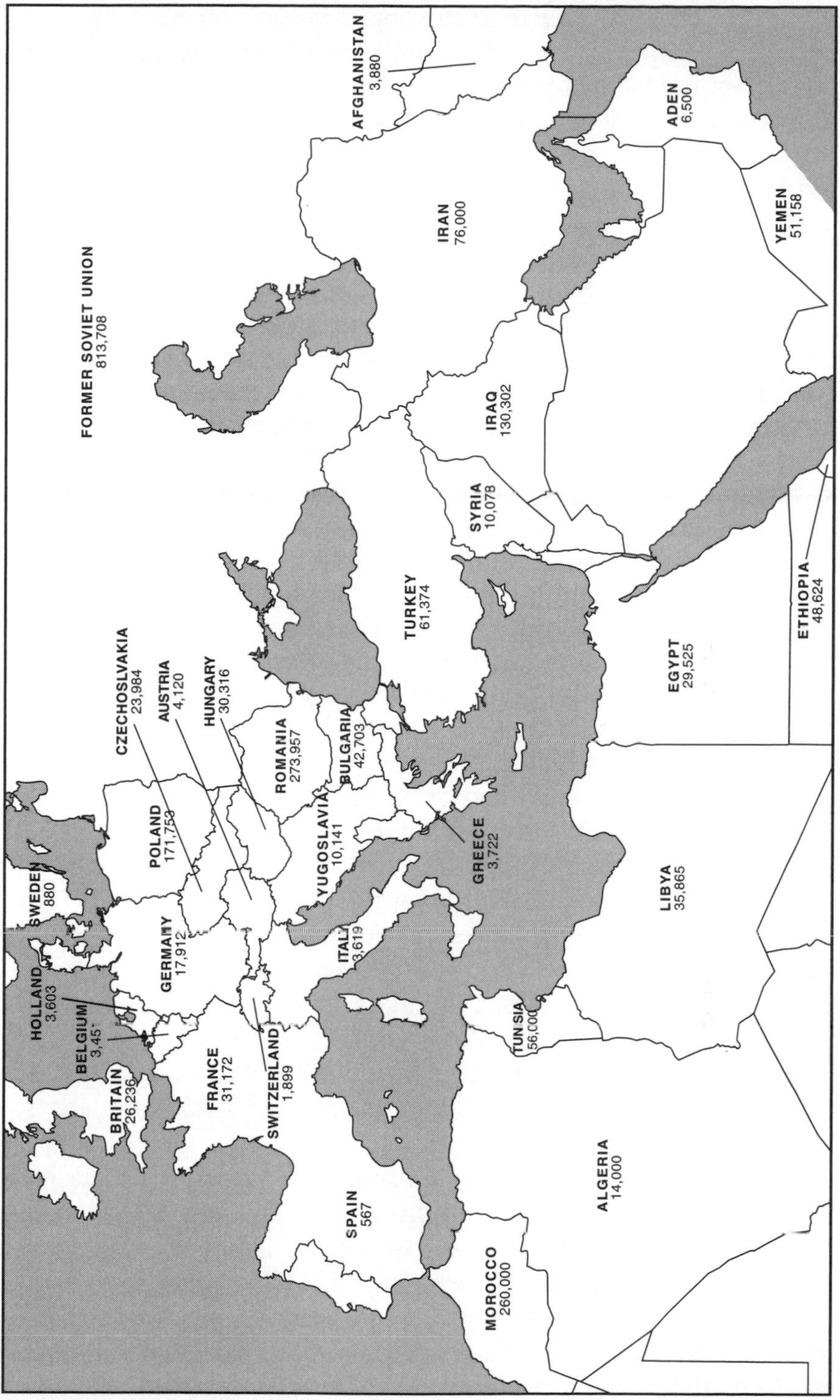

AFGHANISTAN
3,880

ADEN
6,500

IRAN
76,000

YEMEN
51,158

FORMER SOVIET UNION
813,708

IRAQ
130,302

SYRIA
10,078

ETHIOPIA
48,624

TURKEY
61,374

CZECHOSLOVAKIA
23,984

AUSTRIA
4,120

HUNGARY
30,316

EGYPT
29,525

ROMANIA
273,957

BULGARIA
42,703

POLAND
171,753

YUGOSLAVIA
10,141

GREECE
3,722

SWEDEN
880

LIBYA
35,865

GERMANY
17,912

ITALY
3,619

HOLLAND
3,603

BELGIUM
3,451

FRANCE
31,172

SWITZERLAND
1,899

TUNISIA
56,000

BRITAIN
26,236

ALGERIA
14,000

SPAIN
567

MOROCCO
260,000

holy war if the shrines are threatened. No issue more quickly inflames the Arab world than this religious one.

That is also true for the Jews. The Western Wall and, ultimately, the entire Temple Mount constitute the center of their whole ritual system. That site, originally purchased by David, became the nonreplaceable hub of Israel's religion. Though the Muslim claim to Jerusalem is more politically passionate, the Jewish claim has stronger historical support.

Appeals to Abraham

This battle for the land has often been called a war between two books, the Qur'an and the Talmud.[347] In many ways it's a conflict between the Qur'an and the Bible. Two sources of religious authority are pitted against each other, each claiming support from Abrahamic ancestry. The Jews appeal to the detailed story of Abraham in the Old Testament; the Muslims appeal to a reconstructed story of Abraham given by Muhammad in the Qur'an. By any evaluation, the Qur'an is a revision of the Bible with Arabic overtones. It reinterprets and revises both the Old Testament stories of Abraham and Ishmael and the New Testament stories of Jesus. Abraham is transformed into an Arabic sheikh; Jesus' birth and death are completely recast with a Bedouin touch, denying the New Testament emphasis on his death and resurrection and his rightful claim to be the divine Son of God.

This reconstructed history dismisses the sworn word of the Lord to Abraham, Isaac, and Jacob concerning the fulfillment of his covenant. It also seeks to nullify the covenant with David that was declared to be as lasting as the moon in heaven (Psalm 89:33-37). Ultimately, it would destroy the covenant structure of the Word.

The Qur'an fails the basic tests of authenticity. It presumes to confirm itself by its own word and is without miraculous confirmations or prophetic fulfillments demonstrating its divine authority. Both the Old and New Testaments warn of such distortions of God's Word, especially when claiming to come from a messenger or an "angel from heaven," as does the Qur'an (Deuteronomy 18:18-22; Galatians 1:8; Qur'an XCVIII:2).

In evaluating the two claims to Abraham's covenant, one is left in little doubt as to whom the Lord intended as the heir. The Bible emphasizes God's selection of Isaac over Ishmael, even to the chagrin of Abraham (Genesis 17:18-19). Though Ishmael was accorded special blessings, the covenant promises were assigned specifically to Isaac and his seed as "an everlasting covenant." Muslims respond that the children of Israel sinned away their covenantal privileges; their plunge into sin and idolatry resulted in the loss of covenant blessings, as explained by the Qur'an (Sura 155-60).

Such a contention is certainly not unique to Islam. The notion was prominent in the early church and is still popular in many churches today. Church fathers from both East and West excoriated the Jews. In the forefront of this theological faux pas were Chrysostom and Augustine, followed later by reformers Luther and Calvin. As Chapman says, "The crucifixion of the Jew Jesus by order of the whole Jewish community has been made a cornerstone of all Christian theology, supported by the implication that in the eyes of God the Jews are forever accursed."[348]

Using Paul's argument in Romans 2:29 and Galatians 3:7, the early church made itself the heir to all the Abrahamic blessings promised Israel. Even today many see the church as the New Testament fulfillment of Israel.[349] The apostle firmly rejected that idea in Romans 9–11, however, declaring that the Lord will one day restore Israel to its place of favor and will fulfill the Old Testament promises to Abraham.

For the Muslims, the cursing and discarding of the Jews by God is standard doctrine. They believe their mission today is to reoccupy the land first taken by Caliph Omar in 738 and to preserve the sacred shrines of Islam at Jerusalem.[350]

Religious Jews reject such an assessment as blasphemy and consider the Qur'an "an incoherent rhapsody of fable, precept, and declamation" that so distorts history as even to confuse the sister of Moses with Mary the mother of Jesus.[351] The orthodox of Israel doggedly persist in claiming *Eretz Yishrael* as theirs by eternal inheritance from Abraham through the line of Isaac and Jacob.

From this perspective the controversy over the land can ultimately be seen as a clash between two books, the Bible and the Qur'an. Two religious authorities are pitted against each other in the battle for ownership of the land. For Bible believers, the issue would be cut-and-dried if the religious claim were the only consideration.

CURRENT WISDOM IN SEARCH OF A SOLUTION

With the many issues involved, any resolution will require something of a balancing act. Though the historical claims of the Jews to the land are irrefutable, the Palestinians have a hammerlock on the residency issue. They live there, the Abrahamic covenant notwithstanding, and constitute a growing force both in Israel and in the disputed territories. Likewise, appeals to the British mandate agreements are moot, whatever their original intentions. The fact is that both Jews and Arabs defaulted on those agreements. As the Jews violated the property rights of the Palestinians, the Arabs violated the rights of Jews in Arab lands. Yet the most loudly proclaimed issue in the Middle East today is the cry of the Palestinians for justice and repatriation. This they deserve, but not without similar justice on all sides.

A workable solution to the impasse has long baffled the experts, and little sign of a solution is in sight. Many on-the-scene journalists, clergy, psychiatrists, politicians, and military people have suggested all manner of solutions. Although the Likud government in Israel continues to allow some expansion of settlements on the West Bank, others within Israel appear more conciliatory to permanently giving up parts of the West Bank and Gaza Strip to the Palestinians in some kind of agreement. All Israelis agree that the security of Israel's borders is a prerequisite, but many also concede that some concessions to the Palestinians are essential as well. Without such compromise, the uprising threatens to explode into regional war.

From this background, we should consider the options that might bring a measure of peace to the area. Though extremist views continue to be expressed on both sides, a middle ground must be found.

A Fully Independent Palestinian State

The Palestinian Authority demands that Palestinians be given both independence and statehood. It's important to remember that the present Palestinian population in the Middle East is made up of two communities—those in the disputed territories of the West Bank and Gaza (about 3.6 million) and those outside the land in the surrounding Arab countries (about 4.2 million).[352] Both have played significant roles in the conflict. It was the outside community that generated the PLO and mobilized guerrilla forces to agitate for repatriation of its people. But since December 1987, the inside community has been the most active. Both communities today clamor for Israel to restore the pre-1967 borders (based on UN Resolution 242).

Many in Israel respond that a type of independence may be viable and even essential but that such an entity must not be a fully independent sovereign state. Such statehood is unacceptable to Israel for several reasons. First, such an Arab state would greatly endanger the security of Israel. It would pose a potential military threat, allowing weapons and artillery to be positioned within firing range of Israel's heartland.

Second, Israel questions whether Palestinians have the ability to handle full sovereignty. The Palestinians have never incorporated as an independent state. Many have only recently settled there from other Arab regions. Originally a part of southern Syria, the area is made up of people only loosely identified as a nationality. Though

Yasser Arafat is the head of the Palestinian Authority, his track record as a civil and political leader is abysmal. Billions of dollars in aid sent to the Palestinian Authority over the past decade were lost to corruption and mismanagement.

The Palestinian Authority is made up of many splinter groups with widely differing philosophies. They maintain a semblance of unity only in their struggle with Israel. As Harkabi says, past Arab wars with Israel were "really a cover-up for their own internal incohesion and problems."[353] David Grossman quotes a Palestinian as saying, "Arafat is bourgeois. He drives a Mercedes. He doesn't feel the suffering of the refugees. All the Fatah commanders have houses in Syria and the Gulf states. Arafat has no supporters here."[354]

There is little evidence that such a new state could sustain itself, politically, militarily, or economically in the dog-eat-dog world of the Middle East. Surrounded by voracious neighbors, it could shortly become another Lebanon, rife with violent factions each seeking power. The demands of an independent state would likely overwhelm a people lacking the essential ingredients for such sovereignty.

These considerations also suggest the futility of the Western proposals to install a democratically elected government in the West Bank and Gaza Strip. Though noble, it's sheer fantasy in the real world of the Arab East. As Walter Reich has written, "You Americans are trying to impose European notions on the Middle East, and you'll succeed as much as you succeeded when you tried to impose democracy on the Diem regime in South Vietnam. It's foolish to impose such notions here. Are there any democratic countries among the Arab states? Was anybody elected in those countries? Sadat? Mubarak? Assad? Democratic notions are simply irrelevant in this part of the world."[355] In the Palestinian Authority itself, opposition to leadership is unhealthy. Its inner circle rules with an iron fist. Anyone who deviates from the party line to suggest some type of accommodation with Israel is earmarked as a collaborator.

From this perspective, it's absurd to propose a fully independent Palestinian State with a democratically elected government. The Palestinians are not prepared for democratic principles. Under any sponsorship, elections could easily be manipulated by the different factions. And the Palestinian Authority frowns menacingly on anyone undertaking independent action. Likewise, if an independent Arab state were set up there, it would likely be as totalitarian as the other Arab states. And if those in control were to pursue the one-issue agenda of "liberating the remainder of Palestine," the end result would be an inevitable war with Israel that would result in more misery and destruction for the Palestinian people.

Autonomy or Limited Statehood

A more viable and compelling option appears to be Palestinian autonomy under Israeli sovereignty, or limited Palestinian statehood.[356] Under such a plan the resident Palestinians would have a measure of self-rule and also regain some of the prosperity many enjoyed prior to the start of the *intifada*. The plan would give Palestinians the authority to govern and police themselves, building a unique society of their own. But by not allowing them to build an army, Israel could maintain secure borders and world peace might be enhanced. Many variations of this plan have been suggested. Its viability lies in the fact that such an arrangement would fully conform to Palestinian history, for the Palestinians have always enjoyed local autonomy under a larger sovereignty.

The obvious snag in this plan is that any such government, in order to be successful, would need to accept painful choices and compromises that, to this point, they've been unwilling to make. Such a plan would require a government willing to stand against Islamic fundamentalists and their goal of "cleansing" Palestine of the Jews. The plan would also require the Palestinian Authority to stifle the aspirations of many Palestinians living outside of Israel who demand repatriation rather than reparation or compromise. It would require the Palestinians to accept far less land than they were initially offered by the United Nations plan for partition in 1947. And it would require the government to stand against other Arab states that still refuse to accept the very existence of the State of Israel. Except for Egypt and Jordan, most Arab states still hold adamantly to the Khartoum resolution of 1967, which declared: "No peace with Israel, no recognition of Israel, no negotiations with Israel."[357] There is virtually no plan that would satisfy this mind-set short of liquidating Israel.

A second problem is the fact that the Palestinian Authority, the group with whom Israel has been negotiating, has used terrorism to pressure Israel. This directly violates their pledge to renounce terrorism and to negotiate in good faith. Yet the U.S. State Department and much of the liberal community of America and the world urge Israel to negotiate with the Palestinian Authority and work toward the creation of a Palestinian state.[358] Aroused by distorted media images, popular opinion clamors for some kind of a short-term solution. Israel's long-term principles are generally rebuffed in favor of short-term reprieves. That, of course, is the underlying purpose of the *intifada* as orchestrated by the Palestinian Authority, and its persistence was paying off until the events of September 11, 2001, made all forms of terrorism odious to most of the world.

In evaluating the oft-repeated condemnation of Israel by some in the West, we naturally ask what alternative they have in mind. How should Israel respond to suicide bombers or to the leaders who use such atrocities to further their political agenda? To put the shoe on the other foot, how do Egyptians or Syrians respond to civil unrest or terror attacks? Do those in America or Europe who condemn Israel have a more civil way of handling terrorists? On September 11, 2001, the United States experienced firsthand what Israel has endured for more than fifty years. Our response has been to go after those who plotted the attacks. We have invaded nations, captured individuals in other countries, and even launched missile attacks against individual terrorists. While violent reprisals that target innocent civilians are certainly to be condemned, we must make sure that we don't hold to a double standard when it comes to the rights granted to a nation to protect its citizens.

OWNERSHIP RIGHTS SUMMARIZED BY TWO PRINCIPLES

To whom does the land really belong? The evidence seems to point in two directions. It belongs both to the Arabs and the Jews. Personal property justly belongs to those who possess it by rightful purchase or acquisition. Abraham is the one man who both Jews and Arabs would agree was given ownership of the land. But the only piece of land actually purchased by Abraham was the burial cave he purchased for his wife—paying the full asking price to its owner (Genesis 23).

Though many previous generations may have stolen or wrongfully possessed the land, the children can hardly be held responsible for the sins of their fathers (Ezekiel 18:20). The first principle is that tangled history cannot be undone or untangled. Any agreement must begin with things as they are and make reasonable reparations from that point. By this principle, both the Arabs and Jews have a right to the property and local communities in which they live and should be accorded that privilege with all its benefits.

This principle admittedly works a hardship on those in refugee camps because of the policies of the sparring governments. Those governments owe them proper reparation with the help of the world community. They were uprooted by Jews and Arabs both. As the Jewish community has absorbed Jewish refugees from Arab lands, the Arab countries are responsible to absorb those refugees who fled from Israel.

The square mileage of Arab countries is vastly greater than that of Israel. A peaceful solution must deal with the realities of the present, not the tedious recriminations of the past. Justice demands that present property rights of both communities be recognized and respected.

The second principle is the right of sovereignty. Though much of the property in Israel and its territories belongs to the Palestinians, the sovereignty of that land belongs to Israel. The nation acquired that sovereignty in the same way as Britain and the Muslim Turks did before. Though much of the land was not purchased, Israel was forced to possess it for national survival when the world community refused to defend the partitioned allotment given. Israel was forced to carve out secure borders when threatened by hostile neighbors. What nation has not similarly established itself? What Arab nation has not done likewise?

This sovereignty principle is not always palatable to those who find themselves under the sovereign. This is especially true of the Arab population in Israel. It is, however, consistent with the pattern of history. The Muslims, for instance, conquered many lands and held sovereignty over many nationalities. They often gave short shrift to those who resisted that sovereignty. When the sovereignty principle is accepted and applied to all, however, it operates for the good of all.

The outworking of these two principles is indispensable to lasting peace in Israel. Israel, the sovereign, is responsible to protect the property rights and culture of the resident Palestinians, as well as that of the Jews. Likewise, the Arab Palestinians in Israel are responsible to respect the sovereignty of Israel that governs the land for the good and prosperity of all. No one is forced to conform personally, for emigration is always an option. But neither should anyone try to force the sovereign government to relinquish its prerogatives and responsibilities.

These principles are best served and promoted by the democratic process. Though democracy is admittedly a strange notion in the Middle East, it is Israel's chosen model of government. As such it is being agonizingly hammered out through the political process, and must be propagated through the education of both groups living in Israel. The goal of democracy is not to satisfy the whims of all its constituents all the time, but to seek the general welfare of all under its sovereignty. That was also the intent of the Balfour Declaration as approved by the international congress.

The Middle East dilemma reminds us again that politics is the art of the possible, not necessarily the perfect or the ideal. As the grand ideal of a single Arab nation is still a shimmering hope, so Israel's dream of setting up a new Kingdom of David is yet to be realized. That messianic vision has driven Jews to their ancient homeland to set up a political state, but the final restoration of Zionism involves the soul of the nation. That spiritual dimension is another story, the final drama, to which we must now give attention.

Divine Assessment and Promised Restoration

THE MIDDLE EAST has commanded world attention today as a center of military operations. But that's not the whole story. A massive supernatural confrontation is also in the making. Not that God is necessarily on one side or the other, but he is certainly using both to fulfill his purposes. Far from being frustrated or aborted, those purposes are being further highlighted in the unfolding drama. The Lord's invisible chariots have not retired but still patrol the earth (Zechariah 1:10-17).

To appreciate the significance of this spiritual dimension, we need to consider certain biblical promises and their relationship to the current struggle. Without reference to the divine perspective, this review of Israel's perilous journey through church history would be incomplete.

A BIBLICAL ASSESSMENT
The New State Related to Prophecy

For Bible believers, Israel's return to the land often conjures up scenes of anticipation and expectancy. And it should. But since the Zionists have achieved their goal of establishing a homeland, some questions naturally arise. Is this really the return of which the prophets spoke? Those Old Testament seers had much to say of Israel's return to the land in the end times. Most climaxed their prophecies on this note. Likewise, Jesus and the New Testament writers pointed to this return. Are we to assume that those prophecies are now being fulfilled? Or are we being conned by prophetic impostors?

The prophet Ezekiel explicitly describes this future return of Israel to its land (Ezekiel 36–39). After portraying Judah's desolation and scattering for idolatry and obstinacy, the prophet declares the Lord's vow to restore all Israel to the land (Ezekiel 36:5-8, 17-24). That restoration was to begin with a physical regathering that would issue in a final spiritual renewal. The "dry bones" of Ezekiel 37 describe the spiritual deadness of the "whole house of Israel" both in dispersion and while it reassembles in the land in the end times. Following that return, a great northern invasion will take place by "Gog" from the "far north" with its allies (Ezekiel 38:2-13). The confrontation climaxes in the destruction of Israel's enemies, whereupon Israel itself is spiritually renewed (Ezekiel 39:25-29).

The prophet Zechariah predicted that in the final days "Judah will be besieged as well as Jerusalem" (Zechariah 12:2), indicating a Jewish return to the land as a harbinger of the end-time events. The "house of Judah" will occupy the land, and this physical restoration precedes the nation's spiritual restoration (12:10–13:1). Jesus also announced that the Jewish people will be back in the land, with a rebuilt temple, as the final days come to their climactic end. He specifically tells those "in Judea" what to do when they "see standing in the holy place 'the abomination that causes desolation'" (Matthew 24:15-16).

This reminds us that the final restoration of Israel is yet future and will be both total and divinely accomplished. The extremes of optimism and despair that now prevail could well be a part of that initial process of Israel's return in unbelief. New birth does not come without birth pangs.

We might do well, too, to consider how quickly events in the Middle East have moved since World War I. Egypt, for instance, was established as the first modern Arab nation in 1922; that was the same year the Jewish National Home in Palestine was approved by the League of Nations. Three years later, the first universities of both Arabs and Jews were established in Cairo and Jerusalem respectively.[359]

On the scene today are two ancient peoples with fabulous histories demanding a place among the nations, each bringing its own load of cultural baggage. As we've already seen, both claim the same land, and both appeal to their relationship to Abraham to authenticate their rights. Since the question of divine rights through the Abrahamic covenant is a crucial question, let's begin by noting how those promises are being expropriated on the one hand and misappropriated on the other.

The special issue that concerns us here is the Bible's promise to Abraham that his children would inherit the land of Canaan. Both Jews and Arabs believe their relationship to Abraham is the legitimate one, authenticated by a sacred book. The central issue of this conflict is whether the Bible or the Qur'an has divine authority. The issues of the land and its relics are almost incidental to this spiritual core.

THE MUSLIM EXPROPRIATION OF COVENANTAL RIGHTS

The essence of this religious problem may be seen in the struggle over the sacred shrines of Jerusalem. When Caliph Omar took Jerusalem in 638, he immediately built a crude mosque over the temple ruins, which Byzantine Christians had used as a rubbish dump. Umayyad Caliph Abd al-Malik completed this Dome of the Rock in 691, making it a shrine of elegance and splendor. This he did not only to honor Muhammad, but to "instil [sic] a sense of pride in Muslims overawed by the majestic churches of Christendom." It was "intended to make a symbolic statement to both Jews and Christians, the two religions that Islam considered its imperfect predecessors."[360] By building over Solomon's temple, it proclaimed to Jews that Islam had superseded their religion. The heart of Israel's religion was covered over by the religious shrines of the Muslims.

The message to Christians was even more ominous and explicit. Ornaments from Christian Byzantine rulers were used to decorate the inner shrine of the Dome, signifying the spoils of the victor. Islam had risen to supplant Christianity. It also underlined this point in its founding inscription: "O you People of the Book, overstep not bounds in your religion, and of God speak only the truth. The Messiah, Jesus, son of Mary, is only an apostle of God, and His Word which he conveyed unto Mary, and a Spirit proceeding from him. Believe therefore in God and his apostles, and say not Three. It will be better for you. God is only one God. Far be it from his glory that he should have a son."[361]

A more blatant put-down would be hard to find. The beautiful Dome of the Rock, with its golden luster and mathematical rhythm, became a spectacular symbol of Islam's challenge to both Judaism and Christianity. Its very splendor declares its rejection of the Christian doctrines of the Trinity and the divine Sonship of Christ. In this it merely reflects the teachings of the Qur'an, which openly dismiss the Bible's covenantal promises to the "people of the book."

By this distortion the Qur'an bestows upon Muslim Arabs a divine right to the land through Abraham and Ishmael. Muhammad, in fact, made this a cornerstone of Islam.[362] This claim of Abrahamic inheritance compels the Arabs to militancy. "Islam is a militant religion, which makes perpetual war incumbent on the Muslim community until the whole world is subjected to its rule."[363] This, of course, is not loudly proclaimed, except when Muslims are in the majority. Parts of the Qur'an encourage a philosophy of retaliation, justifying *jihad* on unbelievers who obstruct the faith.[364]

THE ISRAELI MISAPPROPRIATION

As the Muslim Arabs have expropriated the biblical promises to the land, so also the Jews have tended to misappropriate them. Some Israeli leaders have appealed to the biblical covenants as grounds for their political right to the land. Others have similarly politicized the Abrahamic covenant, misappropriating it to defend their claims. In so doing they've forgotten to read the fine print. So that we do not make the same mistake, we need to take a closer look at that covenant with its detailed stipulations.

Israel's divine right to the land rests on two Old Testament covenants, as discussed in Chapter 2. The first was that which was given to Abraham, and later confirmed to Isaac and Jacob (Genesis 12:7; 13:15; 17:8; 26:3; 28:13). This covenant was also later used to reaffirm Israel's right to cross the Jordan into Canaan (Deuteronomy 1:8). The second, often called the Palestinian covenant, was given to Moses before the nation entered the Promised Land (Deuteronomy 28–30).[365] This second covenant elaborated on the Abrahamic treaty. In this lengthy treatise the Lord itemized the conditions under which Israel could occupy the land. He reminded them that he was the covenant Lord and they would be his tenants or guests.

Grounded on the Abrahamic covenant, the promise of the land was unconditional; it guaranteed that the land of Canaan would eventually be Israel's forever (Psalm 105:9-11). But related to the Palestinian covenant, its benefits were conditional. The land would be theirs ultimately; but the enjoyment of it by succeeding generations had specific strings attached. Obedience was required of those who would occupy the land.

That this promise and its conditions would be enforced was demonstrated time and again in ancient Israel as the nation moved through cycles of blessing, disobedience, judgment, repentance, and restoration. It almost seemed as if the people became addicted to the pattern. At issue was the Lord's covenant-keeping character. To underscore the certainty of his Word, the Lord twice allowed the temple to be destroyed and the people scattered. From the last calamity in A.D. 70 there has yet to be a complete restoration.

THE BASIS OF DIVINE RESTORATION TO THE LAND

That covenant also outlined specific conditions for Israel's restoration and return to the land. Certain human conditions had to be met by God's people before he would act. Let's briefly trace those conditions as laid out in the Old Testament. These conditions were first expressed in Deuteronomy 30:1-3:

> And it shall come to pass, when all these are come upon you, the blessings and the curses which I have set before you, and you shall call them to mind among all the nations where the Lord your God has driven you, and shall return to the Lord your God and obey his voice according to all that I command you this day, you and your children, with all your heart and with all your soul; then the Lord your God will bring back again your captivity, and have compassion upon you, and will return and gather you from all the nations where the Lord your God has driven you. (Lamsa version)

Those conditions were later repeated in many Old Testament passages, emphasizing that Israel's return to the land was contingent on its "return to the LORD." Even the physical blessings of the covenant were dependent on its spiritual response. Solomon stressed this in his dedicatory prayer at the temple. Envisioning Israel's future scattering when it would depart from the Lord, Solomon implored the Lord to "hear thou in heaven" when the people would pray (1 Kings 8; 2 Chronicles 6). The Lord replied, "If My people who are called by My name will humble themselves, and pray and seek My face, and turn from their wicked ways, then I will hear from heaven, and will forgive their sin and heal their land" (2 Chronicles 7:14, NKJV).

The same conditions were emphasized by the writing prophets. Joel, one of the earliest, presents a paradigm for restoration both historically and prophetically. His key point was that genuine repentance must precede the blessing of restoration (Joel 2:12-19). Deliverance from both locusts and hostile armies depended on the people's genuine turning to the Lord (2:12).

At the close of the Old Testament, Zechariah gets more specific about what that final turning to the Lord means. He is the most messianic of all the prophets, describing both the Lord's first coming and rejection by Israel (9–11), and his second coming and reception (12–14). After portraying the Lord's future deliverance of the remnant from the gentile armies attacking it, the prophet quotes the Lord: "They will look on Me whom they pierced. Yes, they will mourn for Him as one mourns for his only son, and grieve for Him as one grieves for a firstborn" (Zechariah 12:10, NKJV). He defines that piercing as the wounds "with which I was wounded in the house of my friends" (13:6, NKJV). All this relates to the earlier description of Messiah's vicarious offering "as a lamb [led] to the slaughter" in Isaiah 53:5-7 (NKJV).

When Jesus came the first time and was rebuked by the Pharisees for accepting Messianic honor, he reminded them of what the prophet Daniel had said about that "wounding." Daniel had coupled the "cutting off" of Messiah with the destruction of Jerusalem and the temple (Daniel 9:25-26). In Luke 19:44, Jesus related the two when he said the city would be leveled "because you did not recognize the time of your visitation" (NASB). Their failure to recognize and receive their Messianic visitor would bring the judgment of God on the city. And with that judgment would come also their scattering to the ends of the earth.

This was Zechariah's primary point in describing Israel's future repentance or "turning to the LORD." Central to that national mourning would be the acknowledgment they had wounded Messiah in their house. That deep mourning for and reception of him would bring a spiritual revolution to all the families of Israel, resulting in the physical restoration of Israel to the land.

THE DIVINE MEASURE OF ISRAEL TODAY

What happens when we put the divine plumb line to the house of Israel claiming the land today? Has it met the biblical conditions for restoration? By most human standards, the Jewish people stand high in regard to moral character. They appear to enjoy a surplus of intelligence, industry, self-sacrifice, high morals, and religious sincerity. Furthermore, they endured the Holocaust. From that crucible they have emerged to command international attention, doing so under constant threat of extinction. They have dramatically demonstrated the truth of the maxim, "Growth comes through struggle."

Measured by the divine standard, however, another picture emerges. Though modern Israel has a human and international right to the land, its people fall far short of covenant obligations. To put it bluntly, the current generation has no biblical right to possess the covenant land. The nation has never recognized the Messiah God sent, let alone mourned over his wounding. Though many in Israel admit to Jesus' greatness as a Jewish teacher, most adamantly reject him as Messiah. They see him as but one of several prominent pseudo-messiahs.

The State of Israel will allow nearly every deviation from Jewish orthodoxy in its policy of toleration and pluralism. Even Jewish atheists are welcomed as citizens—but not believers in Jesus. Though the Law of Return of 1950 granted citizenship to anyone born Jewish, the Israeli High Court of Justice ruled in 1962 in a case of a man who had been born Jewish but who had converted to Christianity. They decided that "the fundamental conception that 'Jew' and 'Christian' are a contradiction in terms is something which is unreservedly accepted by all."[366] On December 25, 1989, the Israeli Supreme Court ruled that Messianic Jews "cannot claim the right to come to this country as immigrants by virtue of the Law of Return" because those Jews "who believe in Jesus are 'members of a different faith.' "[367]

Judged on biblical grounds, the nation today does not pass divine muster as a nation living in covenant obedience to God. The promise to possess the land is directly tied to the nation's response to Messiah. Though its international right to the land can be well defended, Israel's divine right by covenant to possess it today has only sentiment in its favor.

THE CHURCH'S RESPONSIBILITY TO ISRAEL TODAY

Care must be taken at this point, lest we get the wrong idea of the church's proper attitude toward Israel. As we have noted, a spirit of animosity has clouded relations between Jews and Christians through most of church history. Too often the church has forgotten that it is "'not by might nor by power, but by My Spirit,' says the LORD of hosts" (Zechariah 4:6, NASB). Though the church today cannot repair that damage, it can narrow the breach by rethinking some of the issues in a spirit of reconciliation. Many Jewish-Christian writers have addressed the problem in an attempt to find some ground of rapprochement. Both Catholics and Protestants have anguished over it, seeking areas of dialogue with Jewish leaders. Let's note several monumental problems separating the two camps that need special clarification if a climate for mutual dialogue is to be found.

Supporting Israel's Right to the Land

Historically, Israel's right to possess the land in any given generation is conditioned on the nation's obedience to God. Today most of those living in the State of Israel are there in unbelief. Does that mean the church should not support any of Israel's claims to the land? The answer is no, for two reasons.

First, as indicated earlier, God does announce a regathering of the people to the land in unbelief prior to the coming of the Messiah (Ezekiel 37:1-14; Zechariah 12:1–13:1). The current restoration of the State of Israel seems to be a harbinger of God's end-time program. And if that's the case, then God's hand is in the establishment of Israel.

Second, the Palestinian covenant was established between God and Israel. God, and God alone, has the right to determine the level of blessing or cursing to be meted out to his people. But the Abrahamic covenant does have a component that applies to all the nations. God said, "I will bless those who bless you, and whoever curses you I will curse" (Genesis 12:3). Even when Israel was under God's judgment, God still held nations accountable for their treatment of the Jewish people. God judged the Assyrians and the Babylonians for mistreating his people (Jeremiah 50:17-19). God also announced he would judge nations based on their treatment of his chosen people (Jeremiah 30:16; Obadiah 15-17). The Abrahamic covenant is still operative, and God still holds nations accountable to seek ways to bless the Jewish people. And one way to do that today is to support Israel's right to their God-given land.

Clarifying the Guilt of the Cross

One bitter issue dividing Jews and Christians has long been the responsibility for Jesus' death. Many church theologians from earliest times have viciously denounced the Jews for perpetrating that crime. As Rabbi Eckstein notes, "The deicide charge that Jews killed Christ constituted the very heart of Christian anti-Jewishness."[368] Christians labeled Jews "Christ-killers," contributing to the disease of anti-Semitism in the church and in society. Ironically, the cross, which was meant to "reconcile them both in one body to God" (Ephesians 2:16, NASB), was used to create a gaping chasm between them, blunting its real message. The sad but inevitable result was that the Jews developed contempt for the person of Jesus himself.

It wasn't until October 28, 1965, that the Catholic Church at Vatican Council II officially ended the tragedy. It declared in *Nostra Aetate* that the Jews "should not be presented as rejected by God or accursed," and that the passion of Christ "cannot be charged against all the Jews . . . then . . . or of today."[369]

Although this was a dramatic turnaround, it was only negative, not positive. It contained no admission of error by the church. The deicide stigma still lingers and the Vatican continues to refuse Israel even diplomatic recognition.[370] Though Protestant churches have been divided on the issue, most have taken a similar course by strongly denouncing anti-Semitism, especially since the Holocaust.

In evaluating the deicide charge, we should first acknowledge that Jesus did not die at the hands of Jews, but of Romans. He was tried before both a Jewish tribunal and a Roman court. Both Jews and Gentiles condemned him to die, thus sharing the guilt. The Roman Governor Pilate did so after repeatedly declaring Jesus' innocence, thus incurring greater culpability. Furthermore, the method of Christ's death was not by Jewish stoning, but Roman crucifixion. Though instigated by the Jews, his execution was carried out by the Gentiles.

The biblical impulse for the deicide charge comes from a false inference from the early sermons of Peter (Acts 2:23; 3:15; 4:10; 5:30). Facing the very Jews and council members who had condemned Jesus, Peter called for personal repentance. They had personally participated in the wicked act. This Peter did with a view toward fulfilling the Old Testament prophecy of Israel's national blessing that could only follow national repentance (Acts 4:19–21).

Jesus himself predicted that his death would be at the hands of both Jews and Gentiles (Mark 10:33). The chief priests and scribes would deliver him up to the Gentiles, who would mock, spit upon, scourge, and kill him. That dual responsibility is constantly emphasized in later Scriptures. John, for instance, related the piercing by a Roman soldier to the prophecy that Israel would one day "look on the one they have pierced" (John 19:34–37; Zechariah 12:10). Paul also made no mention of the instigators of Jesus' death, asserting rather that he "was delivered up because of our transgressions" (Romans 4:25, NASB). "Christ died for our sins," he said (1 Corinthians 15:3, NASB). He declared that it was God "who did not spare His own Son, but delivered Him up for us all" (Romans 8:32, NASB). Jesus also said that no one could take his life, "but I lay it down on My own initiative" (John 10:18, NASB). The focus of his death was not on the instigators (though all were certainly guilty), but that, in his death, God "laid on him the iniquity of us all" (Isaiah 53:6). The Bible jealously guards God's sovereign will in the matter.

Ferreting out the culprits of the crucifixion really misses the point. Jesus himself prayed that the Father would forgive those who committed the act (Luke 23:34). Can we believe he expected the church to do otherwise? He had often warned the disciples against an unforgiving spirit, stressing the point with a lengthy parable (Matthew 18:23–35). An unforgiving spirit suggests one has not experienced forgiveness oneself. For the church to assume the role of avenger shows how far amok it has gone.

Making amends, however, does not mean exonerating the Jews for their part in the crucifixion. It simply means admitting our dual responsibility in the crime. It also means confessing in a corporate way the church's additional guilt for two millennia of vilifying the Jews. While we look for that end-time event predicted by Zechariah when the nation of Israel will mourn for Messiah's death (Zechariah 12:10), a penitent church would make a good prelude. It would be only proper for the church to lead the way by mourning for its part in the slaying of millions of Jesus' brethren. Such an admission might help erase some of the stigma and invite further dialogue with those who are open-minded and searching.

Relating Monotheism to the Person of Jesus

Another fundamental issue separating Jews and Christians is the identity of Jesus. Was he the Son of God as the New Testament proclaims? All else is peripheral.[371] It was here the schism began when Jesus assumed the prerogatives of God by forgiving sins, and it is here that the final focus must be. Any continued dialogue on ethical, philosophical, or racial differences can only be incidental apart from this age-old question. It can't be avoided and it won't go away. In light of the biases and powerful feelings on the issue, is any real dialogue possible? Is there any movement toward reconciliation and is there any room for compromise? What are the current Jewish attitudes toward Jesus after their long dispersion and partial regathering?

The name of Jesus was seldom mentioned explicitly in the Talmud or Midrash, though later Mishnaic literature did make various references to him. These were quite derogatory and scandalous.[372] Often they were defensive responses to a hostile Christian community. The last two centuries (especially since Jewish emancipation from ghetto life) have changed much of that, though the bitterness remains. Changes have occurred on both sides of the controversy. Herbert Danby has made the striking observation that the "Jewish attitude has varied with almost mathematical certainty according to the precise degree in which Christians have shown themselves real followers, in spirit and deed, of their Savior."[373]

During recent years there has been a remarkable openness in Israel to speak and write about the historical Jesus. A "Jesus wave" has been noted in present-day Jewish literature.[374] More has been written in Israel about this prophet from Nazareth since 1948 than in all previous centuries. Pinchas Lapide, an Orthodox Jewish professor, represents this group when he writes, "Any Jewish scholar who examines the New Testament will find that Jesus was undoubtedly a Jew—not just a marginal Jew, nor a lukewarm, *proforma* Jew, but a true Jew, whose spiritual roots rose out of the prophetic core of Israel's faith. . . ."[375] Many Jews have come to acknowledge Jesus as one of the greatest Jewish personalities of all time.

That interest, however, relates to the human Jesus, as he is known to liberal thinkers, not to the divine Son of God presented in the Gospels.[376] Some have accepted his characterization as "Son of God" in the sense of being a messenger or prophet from God or as an outstanding "man of God," but not as the Incarnate God of the New Testament. As Eckstein notes, "Jesus remains overwhelmingly rejected by the Jews as the harbinger of the end of days, prophet, Messiah, and certainly, Son of God."[377] Hebrew scholar Samuel Sandmel declares that those who "regard Jesus as more than a man are inconsistent with Judaism and uncongenial to Jews."[378] Judaism regards the Christian doctrine of the Trinity as a later concoction of the early church, especially the Gospel of John and the epistles of Paul.

This uncompromising rejection of Jesus as God Incarnate is almost an article of faith for Rabbinic Judaism and is based on the familiar *Shema* of Deuteronomy 6:4, often called the "Jewish confession of faith." Though the full *Shema* consists of a catena of passages (Deuteronomy 6:4-9; 11:13-21; Numbers 15:37-41), the core is given in its first verse: "Hear, O Israel: The LORD our God, the LORD is one." This declaration is recited daily by the faithful at least every morning and evening. Dr. K. Kohler calls it their "battle-cry of the centuries."[379] Though Judaism requires little active explicit belief in dogma,[380] it especially distinguishes itself by this traditional affirmation of monotheism.

Long debated at least as early as the schools of Hillel and Shamai, this doctrine of a solitary divine being was "developed largely in response to Christian theology and persecution."[381] By it the Jews sought to reiterate their stand against polytheism and idolatry, charging that trinitarianism was a compromise with heathenism.[382] The Babylonian captivity had thoroughly ingrained in them the dangers of idolatry. This charge of idolatry against the early Roman church, in fact, was not without some support, for "the Virgin-Mother with her divine child became adored like the Queen of Heaven of pagan times." And "pagan deities in various lands were transformed into saints of the Church and worshiped by means of images, in order to win the pagan masses for the Christian faith."[383] These idolatrous practices of the apostate church repulsed the Jews, who used them to more adamantly deprecate and refuse the doctrine of the Trinity.

Thus the *Shema* became the Jews' theological defense for rejecting Jesus, who claimed oneness and equality with God. On the surface, that Mosaic command appears clearly to reject any such claim. Maimonides, whose view was adopted into Jewish liturgy, thought these passages expressed the absolute unity and indivisibility of God, which he regarded as "beyond all definition."[384]

How do we answer this? Inasmuch as the *Shema* is part of the

Christian's Bible, it is essential that we understand the point of the passage and reconcile it with the New Testament revelation of Jesus' deity. Does it indeed rule out the doctrine of the Incarnation and the Trinity?

First, we should note that the designation "one" (*echad;* "one Lord") in the *Shema* does not necessarily rule out plurality in the Godhead. The basic meaning of *echad* is "unit" or "unity." Its many usages in the Old Testament reveal a variety of such meanings.[385] Genesis 1:5, for instance, describes the first evening and morning of creation as joined together to become "one day" (NASB), and Genesis 2:24 uses the word to describe the unity of Adam and Eve who became "one flesh." In Exodus 36:18 the word is used to describe the joining together of parts of the tabernacle "that it might be a unit" (NASB). These show that the term includes the possibility of plurality in unity.

Thus the term can hardly be used to prove the absolute indivisibility or solitariness of the Godhead, disallowing the possibility of a Trinity. On the contrary, its basic meaning complements the many suggestions in the Old Testament of plurality of persons in the Godhead. The plural name *Elohim,* for instance, allows for this, more so than the impersonal notion of "divine powers."[386] The many plural conversations within the Godhead certainly imply it (Genesis 1:26; 3:22; 11:7). In Psalm 110:1 the Lord *Yahweh* speaks to the Lord *Adonai,* and in Psalm 2:7, 12 he addresses his Son Messiah. Later in the Prophets the three members of the Godhead are distinguished, as asserted by *Yahweh* himself (Isaiah 48:16).

At the time of the Incarnation of Jesus, the three persons of the Godhead are simply identified, declaring also their oneness in essence and purpose (Luke 3:22; John 10:30). The statement of their equality (John 5:18) does not deny their individuality, but confirms their unique plurality in perfect unity. Though Jesus claimed equality with the Father, he constantly put himself under the central authority of the Father who had sent him (John 5:19–30). This is entirely consistent with the "oneness" of God as proclaimed by Moses in the *Shema.*

There is therefore no exegetical or logical reason to deny the Incarnation and eternal Godhood of Jesus the Son. That doctrine is consistently taught in both the Old Testament and the New. The Christian faith stands or falls on this article of faith. Though dialogue on the issue is certainly appropriate, it should only be on the basis of what the Bible says, not on rabbinic or patristic opinions. Just as the Jews cannot compromise their essential Jewishness, so the Christian cannot negotiate away this essential truth of the Christian faith.

Proselytizing

Another traditional point of irritation between Jews and Christians has been the relish of the church to convert Jews. The problem exists because evangelism is central to the mission of the church and is a major part of its reason for being. Jesus himself commissioned it, and the apostles immediately began carrying it out. Since the first Christians were all Jews, Jews were naturally the church's first field of evangelism.

This mission to bring Jews to Jesus has been called "proselytizing," and quite early became an ugly point of contention. Throughout the Middle Ages, and even into the Renaissance, Jews were hounded by the church to respond to the gospel and convert from Judaism. The problem was that the church often reacted to Jewish rejection by making the task of missions a militant operation. It pursued Jews by every means to wrangle out confessions of "faith."

Such warlike evangelism naturally created much anguish. Various forms of intimidation were used to compel conversions, and the resulting "revivals" produced a crop of counterfeits who melded with their environment in order to survive. These conversion tactics only diluted genuine spirituality in the church and intensified Jewish resentment. Christian conversion became a matter of social prudence and survival, and the targeted Jews simply played games with the overpowering system. Resentments grew on both sides, and the two groups grew further apart. Jews became "cannon shy" to Christian missions.

Though the Jews continue to resent this evangelistic outreach of the church, it should not be forgotten that Israel's religion also had a proselytizing commission (1 Kings 8:43, 60; Isaiah 49:6; 60:3; Matthew 23:15). The church definitely did not invent the seeking of converts. Jews traced their missionary impetus to Abraham, their proto-type, and Josephus notes that later Judaism strongly pursued this work of proselytizing, even with the sword.[387] The noted Hillel, in fact, is said to have devoted his life to missionary activity as an ardent Pharisee.[388] Making converts is indeed part of the very nature of a saving religion, and both Israel and the church were commissioned to pursue that work by the Lord.

The basic irritation of proselytizing is not evangelism itself, but the use of coercion.[389] As Christianity has moved from the militancy of medieval and Reformation times, those intimidating tactics have been rightly condemned and largely abandoned. A new emphasis on the sovereignty of God in evangelism stresses the primacy of in-ner conviction and spiritual birth. Some progress has been made in replacing pushy proselytizing with frank dialogue. Coercion of any stripe is both counterproductive and even destructive to true spiritual relations. And happily, there do appear to be some signs of openness in dialogue.

Such dialogue is wholesome, but should not be misunderstood. It does not mean that the evangelical church should compromise its theology of conversion. Many in the liberal and Catholic wings of the church have waffled in this area by proposing some form of a "double covenant" theory,[390] which presumes that Jews can approach God through the old covenant and the church through the new. One group supposedly finds salvation through the Mosaic legislation and the other through Jesus Christ.

Attractive as that notion might seem, it totally misconceives the message of both the Old Testament and the New. It jauntily dismisses the messianic prophecies in the Old and violates the "one gospel" principle of Paul in the epistles (Galatians 1:6-9). It undercuts the whole New Testament by making Christ an optional Savior. The gospel's message is that Christ died for our sins as the world's only Savior: "For if righteousness comes through the law, then Christ died in vain" (Galatians 2:21, NKJV). He alone was raised from the dead by the Father to accomplish our justification (Romans 3:20-26; 4:25). To reinterpret the covenants by racial relations is to misconstrue both.

The covenants were not parceled out to Jews and Gentiles as two ways of salvation, but were given as progressive developments of one redemptive program. Paul argues from the "one God" declaration of the *Shema* that God has provided but one way of salvation for Jews and Gentiles alike through faith in his Son Jesus Christ (Romans 3:29-30). This exclusiveness has often brought charges of bigotry. But such charges fail to discern the debacle of sin. The gospel is God's only provision for redemption. Nothing else has the power to reverse sin's ravages. The gospel is not a proposition to be negotiated through dialogue and compromise, but is God's good news for all, to be believed and acted upon.

The real irritation, again, is the manner in which church militants carried out their evangelism. Mutual respect was often missing. Many Jews today are still so suspicious of evangelical Christians, they even suspect their goodwill toward modern Israel. They're sure any generosity shown must have ulterior motives.[391] They haven't forgotten how Martin Luther's early good will toward the Jews turned vile and oppressive when they resisted his gospel. The lesson is all-important: It's only through mutual respect and forgiveness that healthy dialogue can thrive.

Rabbi Yechiel Eckstein has offered some insightful counsel by which to approach Jewish-Christian dialogue:

> The Jews will request that Evangelicals regard dialogue as the proper forum in which to "preach the gospel" to Jews and that they abandon the zealous and even cultic techniques often employed in attempts to convert them. For is it not the Christian's commission simply to testify through words and deeds to the truth of the Christian message, while it is the Lord's prerogative to act upon the individual through the Holy Spirit and possibly bring about his conversion? If this is so, is it not reasonable for Jews to ask Evangelicals to fulfill their missionary commission through dialogue, decently and courteously, by model, teaching, and joint cooperation and without the intention of converting them? Certainly Jews will ask responsible Evangelicals to be especially alert to evangelizing efforts that involve any sort of manipulation, deception, or excessively aggressive tactics. . . . [392]

Seeking converts is certainly the goal of Christian missions, but not through any form of coercion. By eliminating such methods, the door of dialogue with the Jews appears to at least stand ajar. Samuel Sandmel concludes his treatise on "Anti-Semitism in the New Testament" with some optimism: "Is it possible that the tragedy of the Holocaust has begun to move the mountain of past misconceptions? This generation of Jews and Christians, receptive to each other, has an opportunity for reconciliation that is without precedent."[393]

Though Sandmel speaks mainly of liberal Catholics and Protestants who buy into his theory, his conclusions may have even broader ramifications for others. Having discerned the error of church-sponsored intimidation, many evangelicals today are welcoming courteous but frank and open dialogue.

Praying for the "Peace of Jerusalem"

Another responsibility of the church concerns David's exhortation to "pray for the peace of Jerusalem" (Psalm 122:6). That verse has long been regarded as a Christian challenge and minimum gesture of goodwill toward the Jews. A personal blessing attaches to it that seems to relate to the Abrahamic covenant, which promises, "I will bless those who bless you."

This exhortation to pray for Jerusalem's peace, however, is so broad and general it seems to lend support for any friendly gesture toward the Jewish people. The early British and American Friends of Zionism, for instance, often saw it as encouraging that movement.[394]

Since the name *Jerusalem* can stand for many things, a host of applications may be suggested.

To pray this prayer intelligently in the will of God, it's important to discern more specifically what "peace" the Psalmist had in mind. Was he speaking of military triumph for the nation? Are we to pray for modern Israel's political dominance over the Arabs? Should we encourage its annexation of the West Bank and Gaza Strip? How about praying that the Muslim Dome of the Rock be replaced by a new Jewish temple? Or should we simply pray for Israel's international prominence and peaceful relations with its neighbors in the Middle East?

The context of this psalm appears to have a very different emphasis. David's concern was for the house of the Lord—that is, the tabernacle in Jerusalem. As Hebrew pilgrims ascended the rugged hills to the city, they especially anticipated a time of fellowship with their covenant Lord, bringing with them various offerings. They came "to give thanks to the name of the LORD" (NASB). Warfare would restrict or deny this privilege, but that was not his main concern. The peace of which he speaks is not primarily outer, but inner peace—not political, but spiritual. "May peace be within you" is his emphasis. His concern through the Psalm is "the house of the LORD" and the spiritual peace that comes through a right relationship with God.

This spiritual peace with the Lord was often the key to Jerusalem's military success and peace with its neighbors. Rarely was it otherwise. Almost invariably, Israel's ancient enemies became powerful when it strayed from the Lord, and they diminished in power as it obeyed. Hence, we should heed the admonition to pray for peace—that is, harmonious relations with the Lord.

That principle is strikingly illustrated in the experience of Jacob returning from Paddan-Aram in Genesis 32–33, and forms an interesting paradigm of Israel's problem today. Jacob had just escaped the wrath of his uncle Laban in faraway Haran when he suddenly found himself approaching the wrath of brother Esau on his return to Canaan. Because he had long ago deceived his brother, Jacob greatly feared meeting Esau with his army of four hundred men. This drove Jacob to prayer, and he developed a plan of action.

After sending his family and servants ahead, Jacob remained north of the Jabbok River. That night he had a crucial meeting with the Lord, a wrestling match with a "man" or theophany of God. After he "struggled with God" and was crippled in the process, Jacob received a new name (Genesis 32:28). That name was Israel, meaning "prince with God," characterizing his new relationship with the Lord.

That meeting, however, had another dimension. It also changed the character of his meeting with Esau the next day. Instead of a wrathful brother coming for revenge, Jacob met a conciliatory brother coming to welcome him and his family with open arms. "Esau ran to meet him and embraced him, and fell on his neck and kissed him, and they wept" (Genesis 33:4, NASB). His restored relationship with God completely changed his relationship with his brother.

The analogy speaks for itself. Israel's basic need today is not peace with the Arabs; it is peace with God. The national turmoil and heartache of both clans is spiritual in nature rather than merely racial. Israel's deepest need is not economic, political, or military, but one it yet firmly resists—a historic tryst with its covenant Lord, similar to that of Jacob returning from exile. That meeting will do what no military victory could accomplish—inaugurate permanent peace and goodwill toward all.

The prophet Zechariah boldly portrays such a meeting, coinciding with Israel's recognition and reception of Messiah (12:10). In the aftermath of that penitential gathering of all the families of Israel, the nation's hostilities will be forever past (Zechariah 12:11-14). At that time the Lord will "extend peace to her like a river," as he restores it to divine favor and international preeminence (Isaiah 66:12; Romans 11:25-27).

For this "peace of Jerusalem" all creation groans, and all God's people are exhorted to pray fervently. It is the grand climax of the biblical drama of Israel, through whom God will bring the full blessing of Abraham to the entire world.

The unfolding of this drama, however, is not meant for Israel alone. It underscores for all the world two essential truths about our God and his prophetic program. The first is that he is a covenant-keeping God. What he has promised will come about, whether with Israel in the end times or with his church in the present age. The second is that the Lord's return could be soon. The rise of Israel on the world scene is climactic in itself, calling to mind the Lord's analogy of the fig tree: "Now when these things begin to happen, look up and lift up your heads, because your redemption draws near" (Luke 21:28, NKJV).

APPENDIX

A
Chronology

ANCIENT ISRAEL

2090 B.C.	Abram receives the covenant
1445 B.C.	Moses leads the Exodus from Egypt
1010 B.C.	King David takes the throne
930 B.C.	Kingdom divided into Israel and Judah after Solomon's death
722 B.C.	Northern Kingdom destroyed by Assyria
586 B.C.	Southern Kingdom, Jerusalem, and temple destroyed by Babylon
537 B.C.	Some Jews return from Babylon to rebuild temple
516 B.C.	Second temple completed
5 B.C.	Birth of John the Baptist and Jesus the Messiah
A.D. 33	Trial, death, and resurrection of Jesus the Messiah
A.D. 70	Destruction of Jerusalem and the temple
A.D. 135	Bar Kochba's revolt and expulsion of Jews from Palestine

MODERN ISRAEL

1882	Persecution in Russia initiates first large Jewish immigration to Palestine. Leon Pinsker writes *Autoemancipation* for return to Palestine
1896	Theodor Herzl writes *Der Judenstaat*
1897	First Zionist Congress at Basle, Switzerland
1917	British Balfour Declaration British conquest of Palestine
1922	Churchill White Paper gives Transjordan to Abdullah, the Hashemite

1924	Adolf Hitler writes *Mein Kampf* in Landsberg prison
1933	Hitler becomes Chancellor of Germany and Jewish emigration begins
1939	MacDonald White Paper seeks to cut off immigration of Jews to Palestine
1945	Truman becomes President of United States; World War II ends
1947	Partitioning of Palestine approved by United Nations
1948	New State of Israel proclaimed by Ben-Gurion followed by War of Independence
1952	Overthrow of Egyptian King Farouk and rise of Nasser
1956	Sinai Campaign "Operation Kadesh"
1961	Adolf Eichmann tried and executed in Israel
1964	PLO founded by Nasser
1967	Arab attack rebuffed in Six-Day War; Israel occupies Jerusalem, West Bank, Gaza, and Golan Heights
1967	Arab Khartoum Resolution of "Three Nos" against Israel
1968	PLO reorganized with Arafat as chairman
1973	Yom Kippur War
1977	Menachem Begin becomes prime minister as Likud Party wins
1978	Camp David talks bring peace treaty between Israel and Egypt
1979	Sinai returned to Egypt
1982	Israel invades Lebanon to clear out PLO terrorists
1987	*Intifada* (uprising) begins in occupied territories
1991	Iraq attacks Israel with Scud missiles in response to Allies' "Operation Desert Storm"
1993	Israel and the PLO approve "Declaration of Principles"
1994	Gaza and Jericho transferred to Palestinian Authority control
1994	Peace treaty signed between Israel and Jordan
1998	Wye River Memorandum signed in which Israel and PLO agree to immediately resume permanent status negotiations
1999	Sharm el-Sheikh Memorandum signed prohibiting parties from changing status of West Bank prior to final agreement
2000	Camp David Summit ends in July without reaching an agreement on final status; al Aqsa *Intifada* begins in September
2003	Mahmoud Abbas (Abu Mazen) appointed as prime minister of the Palestinian Authority, diminishing the authority of Yasser Arafat and paving the way for President Bush to unveil his "Roadmap for Peace" in the Middle East.

International Documents Related to the Land Rights in Palestine

THE BIBLICAL COVENANTS

A. Abrahamic Covenant

Genesis 12:7; 13:14-15; 17:7-8; 26:2-3; 28:13. "Then the LORD appeared to Abram and said, 'To your descendants I will give this land' " (12:7, NKJV). "And the LORD said to Abram . . . 'Lift your eyes now and look from the place where you are—northward, southward, eastward, and westward; for all the land which you see I give to you and your descendants forever' " (13:14-15, NKJV). "And I will establish My covenant between Me and you and your descendants after you in their generations, for an everlasting covenant, to be God to you and your descendants after you. Also I give to you and your descendants after you the land in which you are a stranger, all the land of Canaan, as an everlasting possession" (17:7-8, NKJV).

1. *Reconfirmed to Isaac* (26:2-3, NKJV). "Then the LORD appeared to him and said: 'Do not go down to Egypt; live in the land of which I shall tell you. Dwell in this land, and I will be with you and bless you; for to you and your descendants I give all these lands, and I will perform the oath which I swore to Abraham your father.' "
2. *Reconfirmed to Jacob* (28:13, NKJV). "And behold, the LORD stood above it [Jacob's "ladder to heaven"] and said: 'I am the LORD God of Abraham your father and the God of Isaac; the land on which you lie I will give to you and your descendants.' "

B. Palestinian Covenant to Moses

Leviticus 25–26; Deuteronomy 28–30. Built on the Abrahamic covenant, this covenant elaborated Israel's right to occupy Palestine in two different Mosaic discourses:

1. *Conditions for occupying the land* (Leviticus 25-26, NKJV). "And the LORD spoke to Moses on Mount Sinai, saying, 'Speak to the children of Israel, and say to them: "When you come into the land which I give you, then the land shall keep a sabbath to the LORD" ' " (25:1-2). "The land shall not be sold permanently, for the land is Mine; for you are strangers and sojourners with Me" (25:23). "If you walk in My statutes and keep My commandments, and perform them . . . I will give peace in the land, and you shall lie down, and none will make you afraid. . . . But if you do not obey Me, and do not observe all these commandments, and if you despise My statutes, or if your soul abhors My judgments, so that you do not perform all My commandments, but break My covenant, I also will do this to you" (26:3, 6, 14-16, NKJV). [Seven stages of chastisement are then enumerated, ending in worldwide dispersion.] "I will scatter you among the nations and draw out a sword after you; your land shall be desolate and your cities waste. Then the land shall enjoy its sabbaths as long as it lies desolate and you are in your enemies' land; then the land shall rest and enjoy its sabbaths" (26:33-34, NKJV).

2. *Assurance of final restoration* (Deuteronomy 28-30). Moses' final discourse both anticipated their coming apostasy and itemized the Lord's conditions for their full restoration to the land in the latter days (Deuteronomy 30:1-5, NKJV).

> Now it shall come to pass, when all these things come upon you, the blessing and the curse which I have set before you, and you call them to mind among all the nations where the LORD your God drives you, and you return to the LORD your God and obey His voice, according to all that I command you today, you and your children, with all your heart and with all your soul, that the LORD your God will bring you back from captivity, and have compassion on you, and gather you again from all the nations where the LORD your God has scattered you. If any of you are driven out to the farthest parts under heaven, from there the LORD your God will gather you, and from there He will bring you. Then the LORD your God will bring you to the land which your fathers possessed, and you shall possess it. He will prosper you and multiply you more than your fathers.

THE QUR'ANIC RECONSTRUCTION OF THE COVENANTS

Though the Qur'an does not mention Palestine or Jerusalem directly, it lays the foundation of Islam on the Lord's covenant with Abraham and Ishmael (Sura 2:124-129). In a reconstruction of the biblical account, Muhammad portrayed Abraham's sacrifice of Isaac as a sacrifice of Ishmael, following which the promise of Isaac's coming was also given (37:101-112).[395] Abraham and Ishmael constituted the first "Muslims," having both "submitted" to Allah (3:67; 22:78). At that time they "raised up the foundation of the House" (Ka'ba) in Mecca, where Allah made His covenant with Abraham and Ishmael (2:120-128; 140). Ishmael is included in a list of select heroes of faith in Sura 19:3, with Zechariah, Mary, Abraham, Moses, and Ezra, being described as "one in whom his Lord was well pleased" (19:55).

The Qur'an often speaks of the "People of the Book," Jews and Christians, who are not true believers unless they respond to the injunctions of the further Book of Muhammad (5:18-24; 44-48). Muhammad is seen as the "final Messenger," the "Seal of the Prophets." Though Moses and Jesus were "Messengers," Jesus is said to have announced this final Messenger, "who shall come after me, whose name shall be Ahmad [Muhammad]" (61:5-8; 33:40). He will be the "Apostle" of "true religion" (21:92; 61:9). Had Jews and Christians responded to "the Torah and the Gospel, and what was sent down to you from your Lord" [the Qur'an], they would not be among "those who disbelieve, and cry lies to Our signs—they are the inhabitants of Hell" (5:44-48; 65; 86).

With this reconstructed view of the Abrahamic covenant comes the strong implication that the Jews are no longer heirs of the covenant, having fallen into idolatry. Rather, "they are cursed" for their disbelief, as evident from their present punishment from the Lord (5:60; 62:5-8). The covenant promises to Abraham reverted to the children of Ishmael (Abraham's first son) who receive the message of Muhammad, the final "Messenger." By inference, then, the land also is theirs (5:120), and they are responsible to fight for it (9:29; 22:39).

JEWISH-ARAB AGREEMENTS[396]
A. The Feisal-Weizmann Agreement
January 3, 1919

His Royal Highness the Emir Feisal, representing and acting on behalf of the Arab Kingdom of Hedjaz, and Dr. Chaim Weizmann, representing and acting on behalf of the Zionist Organization, mindful of the racial kinship and ancient bonds existing between the Arabs and the Jewish people, and realizing that the surest means of working out the consummation of their national aspirations is through the closest possible collaboration in the development of the Arab State and Palestine, and being desirous further of confirming the good understanding which exists between them, have agreed upon the following Articles:

ARTICLE I

The Arab State and Palestine in all their relations and undertaking shall be controlled by the most cordial goodwill and understanding, and to this end Arab and Jewish duly accredited agents shall be established and maintained in the respective territories.

ARTICLE II

Immediately following the completion of the deliberations of the Peace Conference, the definite boundaries between the Arab State and Palestine shall be determined by a Commission to be agreed upon by the parties hereto.

ARTICLE III

In the establishment of the Constitution and Administration of Palestine all such measures shall be adopted as will afford the fullest guarantees for carrying into effect the British Government's Declaration of the 2nd of November 1917.

ARTICLE IV

All necessary measures shall be taken to encourage and stimulate immigration of Jews into Palestine on a large scale, and as quickly as possible to settle Jewish immigrants upon the land through closer settlement and intensive cultivation of the soil. In taking such measures the Arab peasant and tenant farmers shall be protected in their rights, and shall be assisted in forwarding their economic development.

ARTICLE V

No regulation or law shall be made prohibiting or interfering in any way with the free exercise of religion; and further the free exercise and enjoyment of religious profession and worship without discrimination or reference shall forever be allowed. No religious test shall ever be required for the exercise of civil or political rights.

ARTICLE VI

The Mohammedan Holy Places shall be under Mohammedan control.

ARTICLE VII

The Zionist Organization proposes to send to Palestine a commission of experts to make a survey of the economic possibilities of the country, and to report upon the best means for its development. The Zionist Organization will place aforementioned Commission at the disposal of the Arab State for the purpose of a survey of the economic possibilities of the Arab State and to report upon the best means for its development. The Zionist Organization will use its best effort to assist the Arab State in providing the means for developing the natural resources and economic possibilities thereof.

ARTICLE VIII

The parties hereto agree to act in complete accord and harmony on all matters embraced herein before the Peace Congress.

ARTICLE IX

Any matters of dispute which may arise between the contracting parties shall be referred to the British Government for arbitration.

Given under our hand at London, England, the third of January, one thousand nine hundred and nineteen.

Chaim Weizmann
Feisal ibn-Hussein

RESERVATION BY THE EMIR FEISAL

If the Arabs are established as I have asked in my manifesto of January 4th addressed to the British Secretary of State for Foreign

Affairs, I will carry out what is written in this agreement. If changes are made, I cannot be answerable for failure to carry out this agreement.

Feisal ibn-Hussein

B. The Feisal-Frankfurter Correspondence
Written by Feisal ibn-Hussein to American jurist Felix Frankfurter (Paris, March 3, 1919)

We feel that the Arabs and Jews are cousins in race, having suffered similar oppressions at the hands of powers stronger than themselves, and by a happy coincidence have been able to take the first step towards the attainment of their national ideals together.

We Arabs, especially the educated among us, look with the deepest sympathy on the Zionist movement. Our deputation here in Paris is fully acquainted with the proposals submitted yesterday by the Zionist Organization to the Peace Conference, and we regard them as moderate and proper. We will do our best, in so far as we are concerned, to help them through; we will wish the Jews a most hearty welcome home.

With the chiefs of your movement, especially with Dr. Weizmann, we have had and continue to have the closest relations. He has been a great helper of our cause, and I hope the Arabs may soon be in a position to make the Jews some returns for their kindness. We are working together for a reformed and revived Near East, and our two movements complete one another. The Jewish movement is national and not imperialist. Our movement is national and not imperialist, and there is room in Syria for us both. Indeed I think that neither can be a real success without the other.

People less informed and less responsible than our leaders and yours, ignoring the need for cooperation of the Arabs and Zionists, have been trying to exploit the local difficulties that must necessarily arise in Palestine in the early stages of our movements. Some of them have, I am afraid, misrepresented your aims to the Arab peasantry, with the result that interested parties have been able to make capital out of what they call our differences.

I wish to give you my firm conviction that these differences are not on questions of principle, but on matters of detail such as must inevitably occur in every contact of neighbouring peoples, and as are easily adjusted by mutual goodwill. Indeed nearly all of them will disappear with fuller knowledge.

I look forward, and my people with me look forward, to a future in which we will help you and you will help us, so that the countries in which we are mutually interested may once again take their places in the community of civilized peoples of the world.

Feisal

Response by Felix Frankfurter (March 1919)

Royal Highness:

Allow me, on behalf of the Zionist Organization, to acknowledge your recent letter with deep appreciation.

Those of us who come from the United States have already been gratified by the friendly relations and the active cooperation maintained between you and the Zionist leaders, particularly Dr. Weizmann. We knew it could not be otherwise; we knew that the aspirations of the Arab and the Jewish peoples were parallel, that each aspired to reestablish its nationality in its own homeland, each making its own distinctive contribution to civilization, each seeking its own peaceful mode of life.

The Zionist leaders and the Jewish people for whom they speak have watched with satisfaction the spiritual vigour of the Arab movement. Themselves seeking justice, they are anxious that the just national aims of the Arab people be confirmed and safeguarded by the Peace Conference.

We knew from your acts and your past utterances that the Zionist movement—in other words, the national aims of the Jewish people—had your support and the support of the Arab people for whom you speak. These aims are now before the Peace Conference as definite proposals by the Zionist Organizations. We are happy indeed that you consider these proposals "moderate and proper," and that we have in you a staunch supporter for their realization. For both the Arab and the Jewish peoples there are difficulties ahead—difficulties that challenge the united statesmanship of Arab and Jewish leaders. For it is no easy task to rebuild two great civilizations that have been suffering oppression and misrule for centuries. We each have our difficulties we shall work out as friends, friends who are animated by similar purposes, seeking a free and full development for the two neighbouring peoples. The Arabs and Jews are neighbours in territory; we cannot but live side by side as friends.

Very respectfully,
Felix Frankfurter

BRITISH DOCUMENTS ON PALESTINE DURING AND AFTER WORLD WAR I
A. The McMahon-Hussein Letter
From Sir Henry McMahon, British High Commissioner in Cairo to Husain ibn Ali, the Sherif of Mecca on October 24, 1915, concerning the setting up of an Arab state

> The two districts of Mersina and Alexandretta [southern Turkey] and portions of Syria lying west of the districts of Damascus, Homs, Hamma and Allepo cannot be said to be purely Arab, and should be excluded from the limits demanded.
>
> As for those regions lying within these frontiers wherein Great Britain is free to act without detriment to the interests of her ally, France, I am empowered in the name of the Government of Great

Britain to give the following assurances and make the following reply to your letter:

1. Subject to the above modifications, Great Britain is prepared to recognize and support the independence of Arabs in all the regions within the limits demanded by the Sherif of Mecca.
2. Great Britain will guarantee the Holy Places against external aggression and will recognize their inviolability.
3. When the situation admits, Great Britain will give to the Arabs her advice and will assist them to establish what may appear to be the most suitable forms of government in those various territories.

A further letter by the British, printed in the *London Times* in 1937, denied the Arab claim that Palestine was included in this exchange.[397]

B. The British Balfour Declaration
Letter from Lord Arthur James Balfour, British Foreign Minister, to Baron de Rothschild of Paris on November 2, 1917, which became the "Balfour Declaration"

His Majesty's Government view with favour the establishment in Palestine of a national home for the Jewish people, and will use their best endeavours to facilitate the achievement of this object, it being clearly understood that nothing shall be done which may prejudice the civil and religious rights of existing non-Jewish communities in Palestine, or the right and political status enjoyed by Jews in any other country.

C. The Churchill White Paper
By British Secretary of State, Winston Churchill, qualifying the Balfour Declaration, June 1922

The Secretary of State for the Colonies has given renewed consideration to the existing political situation in Palestine, with a very earnest desire to arrive at a settlement of the outstanding questions which have given rise to uncertainty and unrest among certain sections of the population. After consultation with the High Commissioner for Palestine, the following statement has been drawn up. It summarizes the essential parts of the correspondence that has already taken place between the Secretary of State and a Delegation from the Moslem Christian Society of Palestine, which has been for some time in England, and it states the further conclusions which have since been reached.

The tension which has prevailed from time to time in Palestine is mainly due to apprehensions, which are entertained both by sections of the Arab and by sections of the Jewish population. These apprehensions, so far as the Arabs are concerned, are partly based upon exaggerated interpretations of the meaning of the Declaration favouring the establishment of a Jewish National Home in Palestine, made on behalf of His Majesty's Government on 2nd November, 1917. Unauthorized statements have been made to the effect that the purpose in view is to create a wholly Jewish Palestine. Phrases have been used such as that Palestine is to become "as Jewish as England is English." His Majesty's Government regard any such expectation as impracticable and have no such aim in view. . . . They would draw attention to the fact that the terms of the Declaration referred to do not contemplate that Palestine as a whole should be converted into a Jewish National Home, but that such a Home should be founded "in Palestine."

With reference to the Constitution which it is now intended to establish in Palestine, the draft of which has already been published, it is desirable to make certain points clear. In the first place, it is not the case, as has been represented by the Arab Delegation, that during the war His Majesty's Government gave an undertaking that an independent national government should be at once established in Palestine. This representation mainly rests upon a letter dated the 24th October, 1915, from Sir Henry McMahon, then His Majesty's High Commissioner in Egypt, to the Sherif of Mecca, now King Hussein of the Kingdom of the Hejaz. That letter is quoted as conveying the promise to the Sherif of Mecca to recognize and support the independence of the Arabs within the territories proposed by him. But this promise was given subject to a reservation made in the same letter, which excluded from its scope, among other territories, the portions of Syria lying to the west of the district of Damascus. This reservation has always been regarded by His Majesty's Government as covering the vilayet of Beirut and the independent Sanjak of Jerusalem. The whole of Palestine west of the Jordan was thus excluded from Sir H. McMahon's pledge.

D. The MacDonald White Paper of 1939
Revision of the Immigration policy of the Balfour Declaration by the British Chamberlain Government, May 17, 1939

After the failure of the partition scheme and a subsequent attempt to work out an agreed solution at a Conference in London (February–March 1939), the British government announced its new policy in a White Paper published on May 17, 1939. The Arab demands were largely met; Jewish immigration was to continue at a maximum rate of 15,000 for another five years. After that it was to cease altogether unless the Arabs would accept it.

Article 14 spelled out its revised immigration policy:

Article 14. It has been urged that all further Jewish immigration into Palestine should be stopped forthwith. His Majesty's Government cannot accept such a proposal. It would damage the whole of the financial and economic system of Palestine and thus affect adversely the interests of Arabs and Jews alike. Moreover, in the view of His Majesty's Government, abruptly to stop further immigration would be unjust to the Jewish National Home. But above all, His Majesty's Government are conscious of the present unhappy plight of large number of Jews who seek a refuge from certain European countries, and they believe that Palestine can and should make a further contribution to the solution of this pressing world problem. In all these circumstances, they believe that they will be acting consistently with their

Mandatory obligations to both Arabs and Jews, and in the manner best calculated to serve the interests of the whole people of Palestine, by adopting the following proposals regarding immigration:

1. Jewish immigration during the next five years will be at a rate which, if economic absorptive capacity permits, will bring the Jewish population up to approximately one-third of the total population of the country. Taking into account the expected natural increase of the Arab and Jewish populations, and the number of illegal Jewish immigrants now in the country, this would allow the admission, as from the beginning of April this year, of some 75,000 immigrants over the next five years. These immigrants would, subject to the criterion of economic absorptive capacity, be admitted as follows:

    (a) For each of the next five years a quota of 10,000 Jewish immigrants will be allowed on the understanding that a shortage in any one year may be added to the quotas for subsequent years, within the five-year period, if economic absorptive capacity permits.

    (b) In addition, as a contribution towards the solution of the Jewish refugee problem, 25,000 refugees will be admitted as soon as the High Commissioner is satisfied that adequate provision for their maintenance is ensured, special consideration being given to refugee children and dependents.

2. The existing machinery for ascertaining economic absorptive capacity will be retained, and the High Commissioner will have the ultimate responsibility for deciding the limits of economic capacity. Before each periodic decision is taken, Jewish and Arab representatives will be consulted.

3. After the period of five years no further Jewish immigration will be permitted unless the Arabs of Palestine are prepared to acquiesce in it.

4. His Majesty's Government are determined to check illegal immigration, and further preventive measures are being adopted. The numbers of Jewish illegal immigrants who, despite these measures, may succeed in coming into the country and cannot be deported will be deducted from the yearly quota.

STATE OF ISRAEL PROCLAMATION OF INDEPENDENCE
Delivered by David Ben-Gurion in Tel Aviv on May 14, 1948

The Land of Israel was the birthplace of the Jewish people. Here their spiritual, religious and national identity was formed. Here they achieved independence and created a culture of national and universal significance. Here they wrote and gave the Bible to the world.

Exiled from the Land of Israel the Jewish people remained faithful to it in all the countries of their dispersion, never ceasing to pray and hope for their return and the restoration of their national freedom.

Impelled by this historic association, Jews strove throughout the centuries to go back to the land of their fathers and regain their statehood. In recent decades they returned in masses. They reclaimed the wilderness, revived their language, built cities and villages, and established a vigorous and ever-growing community, with its own economic and cultural life. They sought peace yet were prepared to defend themselves. They brought the blessings of progress to all inhabitants of the country and looked forward to sovereign independence.

In the year 1897 the first Zionist Congress, inspired by Theodor Herzl's vision of the Jewish State, proclaimed the right of the Jewish people to national revival in their own country.

This right was acknowledged by the Balfour Declaration of November 2, 1917, and reaffirmed by the Mandate of the League of Nations, which gave explicit international recognition to the historic connection of the Jewish people with Palestine and their right to reconstitute their National Home.

The recent holocaust, which engulfed millions of Jews in Europe, proved anew the need to solve the problem of the homelessness and lack of independence of the Jewish people by means of the re-establishment of the Jewish State, which would open the gates to all Jews and endow the Jewish people with equality of status among the family of nations.

The survivors of the disastrous slaughter in Europe and also Jews from other lands, have not desisted from their efforts to reach Eretz-Yishrael in face of difficulties, obstacles and perils; and have not ceased to urge their right to a life of dignity, freedom and honest toil in their ancestral land.

In the Second World War the Jewish people in Palestine made their full contribution to the struggle of the freedom-loving nations against the Nazi evil. The sacrifices of their soldiers and their war effort gained them the right to rank with the nations which founded the United Nations.

On November 29, 1947, the General Assembly of the United Nations adopted a Resolution requiring the establishment of the Jewish State in Palestine. The General Assembly called upon the inhabitants of the country to take all the necessary steps on their part to put the plan into effect. This recognition by the United Nations of the right of the Jewish people to establish their independent State is unassailable.

It is the natural right of the Jewish people to lead, as do all other nations, an independent existence in its sovereign State.

Accordingly we, the members of the National Council, representing the Jewish people in Palestine and the World Zionist Movement, are met together in solemn assembly today, the day of the termination of the British Mandate for Palestine; and by virtue of the natural and historic right of the Jewish people and of the Resolution of the General Assembly of the United Nations.

We hereby proclaim the establishment of the Jewish State in Palestine, to be called Medinath Yisrael (The State of Israel).

We hereby declare that, as from the termination of the Mandate at midnight, May 14-15, 1948, and pending the setting up of the duly elected bodies of the State in accordance with a Constitution, to be drawn up by the Constituent Assembly not later than October 1, 1948, the National Council shall act as the Provisional State Council and that the National Administration shall constitute the Provisional Government of the Jewish State, which shall be known as Israel.

The State of Israel will be open to the immigration of Jews from all countries of their dispersion; will promote the development of the country for the benefit of all its inhabitants; will be based on the principles of liberty, justice and peace as conceived by the Prophets of Israel; will uphold the full social and political equality of all its citizens, without distinction of religion, race, or sex; will guarantee freedom of religion, conscience, education and culture; will safeguard the Holy Places of all religions; and will loyally uphold the principles of the United Nations Charter.

The State of Israel will be ready to cooperate with the organs and representatives of the United Nations in the implementation of the Resolution of the Assembly of November 29, 1947, and will take steps to bring about the Economic Union over the whole of Palestine.

We appeal to the United Nations to assist the Jewish people in the building of its State and to admit Israel into the family of nations.

In the midst of wanton aggression, we yet call upon the Arab inhabitants of the State of Israel to preserve the ways of peace and play their part in the development of the State, on the basis of full and equal citizenship and due representation in all its bodies and institutions—provisional and permanent.

We extend our hand in peace and neighbourliness to all the neighbouring states and the peoples, and invite them to cooperate with the independent Jewish nation for the common good of all. The State of Israel is prepared to make its contribution to the progress of the Middle East as a whole.

Our call goes out to the Jewish people all over the world to rally to our side in the task of immigration and development and to stand by us in the great struggle for the fulfillment of the dream of generations for the redemption of Israel.

With trust in Almighty God, we set our hand to this Declaration at this Session of the Provisional State Council, on the soil of the Homeland, in the city of Tel Aviv, on this Sabbath eve, the fifth of Iyar, 5708, the fourteenth day of May, 1948.

UNITED NATIONS RESOLUTIONS 242 AND 338
A. Resolution 242
United Nations Security Council, November 22, 1967

The Security Council—

Expressing its continuing concern with the grave situation in the Middle East,

Emphasizing the inadmissibility of the acquisition of territory by war and the need to work for a just and lasting peace in which every State in the area can live in security,

Emphasizing further that all Member States in their acceptance of the Charter of the United Nations have undertaken a commitment to act in accordance with Article 2 of the Charter,

1. Affirms that the fulfillment of Charter principles requires the establishment of a just and lasting peace in the Middle East which should include the application of both the following principles:
   (a) Withdrawal of Israel armed forces from territories occupied in the recent conflict;
   (b) Termination of all claims or states of belligerency and respect for and acknowledgment of the sovereignty, territorial integrity and political independence of every State in the area and their right to live in peace within secure and recognized boundaries free from threats or acts of force;
2. Affirms further the necessity:
   (a) For guaranteeing freedom of navigation through international waterways in the area;
   (b) For achieving a just settlement of the refugee problem;
   (c) For guaranteeing the territorial inviolability and political independence of every state in the area, through measures including the establishment of demilitarized zones;
3. Requests the Secretary-General to designate a Special Representative to proceed to the Middle East to establish and maintain contacts with the States concerned in order to promote agreement and assist efforts to achieve a peaceful and accepted settlement in accordance with the provisions and principles in this resolution;
4. Requests the Secretary-General to report to the Security Council on the progress of the efforts of the Special Representative as soon as possible.

B. Resolution 338
United Nations Security Council, October 21, 1973

The Security Council—

1. Calls upon all parties to the present fighting to cease all firing and terminate all military activity immediately, no later than 12 hours after the moment of the adoption of this decision, in the positions they now occupy;
2. Calls upon the parties concerned to start immediately after the cease-fire the implementation of Security Council resolution 242 (1967) in all its parts;
3. Decides that, immediately and concurrently with the cease-fire, negotiations start between the parties concerned under appropriate auspices aimed at establishing a just and durable peace in the Middle East.

AGREEMENTS BETWEEN ISRAEL AND THE PALESTINIANS
A. Exchange of Letters between Arafat, Rabin, and the Foreign Minister of Norway

September 9, 1993

Yitzhak Rabin
Prime Minister of Israel

Mr. Prime Minister,

The signing of the Declaration of Principles marks a new era in the history of the Middle East. In firm conviction thereof, I would like to confirm the following PLO commitments:

The PLO recognizes the right of the State of Israel to exist in peace and security.

The PLO accepts United Nations Security Council Resolutions 242 and 338.

The PLO commits itself to the Middle East peace process, and to a peaceful resolution of the conflict between the two sides and declares that all outstanding issues relating to permanent status will be resolved through negotiations.

The PLO considers that the signing of the Declaration of Principles constitutes a historic event, inaugurating a new epoch of peaceful coexistence, free from violence and all other acts which endanger peace and stability. Accordingly, the PLO renounces the use of terrorism and other acts of violence and will assume responsibility over all PLO elements and personnel in order to assure their compliance, prevent violations and discipline violators.

In view of the promise of a new era and the signing of the Declaration of Principles and based on Palestinian acceptance of Security Council Resolutions 242 and 338, the PLO affirms that those articles of the Palestinian Covenant which deny Israel's right to exist, and the provisions of the Covenant which are inconsistent with the commitments of this letter are now inoperative and no longer valid. Consequently, the PLO undertakes to submit to the Palestinian National Council for formal approval the necessary changes in regard to the Palestinian Covenant.

> *Sincerely,*
> *Yasser Arafat*
> *Chairman*
> *The Palestine Liberation Organization*

September 9, 1993

His Excellency
Johan Jorgen Holst
Foreign Minister of Norway

Dear Minister Holst,

I would like to confirm to you that, upon the signing of the Declaration of Principles, the PLO encourages and calls upon the Palestinian people in the West Bank and Gaza Strip to take part in the steps leading to the normalization of life, rejecting violence and terrorism, contributing to peace and stability and participating actively in shaping reconstruction, economic develoment and cooperation.

Sincerely,
Yasser Arafat
Chairman
The Palestine Liberation Organization

September 9, 1993

Yasser Arafat
Chairman
The Palestinian Liberation Organization

Mr. Chairman,

In response to your letter of September 9, 1993, I wish to confirm to you that, in light of the PLO commitments included in your letter, the Government of Israel has decided to recognize the PLO as the representative of the Palestinian people and commence negotiations with the PLO within the Middle East peace process.

Yitzhak Rabin
Prime Minister of Israel

B. Declaration of Principles on Interim Self-Government Arrangements September 13, 1993

The Government of the State of Israel and the P.L.O. team (in the Jordanian–Palestinian delegation to the Middle East Peace Conference) (the "Palestinian Delegation"), representing the Palestinian people, agree that it is time to put an end to decades of confrontation and conflict, recognize their mutual legitimate and political rights, and strive to live in peaceful coexistence and mutual dignity and security and achieve a just, lasting and comprehensive peace settlement and historic reconciliation through the agreed political process. Accordingly, the two sides agree to the following principles:

ARTICLE I: AIM OF THE NEGOTIATIONS

The aim of the Israeli-Palestinian negotiations within the current Middle East peace process is, among other things, to establish a Palestinian Interim Self-Government Authority, the elected Council (the "Council"), for the Palestinian people in the West Bank and the Gaza Strip, for a transitional period not exceeding five years, leading to a permanent settlement based on Security Council Resolutions 242 and 338.

It is understood that the interim arrangements are an integral part of the whole peace process and that the negotiations on the permanent status will lead to the implementation of Security Council Resolutions 242 and 338.

ARTICLE II: FRAMEWORK FOR THE INTERIM PERIOD

The agreed framework for the interim period is set forth in this Declaration of Principles.

ARTICLE III: ELECTIONS

1. In order that the Palestinian people in the West Bank and Gaza Strip may govern themselves according to democratic principles, direct, free and general political elections will be held for the Council under agreed supervision and international observation, while the Palestinian police will ensure public order.
2. An agreement will be concluded on the exact mode and conditions of the elections in accordance with the protocol attached as Annex I, with the goal of holding the elections not later than nine months after the entry into force of this Declaration of Principles.
3. These elections will constitute a significant interim preparatory step toward the realization of the legitimate rights of the Palestinian people and their just requirements.

ARTICLE IV: JURISDICTION

Jurisdiction of the Council will cover West Bank and Gaza Strip territory, except for issues that will be negotiated in the permanent status negotiations. The two sides view the West Bank and the Gaza Strip as a single territorial unit, whose integrity will be preserved during the interim period.

ARTICLE V: TRANSITIONAL PERIOD AND PERMANENT STATUS NEGOTIATIONS

1. The five-year transitional period will begin upon the withdrawal from the Gaza Strip and Jericho area.
2. Permanent status negotiations will commence as soon as possible, but not later than the beginning of the third year of the interim period, between the Government of Israel and the Palestinian people representatives.
3. It is understood that these negotiations shall cover remaining issues, including: Jerusalem, refugees, settlements, security arrangements, borders, relations and cooperation with other neighbors, and other issues of common interest.
4. The two parties agree that the outcome of the permanent status negotiations should not be prejudiced or preempted by agreements reached for the interim period.

ARTICLE VI: PREPARATORY TRANSFER OF POWERS AND RESPONSIBILITIES

1. Upon the entry into force of this Declaration of Principles and the withdrawal from the Gaza Strip and the Jericho area, a transfer of authority from the Israeli military government and its Civil Administration to the authorised Palestinians for this task, as detailed herein, will commence. This transfer of authority will be of a preparatory nature until the inauguration of the Council.
2. Immediately after the entry into force of this Declaration of Princi-

ples and the withdrawal from the Gaza Strip and Jericho area, with the view to promoting economic development in the West Bank and Gaza Strip, authority will be transferred to the Palestinians on the following spheres: education and culture, health, social welfare, direct taxation, and tourism. The Palestinian side will commence in building the Palestinian police force, as agreed upon. Pending the inauguration of the Council, the two parties may negotiate the transfer of additional powers and responsibilities, as agreed upon.

ARTICLE VII: INTERIM AGREEMENT

1. The Israeli and Palestinian delegations will negotiate an agreement on the interim period (the "Interim Agreement").
2. The Interim Agreement shall specify, among other things, the structure of the Council, the number of its members, and the transfer of powers and responsibilities from the Israeli military government and its Civil Administration to the Council. The Interim Agreement shall also specify the Council's executive authority, legislative authority in accordance with Article IX below, and the independent Palestinian judicial organs.
3. The Interim Agreement shall include arrangements, to be implemented upon the inauguration of the Council, for the assumption by the Council of all of the powers and responsibilities transferred previously in accordance with Article VI above.
4. In order to enable the Council to promote economic growth, upon its inauguration, the Council will establish, among other things, a Palestinian Electricity Authority, a Gaza Sea Port Authority, a Palestinian Development Bank, a Palestinian Export Promotion Board, a Palestinian Environmental Authority, a Palestinian Land Authority and a Palestinian Water Administration Authority, and any other Authorities agreed upon, in accordance with the Interim Agreement that will specify their powers and responsibilities.
5. After the inauguration of the Council, the Civil Administration will be dissolved, and the Israeli military government will be withdrawn.

ARTICLE VIII: PUBLIC ORDER AND SECURITY

In order to guarantee public order and internal security for the Palestinians of the West Bank and the Gaza Strip, the Council will establish a strong police force, while Israel will continue to carry the responsibility for defending against external threats, as well as the responsibility for overall security of Israelis for the purpose of safeguarding their internal security and public order.

ARTICLE IX: LAWS AND MILITARY ORDERS

1. The Council will be empowered to legislate, in accordance with the Interim Agreement, within all authorities transferred to it.
2. Both parties will review jointly laws and military orders presently in force in remaining spheres.

ARTICLE X: JOINT ISRAELI-PALESTINIAN LIAISON COMMITTEE

In order to provide for a smooth implementation of this Declaration of Principles and any subsequent agreements pertaining to the interim period, upon the entry into force of this Declaration of Principles, a Joint Israeli-Palestinian Liaison Committee will be established in order to deal with issues requiring coordination, other issues of common interest, and disputes.

ARTICLE XI: ISRAELI-PALESTINIAN COOPERATION IN ECONOMIC FIELDS

Recognizing the mutual benefit of cooperation in promoting the development of the West Bank, the Gaza Strip and Israel, upon the entry into force of this Declaration of Principles, an Israeli-Palestinian Economic Cooperation Committee will be established in order to develop and implement in a cooperative manner the programs identified in the protocols attached as Annex III and Annex IV.

ARTICLE XII: LIAISON AND COOPERATION WITH JORDAN AND EGYPT

The two parties will invite the Governments of Jordan and Egypt to participate in establishing further liaison and cooperation arrangements between the Government of Israel and the Palestinian representatives, on the one hand, and the Governments of Jordan and Egypt, on the other hand, to promote cooperation between them. These arrangements will include the constitution of a Continuing Committee that will decide by agreement on the modalities of admission of persons displaced from the West Bank and Gaza Strip in 1967, together with necessary measures to prevent disruption and disorder. Other matters of common concern will be dealt with by this Committee.

ARTICLE XIII: REDEPLOYMENT OF ISRAELI FORCES

1. After the entry into force of this Declaration of Principles, and not later than the eve of elections for the Council, a redeployment of Israeli military forces in the West Bank and the Gaza Strip will take place, in addition to withdrawal of Israeli forces carried out in accordance with Article XIV.
2. In redeploying its military forces, Israel will be guided by the principle that its military forces should be redeployed outside populated areas.
3. Further redeployments to specified locations will be gradually implemented commensurate with the assumption of responsibility for public order and internal security by the Palestinian police force pursuant to Article VIII above.

ARTICLE XIV: ISRAELI WITHDRAWAL FROM THE GAZA STRIP AND JERICHO AREA

Israel will withdraw from the Gaza Strip and Jericho area, as detailed in the protocol attached as Annex II.

ARTICLE XV: RESOLUTION OF DISPUTES

1. Disputes arising out of the application or interpretation of this Declaration of Principles or any subsequent agreements pertaining to the interim period, shall be resolved by negotiations through the Joint Liaison Committee to be established pursuant to Article X above.
2. Disputes which cannot be settled by negotiations may be resolved by a mechanism of conciliation to be agreed upon by the parties.
3. The parties may agree to submit to arbitration disputes relating to the interim period, which cannot be settled through conciliation. To this end, upon the agreement of both parties, the parties will establish an Arbitration Committee.

ARTICLE XVI: ISRAELI–PALESTINIAN COOPERATION CONCERNING REGIONAL PROGRAMS

Both parties view the multilateral working groups as an appropriate instrument for promoting a "Marshall Plan," the regional programs and other programs, including special programs for the West Bank and Gaza Strip, as indicated in the protocol attached as Annex IV.

ARTICLE XVII: MISCELLANEOUS PROVISIONS

1. This Declaration of Principles will enter into force one month after its signing.
2. All protocols annexed to this Declaration of Principles and Agreed Minutes pertaining thereto shall be regarded as an integral part hereof.

Done at Washington, D.C., this thirteenth day of September, 1993.
For the Government of Israel
For the P.L.O.
Witnessed By:
The United States of America
The Russian Federation

C. The Wye River Memorandum
October 23, 1998

The following are steps to facilitate implementation of the Interim Agreement on the West Bank and Gaza Strip of September 28, 1995 (the "Interim Agreement") and other related agreements including the Note for the Record of January 17, 1997 (hereinafter referred to as "the prior agreements") so that the Israeli and Palestinian sides can more effectively carry out their reciprocal responsibilities, including those relating to further redeployments and security respectively. These steps are to be carried out in a parallel phased approach in accordance with this Memorandum and the attached time line. They are subject to the relevant terms and conditions of the prior agreements and do not supersede their other requirements.

I. FURTHER REDEPLOYMENTS

A. Phase One and Two Further Redeployments

1. Pursuant to the Interim Agreement and subsequent agreements, the Israeli side's implementation of the first and second F.R.D. will consist of the transfer to the Palestinian side of 13% from Area C as follows:

   1% to Area (A)
   12% to Area (B)

   The Palestinian side has informed that it will allocate an area/areas amounting to 3% from the above Area (B) to be designated as Green Areas and/or Nature Reserves. The Palestinian side has further informed that they will act according to the established scientific standards, and that therefore there will be no changes in the status of these areas, without prejudice to the rights of the existing inhabitants in these areas including Bedouins; while these standards do not allow new construction in these areas, existing roads and buildings may be maintained.
   The Israeli side will retain in these Green Areas/Nature Reserves the overriding security responsibility for the purpose of protecting Israelis and confronting the threat of terrorism. Activities and movements of the Palestinian Police forces may be carried out after coordination and confirmation; the Israeli side will respond to such requests expeditiously.

2. As part of the foregoing implementation of the first and second F.R.D., 14.2% from Area (B) will become Area (A).

B. Third Phase of Further Redeployments

With regard to the terms of the Interim Agreement and of Secretary Christopher's letters to the two sides of January 17, 1997 relating to the further redeployment process, there will be a committee to address this question. The United States will be briefed regularly.

II. SECURITY

In the provisions on security arrangements of the Interim Agreement, the Palestinian side agreed to take all measures necessary in order to prevent acts of terrorism, crime and hostilities directed against the Israeli side, against individuals falling under the Israeli side's authority and against their property, just as the Israeli side agreed to take all measures necessary in order to prevent acts of terrorism, crime and hostilities directed against the Palestinian side, against individuals falling under the Palestinian side's authority and against their property. The two sides also agreed to take legal measures against offenders within their jurisdiction and to prevent incitement against each other by any organizations, groups or individuals within their jurisdiction.
Both sides recognize that it is in their vital interests to combat ter-

rorism and fight violence in accordance with Annex I of the Interim Agreement and the Note for the Record. They also recognize that the struggle against terror and violence must be comprehensive in that it deals with terrorists, the terror support structure, and the environment conducive to the support of terror. It must be continuous and constant over a long-term, in that there can be no pauses in the work against terrorists and their structure. It must be cooperative in that no effort can be fully effective without Israeli-Palestinian cooperation and the continuous exchange of information, concepts, and actions.

Pursuant to the prior agreements, the Palestinian side's implementation of its responsibilities for security, security cooperation, and other issues will be as detailed below during the time periods specified in the attached time line:

A. Security Actions
1. Outlawing and Combating Terrorist Organizations
    a. The Palestinian side will make known its policy of zero tolerance for terror and violence against both sides.
    b. A work plan developed by the Palestinian side will be shared with the U.S. and thereafter implementation will begin immediately to ensure the systematic and effective combat of terrorist organizations and their infrastructure.
    c. In addition to the bilateral Israeli-Palestinian security cooperation, a U.S.-Palestinian committee will meet biweekly to review the steps being taken to eliminate terrorist cells and the support structure that plans, finances, supplies and abets terror. In these meetings, the Palestinian side will inform the U.S. fully of the actions it has taken to outlaw all organizations (or wings of organizations, as appropriate) of a military, terrorist or violent character and their support structure and to prevent them from operating in areas under its jurisdiction.
    d. The Palestinian side will apprehend the specific individuals suspected of perpetrating acts of violence and terror for the purpose of further investigation, and prosecution and punishment of all persons involved in acts of violence and terror.
    e. A U.S.-Palestinian committee will meet to review and evaluate information pertinent to the decisions on prosecution, punishment or other legal measures which affect the status of individuals suspected of abetting or perpetrating acts of violence and terror.

2. Prohibiting Illegal Weapons
    a. The Palestinian side will ensure an effective legal framework is in place to criminalize, in conformity with the prior agreements, any importation, manufacturing or unlicensed sale, acquisition or possession of firearms, ammunition or weapons in areas under Palestinian jurisdiction.
    b. In addition, the Palestinian side will establish and vigorously and continuously implement a systematic program for the collection and appropriate handling of all such illegal items in

accordance with the prior agreements. The U.S. has agreed to assist in carrying out this program.

c. A U.S.-Palestinian-Israeli committee will be established to assist and enhance cooperation in preventing the smuggling or other unauthorized introduction of weapons or explosive materials into areas under Palestinian jurisdiction.

3. Preventing Incitement

a. Drawing on relevant international practice and pursuant to Article XXII (1) of the Interim Agreement and the Note for the Record, the Palestinian side will issue a decree prohibiting all forms of incitement to violence or terror, and establishing mechanisms for acting systematically against all expressions or threats of violence or terror. This decree will be comparable to the existing Israeli legislation which deals with the same subject.

b. A U.S.-Palestinian-Israeli committee will meet on a regular basis to monitor cases of possible incitement to violence or terror and to make recommendations and reports on how to prevent such incitement. The Israeli, Palestinian and U.S. sides will each appoint a media specialist, a law enforcement representative, an educational specialist and a current or former elected official to the committee.

B. Security Cooperation

The two sides agree that their security cooperation will be based on a spirit of partnership and will include, among other things, the following steps:

1. Bilateral Cooperation

There will be full bilateral security cooperation between the two sides which will be continuous, intensive and comprehensive.

2. Forensic Cooperation

There will be an exchange of forensic expertise, training, and other assistance.

3. Trilateral Committee

In addition to the bilateral Israeli-Palestinian security cooperation, a high-ranking U.S.-Palestinian-Israeli committee will meet as required and not less than biweekly to assess current threats, deal with any impediments to effective security cooperation and coordination and address the steps being taken to combat terror and terrorist organizations. The committee will also serve as a forum to address the issue of external support for terror. In these meetings, the Palestinian side will fully inform the members of the committee of the results of its investigations concerning terrorist suspects already in custody and the participants will exchange additional relevant information. The committee will report regularly to the leaders of the two sides on the status of cooperation, the results of the meetings and its recommendations.

C. Other Issues
1. Palestinian Police Force
   a. The Palestinian side will provide a list of its policemen to the Israeli side in conformity with the prior agreements.
   b. Should the Palestinian side request technical assistance, the U.S. has indicated its willingness to help meet these needs in cooperation with other donors.
   c. The Monitoring and Steering Committee will, as part of its functions, monitor the implementation of this provision and brief the U.S.

2. PLO Charter
   The Executive Committee of the Palestine Liberation Organization and the Palestinian Central Council will reaffirm the letter of 22 January 1998 from PLO Chairman Yasir Arafat to President Clinton concerning the nullification of the Palestinian National Charter provisions that are inconsistent with the letters exchanged between the PLO and the Government of Israel on 9/10 September 1993. PLO Chairman Arafat, the Speaker of the Palestine National Council, and the Speaker of the Palestinian Council will invite the members of the PNC, as well as the members of the Central Council, the Council, and the Palestinian Heads of Ministries to a meeting to be addressed by President Clinton to reaffirm their support for the peace process and the aforementioned decisions of the Executive Committee and the Central Council.

3. Legal Assistance in Criminal Matters
   Among other forms of legal assistance in criminal matters, the requests for arrest and transfer of suspects and defendants pursuant to Article II (7) of Annex IV of the Interim Agreement will be submitted (or resubmitted) through the mechanism of the Joint Israeli-Palestinian Legal Committee and will be responded to in conformity with Article II (7) (f) of Annex IV of the Interim Agreement within the twelve-week period. Requests submitted after the eighth week will be responded to in conformity with Article II (7) (f) within four weeks of their submission. The U.S. has been requested by the sides to report on a regular basis on the steps being taken to respond to the above requests.

4. Human Rights and the Rule of Law
   Pursuant to Article XI (1) of Annex I of the Interim Agreement, and without derogating from the above, the Palestinian Police will exercise powers and responsibilities to implement this Memorandum with due regard to internationally accepted norms of human rights and the rule of law, and will be guided by the need to protect the public, respect human dignity, and avoid harassment.

III. INTERIM COMMITTEES AND ECONOMIC ISSUES
1. The Israeli and Palestinian sides reaffirm their commitment to enhancing their relationship and agree on the need actively to promote economic development in the West Bank and Gaza. In this regard, the parties agree to continue or to reactivate all standing committees established by the Interim Agreement,

including the Monitoring and Steering Committee, the Joint Economic Committee (JEC), the Civil Affairs Committee (CAC), the Legal Committee, and the Standing Cooperation Committee.

2. The Israeli and Palestinian sides have agreed on arrangements which will permit the timely opening of the Gaza Industrial Estate. They also have concluded a "Protocol Regarding the Establishment and Operation of the International Airport in the Gaza Strip During the Interim Period."

3. Both sides will renew negotiations on Safe Passage immediately. As regards the southern route, the sides will make best efforts to conclude the agreement within a week of the entry into force of this Memorandum. Operation of the southern route will start as soon as possible thereafter. As regards the northern route, negotiations will continue with the goal of reaching agreement as soon as possible. Implementation will take place expeditiously thereafter.

4. The Israeli and Palestinian sides acknowledge the great importance of the Port of Gaza for the development of the Palestinian economy, and the expansion of Palestinian trade. They commit themselves to proceeding without delay to conclude an agreement to allow the construction and operation of the port in accordance with the prior agreements. The Israeli-Palestinian Committee will reactivate its work immediately with a goal of concluding the protocol within sixty days, which will allow commencement of the construction of the port.

5. The two sides recognize that unresolved legal issues adversely affect the relationship between the two peoples. They therefore will accelerate efforts through the Legal Committee to address outstanding legal issues and to implement solutions to these issues in the shortest possible period. The Palestinian side will provide to the Israeli side copies of all of its laws in effect.

6. The Israeli and Palestinian sides also will launch a strategic economic dialogue to enhance their economic relationship. They will establish within the framework of the JEC an Ad Hoc Committee for this purpose. The committee will review the following four issues: (1) Israeli purchase taxes; (2) cooperation in combating vehicle theft; (3) dealing with unpaid Palestinian debts; and (4) the impact of Israeli standards as barriers to trade and the expansion of the A1 and A2 lists. The committee will submit an interim report within three weeks of the entry into force of this Memorandum, and within six weeks will submit its conclusions and recommendations to be implemented.

7. The two sides agree on the importance of continued international donor assistance to facilitate implementation by both sides of agreements reached. They also recognize the need for enhanced donor support for economic development in the West Bank and Gaza. They agree to jointly approach the donor community to organize a Ministerial Conference before the end of 1998 to seek pledges for enhanced levels of assistance.

IV. PERMANENT STATUS NEGOTIATIONS

The two sides will immediately resume permanent status negotiations on an accelerated basis and will make a determined effort to achieve the mutual goal of reaching an agreement by May 4, 1999. The negotiations will be continuous and without interruption. The U.S. has expressed its willingness to facilitate these negotiations.

V. UNILATERAL ACTIONS

Recognizing the necessity to create a positive environment for the negotiations, neither side shall initiate or take any step that will change the status of the West Bank and the Gaza Strip in accordance with the Interim Agreement.

This Memorandum will enter into force ten days from the date of signature.

Done at Washington, D.C. this 23d day of October 1998.
For the Government of the State of Israel:
Benjamin Netanyahu
For the PLO:
Yasser Arafat
Witnessed by:
William J. Clinton
The United States of America

D. Trilateral Statement on the Middle East Peace Summit Camp David, July 25, 2000

President William J. Clinton
Israeli Prime Minister Ehud Barak
Palestinian Authority Chairman Yasser Arafat

Between July 11 and 24, under the auspices of President Clinton, Prime Minister Barak and Chairman Arafat met at Camp David in an effort to reach an agreement on permanent status. While they were not able to bridge the gaps and reach an agreement, their negotiations were unprecedented in both scope and detail. Building on the progress achieved at Camp David, the two leaders agreed on the following principles to guide their negotiations:

1. The two sides agreed that the aim of their negotiations is to put an end to decades of conflict and achieve a just and lasting peace.
2. The two sides commit themselves to continue their efforts to conclude an agreement on all permanent status issues as soon as possible.
3. Both sides agree that negotiations based on UN Security Council Resolutions 242 and 338 are the only way to achieve such an agreement and they undertake to create an environment for negotiations free from pressure, intimidation and threats of violence.
4. The two sides understand the importance of avoiding unilateral

actions that prejudge the outcome of negotiations and that their differences will be resolved only by good faith negotiations.

5. Both sides agree that the United States remains a vital partner in the search for peace and will continue to consult closely with President Clinton and Secretary Albright in the period ahead.

Endnotes

Chapter 1: Contours of Conflict
1 Harold S. Kushner, *When Bad Things Happen to Good People*, 56.

Chapter 2: A Family Feud Rekindled
2 Charles Singer, "Science and Judaism," in *The Jews, Their History, Culture, and Religion*, ed. Louis Finkelstein, 1:1427; cf. Max Dimont, *Jews, God, and History*, 18, 252.

3 Ibid., 1:1415–27.

4 Others don't see this as a separate covenant but rather as the stipulations of the Mosaic covenant (cf. Leviticus 26). In either case, the chapters focus on God's blessings and cursings to Israel, based on their obedience or disobedience to God's covenant. The ultimate curse of the covenant was forfeiture of their right to live in the land (Leviticus 26:27-43; Deuteronomy 28:58-68). But God goes on to announce that this final curse does not make his promise null and void (Leviticus 26:44-45). When those in captivity turn back to seek the Lord, he promises to restore them to the land (Deuteronomy 30:1-5).

Chapter 3: The Jews in Worldwide Dispersion
5 Max Dimont, *Jews, God, and History*, 105.

6 Flavius Josephus, *The Wars of the Jews*, 5.3.1; 6.9.3. Josephus wrote his *Jewish War, Jewish Antiquities*, and *Life in Rome* between A.D. 70 and 80.

7 Heinrich Graetz, *History of the Jews*, 2:308.

8 Josephus, *Wars of the Jews*, 6.9.4.

9 Ibid., 7.1.1. The one exception to this destruction was the Western Wall.

10 Heinrich Graetz, *History of the Jews*, 2:312.

11 Ibid., 2:312-313.

12 Josephus, *Wars of the Jews*, 7.8.1.

13 Dimont, *Jews, God, and History*, 105.

14 Richard E. Gade, *A Historical Survey of Anti-Semitism*, 16.

15 Abba Hillel Silver, *Messianic Speculation in Israel*, 20.

16 F. J. Foakes Jackson, *Josephus and the Jews*, 86; Cecil Roth, *A History of the Jews*, 114.

17 Dimont, *Jews, God, and History*, 110–11.

18 Eli Sanders, "Two Peoples, One Land: Understanding the Israeli-Palestinian Conflict," *The Seattle Times*, 12 May 2002. The *Encyclopedia Britannica* says that following the bar Kochba revolt, "the province of Judaea was renamed Syria Palaestina (later simply called Palaestina), and, according to Eusebius (*Historia*

Ecclesiastica iv. 6), no Jew was thenceforth allowed to set foot in Jerusalem or the surrounding district" (s.v., "Palestine, history of").

[19] Gade, *Historical Survey*, 17.
[20] Roth, *History of the Jews*, 115.
[21] Silver, *Messianic Speculation*, 28.
[22] Gade, *Historical Survey*, 19.
[23] Graetz, *History of the Jews*, 2:562 ff.
[24] Dimont, *Jews, God, and History*, 168.
[25] Roth, *History of the Jews*, 126.
[26] Dimont, *Jews, God, and History*, 75–83.
[27] Max Dimont, *The Jews in America*, 153.
[28] William L. Hull, *The Fall and Rise of Israel*, 41.
[29] Dimont, *Jews in America*, 152; cf. *The Jews, Their History*, ed. Louis Finkelstein, 1796; (cf. 1355, relating to the human body).
[30] Dimont, *Jews in America*, 152.
[31] Dimont, *Jews, God, and History*, 171.
[32] Roth, *History of the Jews*, 153; cf. Finkelstein, *The Jews, Their History*, 191–194.
[33] Cecil Roth, ed., *The Concise Jewish Encyclopedia*, 303.
[34] Ibid., 303; Dimont, *Jews, God, and History*, 204–208.
[35] Dimont, *Jews, God, and History*, 182–183.

Chapter 4: Jewish Migrations and Expulsions

[36] Wm. H. Harris and Judith S. Levy, eds., *The New Columbia Encyclopedia*, 1854.
[37] Kenneth Cragg, *The House of Islam*, 20.
[38] Gade, *Historical Survey*, 22.
[39] *Qur'an*, Sura 3:67.
[40] Dimont, *Jews, God, and History*, 193; cf. Roth, *History of the Jews*, 151.
[41] *Qur'an*, Sura 19:15–35.
[42] Ibid., Sura 4:157.
[43] John Elder, *The Biblical Approach to Muslims*, 26. A variety of interpretations are given for this verse by Arab interpreters.
[44] Arthur Jeffery, *Islam, Muhammad and His Religion*, 39.
[45] Elizabeth and Robert Fernea, *The Arab World*, 83; cf. Wesley G. Pippert, *Land of Promise, Land of Strife*, 191.
[46] Cragg, *House of Islam*, 64.
[47] S. D. Goiten, *Jews and Arabs*, 21–23, discusses the questionable descendancy of Arabs from Ishmael, though Muhammad made this a "cornerstone of his new faith"; cf. Helmet Gatje, *The Qur'an and Its Exegesis*, 127–128. For a complete history of the Arab people, see Tony Maalouf, *Arabs in the Shadow of Israel*, 8–9, 106–111.
[48] *Qur'an*, Sura 2:135.
[49] Some believe that archaeological evidence shows that the "Rock" (or spot of the inner altar of the temple) is actually located 343 feet northwest of the Dome (cf. Asher S. Kaufman, "Where the Ancient Temple of Jerusalem Stood," *Biblical Archaeological Review*, March/April 1983). However, others argue that the inner altar and ark stood where the Dome of the Rock now sits (cf. Leen Ritmeyer, "The Ark of the Covenant: Where It Stood in Solomon's Temple," *Biblical Archaeological Review*, January/February 1996). Leen and Kathleen Ritmeyer have published their most recent findings in *Secrets of Jerusalem's Temple Mount* (Washington, DC: Biblical Archaeology Society, 1998).
[50] *Qur'an*, Sura 2:172 ff.
[51] Dimont, *Jews, God, and History*, 193; cf. Roth, *History of the Jews*, 151.
[52] Philip K. Hitti, *Islam: A Way of Life*, 106–20.
[53] Dimont, *Jews, God, and History*, 95.
[54] Jack Finegan, *Discovering Israel*, 73.

55 William L. Hull, *The Fall and Rise of Israel*, 51.
56 Ibid., 92.
57 Finkelstein, *The Jews, Their History*, 1:224.
58 Hull, *Fall and Rise*, 52.
59 Ibid., 53.
60 Ibid., 52.
61 Dimont, *Jews, God, and History*, 221.
62 Ibid., 222.
63 Roth, *History of the Jews*, 180.
64 Hull, op cit., 94.
65 Roth, op cit., 213.
66 Harris and Levy, *New Columbia Encyclopedia*, 2161.
67 Hull, *Fall and Rise*, 55.
68 Graetz, *History of the Jews*, 4:101.
69 Ibid., 101.
70 Finkelstein, *The Jews, Their History*, 1:233.
71 Gade, *Historical Survey*, 36.
72 Dimont, *Jews, God, and History*, 226.
73 Hull, *Fall and Rise*, 61.
74 Ibid., 61.
75 Dimont, *Jews, God, and History*, 230.
76 Max L. Margolis and Alexander Marx, *History of the Jewish People*, 485.
77 Graetz, *History of the Jews*, 4:550–52.
78 Ibid., 552.
79 Finkelstein, *The Jews, Their History*, 291.
80 Margolis and Marx, *History of Jewish People*, 525–26.
81 Ibid., 526 ff.; Dimont, *Jews, God, and History*, 202.
82 D. M. Dunlop in his *History of the Jewish Khazars* has traced the many sources of the ancient Khazars and has given one of the most reliable accounts of the Kingdom of Khazaria in the English language, showing their significance in halting the Islamic conquest in the north.
83 Dimont, *Jews, God, and History*, 230.
84 Ibid., 244; Finkelstein, *The Jews, Their History*, 250–51.
85 Ibid., 244–45.
86 Arnold White, *World's Great Events*, VII, 343–44.
87 Dimont, *Jews, God, and History*, 254–58.
88 Ibid., 310.
89 Ibid., 313–17.
90 Ibid., 320–24.
91 Ibid., 322–23.
92 Dennis Prager and Joseph Telushkin, *Why the Jews?*, 202.
93 Ibid., 8; cf. Prager and Telushkin, *Why the Jews?*, 202; Roth, *Jewish Encyclopedia*, 160.
94 Ibid., 202.
95 "Saudi Hand Behind Egypt's Anti-Jewish TV Serial," DEBKAfile, 4 November 2002.
96 Henry Ford Sr., *The International Jew*, 163, 202.
97 Gade, *Historical Survey*, 34.
98 Ibid., 54.
99 Dimont, *Jews, God, and History*, 17.
100 Ibid., 264–65.
101 Ibid., 264.
102 Ibid., 20.
103 Ibid., 124.

Chapter 5: Zionism: Turning Dreams into Drama

[104] Dimont, *Jews, God, and History*, 393.

[105] Ibid.

[106] Harris and Levy, *New Columbia Encyclopedia*, 1014.

[107] James A. Rudin, *Israel for Christians*, 24.

[108] Abram Leon Sachar, *A History of the Jews*, 353.

[109] Ibid., 354.

[110] Ibid., 451.

[111] Dimont, *Jews, God, and History*, 399; Hull, *Fall and Rise*, 122 (see note 113).

[112] Alan R. Taylor, *Prelude to Israel*, 15.

[113] Hull, *Fall and Rise*, 129.

[114] Finkelstein, *The Jews, Their History*, 691.

[115] Taylor, *Prelude*, 34–35; Howard M. Sachar, *A History of Israel*, 128–29.

[116] Rudin, *Israel for Christians*, 7.

[117] Ibid., 8; Abba Eban, *My Country: The Story of Modern Israel*, 33; Sachar, *History of the Jews*, 413.

[118] Hagop A. Chakmakjian, *In Quest of Justice and Peace in the Middle East*, 28–29.

[119] Sachar, *History of the Jews*, 412–14.

[120] Ibid., 413.

[121] Ibid., 414.

[122] Hull, *Fall and Rise*, 149.

[123] Michael Cohen, *Palestine and the Great Powers*, 184.

[124] Peter Mansfield, *The Arab World*, 48; Hull, *Fall and Rise*, 142.

[125] Cohen, *Great Powers*, 7; Hull, *Fall and Rise*, 204.

[126] Hull, *Fall and Rise*, 205.

[127] Ibid.

Chapter 6: World War II and the Holocaust

[128] James Korting, *An Outline of German History from 1890 to 1945*, 67.

[129] Sachar, *History of the Jews*, 373.

[130] Adolf Hitler, *Mein Kampf*, 906.

[131] Ibid., 441–42.

[132] Ibid., 83.

[133] Ibid., 84.

[134] Ibid., 84; 118.

[135] The writings of Count de Gobineau, a Frenchman; Friedrich Nietzsche, a German; and Houston S. Chamberlain, an Englishman living in Germany, all contributed to this early nineteenth-century anti-Semitism. The two-volume work by Chamberlain (not to be confused with Neville Chamberlain), *Foundations of the Nineteenth Century*, saturated Europe with a quarter million copies of this Aryan superrace philosophy. See brief sketch by Dimont, *Jews, God, and History*, 313–28.

[136] Hitler, *Mein Kampf*, 14, 17.

[137] Ibid., 160–61.

[138] Ibid., 137.

[139] Harris and Levy, *New Columbia Encyclopedia*, 757.

[140] Hitler, *Mein Kampf*, 99–103.

[141] Ibid., 80–81.

[142] Ibid., 81.

[143] Ibid., 406, 412 ff., 994.

[144] Marc Hillel and Clarissa Henry in *Of Pure Blood* have documented and described the "maternity homes or stud-farms" developed by Hitler and Himmler by which they kidnapped selected girls to mate with selected males to "bear children for the Führer."

[145] Korting, *German History*, 99.

[146] Friedrich Meinecke, *The German Catastrophe*, 81 ff.
[147] Ibid., 86.
[148] Korting, *German History*, 142.
[149] Ibid., 144.
[150] Ibid., 148.
[151] Meinecke, *German Catastrophe*, 82.
[152] Prager and Telushkin, *Why the Jews?*, 160; Hitler, *Mein Kampf*, 117.
[153] Dimont, *Jews, God, and History*, 377-379.
[154] Ibid., 373.
[155] Martha Dodd, *Through Embassy Eyes*, 228.
[156] Dimont, *Jews, God, and History*, 378–79.
[157] Sachar, *History of the Jews*, 376; Roth, *History of the Jews*, 392.
[158] Korting, *German History*, 148.
[159] Sachar, *History of the Jews*, 379.
[160] Yehuda Bauer, *The Holocaust in Historical Perspective*, 103 ff.
[161] Ibid., 109, 126.
[162] Dimont, *Jews, God, and History*, 380.
[163] Korting, *German History*, 174.
[164] Martin Gilbert, *Jewish History Atlas*, 96; Rudin, *Israel for Christians*, 45.
[165] Gade, *Historical Survey*, 108.
[166] Prager and Telushkin, *Why the Jews?*, 155.
[167] Finkelstein, *The Jews, Their History*, 1532.
[168] Dimont, *Jews, God, and History*, 373, 387.
[169] A large literature on the Holocaust has been produced in recent years, among which is the excellent survey by David M. Rausch, *Legacy of Hatred*. He identifies many anti-Semitic groups of White Supremacists continuing in both Europe and America today (185 ff.).
[170] Korting, *German History*, 169.
[171] Ibid., 171–72.
[172] This is not to suggest that the virus of anti-Semitism was extinguished, for it has experienced a persistent resurgence in Neo-Nazism and other forms in recent years; cf. Rausch, *Legacy*, 211 ff.

Chapter 7: The Tattered Remnant and the New State of Israel
[173] Hull, *Fall and Rise*, 234.
[174] Michael Pragai, *Faith and Fulfillment*, 175.
[175] Ibid., 232.
[176] Ibid.
[177] Finkelstein, *The Jews, Their History*, 1575–78.
[178] Taylor, *Prelude*, 56–57.
[179] Cohen, *Great Powers*, 20.
[180] Hull, *Fall and Rise*, 235.
[181] Taylor, *Prelude*, 94–95.
[182] Pragai, *Faith and Fulfillment*, 135.
[183] Richard Ward, Don Peretz, and Evan M. Wilson, *The Palestine State*, 9.
[184] Cohen, *Great Powers*, 186; Hull, *Fall and Rise*, 213, 217.
[185] Cohen, *Great Powers*, 45.
[186] Sachar, *History of Israel*, 255.
[187] Pragai, *Faith and Fulfillment*, 223–24.
[188] Cohen, *Great Powers*, 43–46.
[189] Ibid., 55.
[190] Pragai, *Faith and Fulfillment*, 137.
[191] Taylor, *Prelude*, 87–90.
[192] Sachar, *History of Israel*, 264.
[193] Ibid., 257.

194 Ibid., 268.
195 Hull, *Fall and Rise*, 263.
196 Taylor, *Prelude*, 98.
197 Sachar, *History of Israel*, 267.
198 Ibid., 278.
199 Cohen, *Great Powers*, 274.
200 Taylor, *Prelude*, 102.
201 Sachar, *History of Israel*, 289.
202 Ibid., 291.
203 Ibid., 292.
204 Ibid., 297.
205 Cohen, *Great Powers*, 20, 305–6.
206 Sachar, *History of Israel*, 306.
207 Ibid., 317.
208 Cohen, *Great Powers*, 322.
209 Ibid., 331.
210 Ibid., 331–34.
211 Golda Meir, "Name of Article," *Life,* 3 October 1969, 32.
212 Finegan, *Discovering Israel*, 70.
213 Francis L. Lowenheim, "Israel's Recognition Didn't Come Easy," *The Oregonian,* 8 December 1989.
214 Pragai, *Faith and Fulfillment*, 224.
215 Hull, *Fall and Rise*, 333; Sachar, *History of the Jews*, 444.
216 Hull, *Fall and Rise*, 333, 340.
217 Sachar, *History of the Jews*, 444.
218 Hull, *Fall and Rise*, 336.
219 Sachar, *History of the Jews*, 318.
220 Ibid., 330.
221 Hull, *Fall and Rise*, 342.
222 Sachar, *History of the Jews*, 345.
223 Hull, *Fall and Rise*, 342.
224 Ibid.
225 Sachar, *History of the Jews*, 353.

Chapter 8: Israel's Defense and Expansion

226 Dimont, *Jews, God, and History*, 409.
227 Roth, *History of the Jews*, 432.
228 Sachar, *History of Israel*, 620.
229 Ibid., 633.
230 Ibid., 640.
231 Ibid.
232 Sachar, *History of Israel*, 656.
233 Roth, *History of the Jews*, 436.
234 Roth, *Jewish Encyclopedia*, 493.
235 Sachar, *History of Israel*, 667.
236 Ibid., 666.
237 Ibid., 747.
238 Ibid., 676.
239 Ibid., 689.
240 Ibid., 695.
241 Ibid., 750.
242 Ibid., 759.
243 Ibid.
244 Ibid., 758.
245 Ibid., 768–70. According to Seymour Hersh, another reason the United States

agreed to resupply Israel is that the Israelis, fearing a catastrophic military defeat, were prepared to use their recently developed nuclear weapons (Seymour Hersh, *The Samson Option*, 225–40).

246 Gilbert, *Jewish History Atlas*, 120.
247 Sachar, *History of Israel*, 766.
248 Ibid., 781.
249 Ibid., 787.
250 Ibid., 786.
251 Ibid., 812.
252 Ibid., 791.

Chapter 9: Convulsions from Within: *Intifada*

253 Amos Perlmutter, *Israel: The Partitioned State: A Political History Since 1900*, 22.
254 Sachar, *History of Israel*, 3.
255 Ibid., 25.
256 Ibid., 26.
257 Perlmutter, *Partitioned State*, 262.
258 Sachar, *History of Israel*, 137.
259 Perlmutter, *Partitioned State*, 298.
260 Ibid., 281.
261 Sachar, *History of Israel*, 52, 67, 128.
262 Yehoshafat Harkabi, *Israel's Fateful Hour*, 92.
263 Sachar, *History of Israel*, 210.
264 Harkabi, *Fateful Hour*, 13.
265 Thomas Kiernan, *Arafat: The Man and the Myth*, 114.
266 Ibid., 114; Walter Reich, *Stranger in My House: Jews and Arabs in the West Bank*, 2–3.
267 Perlmutter, *Partitioned State*, 34.
268 Kiernan, *Man and Myth*, 114, 116.
269 Ibid., 14.
270 Alan Hart, *Arafat: Terrorist or Peacemaker?* 68.
271 Kiernan, *Man and Myth*, 99
272 Ibid., 113.
273 Ibid., 160–61, 235.
274 Hart, *Terrorist or Peacemaker?* 162.
275 Sachar, *History of Israel*, 519–22.
276 Hart, *Terrorist or Peacemaker?* 163.
277 Ibid., 118.
278 Ibid., 127.
279 Ibid., 25.
280 Ibid., 202.
281 Ibid., 235.
282 Hart, *Terrorist or Peacemaker?* 321.
283 Kiernan, *Man and Myth*, 231.
284 Hart, *Terrorist or Peacemaker?* 29.
285 Kiernan, *Man and Myth*, 264.
286 Hart, *Terrorist or Peacemaker?* 203.
287 Harkabi, *Fateful Hour*, 14–22.
288 David K. Shipler, *Arab and Jew*, 84.
289 Kiernan, *Man and Myth*, 70.
290 Ibid., 33, 51.
291 Shipler, *Arab and Jew*, 169.
292 Hart, *Terrorist or Peacemaker?* 170.
293 Ward, Peretz, and Wilson, *Palestine State*, 53 ff.

294 Hart, *Terrorist or Peacemaker?* 325.

295 Mona Charen, "Films on Palestinians Mug History." *The Oregonian*, 11 September 1989.

296 Allyn Fisher, "Sharon to form hard-line faction in Likud bloc," *The Oregonian*, 15 February 1990.

297 Hussein Agha and Robert Malley, "Camp David: The Tragedy of Errors," *The New York Review of Books*, 9 August 2001.

298 "Arafat says he is ready, but stops short of committing to cease-fire," *Jerusalem Post Internet Edition*, 1 January 2003.

299 Shipler, *Arab and Jew*, 79–137.

300 George Will, "White House Ready to Dance with PLO," *The Oregonian*, 17 September 1989.

301 Shipler, *Arab and Jew*, 117.

302 David Grossman, *The Yellow Wind*, 83–84.

303 Ibid., 151.

304 Shipler, *Arab and Jew*, 144 ff.

305 Ibid., 110.

306 Charen, "Films."

307 Grossman, *Yellow Wind*, 151.

308 Ibid., 63.

309 Ibid., 194.

310 Ibid., 74.

311 Shipler, *Arab and Jew*, 292–97.

312 Ibid., 503.

313 Ibid., 64.

314 Ibid., 502.

315 *Encyclopedia Britannica*, 2003 Deluxe Edition CD-ROM, s.v., "Israel." They note that "the Israelis left the Temple Mount in Jerusalem, the local Arab institutions, and indeed the Jordanian legal code throughout the West Bank in the hands of the Palestinians, just as they left Egyptian regulations in place in Gaza."

Chapter 10: To Whom Does the Land Really Belong?

316 Avi Shlaim, *Collusion Across the Jordan*, 23; Colin Chapman, *Whose Promised Land?* 55 ff.

317 Reich, *Stranger in House*, 48.

318 Grossman, *Yellow Wind*, 8.

319 Hart, *Terrorist or Peacemaker?* 98; Schlaim, *Collusion*, 476.

320 Shipler, *Arab and Jew*, 55.

321 Goiten, *Jews and Arabs*, 121–22; Shipler, *Arab and Jew*, 152.

322 *Qur'an*, Sura 3:60.

323 Ibid., 2:110.

324 Ibid., 6:85.

325 Shipler, *Arab and Jew*, 258; Cragg, *House of Islam*, 46.

326 Cragg, *House of Islam*, 46.

327 Ward, Peretz, and Wilson, *Palestine State*, 63–64.

328 Ibid., 62 ff.

329 Albert Memmi, *Jews and Arabs*, 21.

330 Ward, Peretz, and Wilson, *Palestine State*, 7.

331 Harkabi, *Fateful Hour*, 146.

332 Eban, *My Country*, 33.

333 Schlaim, *Collusion*, 3.

334 Sachar, *History of Israel*, 436.

335 Ibid., 437.

336 Ibid., 438.

337 Shipler, *Arab and Jew*, 32–36.

338 Ibid., 439.
339 Ibid.
340 Schlaim, *Collusion*, 3.
341 Sachar, *History of Israel*, 438.
342 Eban, *My Country*, 97.
343 Shipler, *Arab and Jew*, 140–76.
344 See Chapter 4, note 49.
345 Samuel Naaman, "The Future of Islamic Fundamentalism," in *Prophecy in Light of Today*, Charles Dyer, ed., p. 56.
346 Harold Fisch, *The Zionist Revolution: A New Perspective*, 10; Charles Gulston, *Jerusalem: The Tragedy and the Triumph*, 59.
347 Shipler, *Arab and Jew*, 174–75.
348 Chapman, *Whose Promised Land?*, 30.
349 Manfred Waldemar Kohl, "Towards a Theology of Land: A Christian Answer to the Hebrew-Arab Conflict," *International Congregational Journal* 2 (August 2002): 165–78.
350 Fernea and Fernea, *The Arab World*, 83.
351 Sachar, *History of the Jews*, 157; *Qur'an*, Sura 19:28.
352 Khaled Abu Toameh, "PA Population to Double in 19 Years," *Jerusalem Post Internet Edition*, 9 January 2003.
353 Harkabi, *Fateful Hour*.
354 Grossman, *Yellow Wind*, 22–23.
355 Reich, *Stranger in House*, 29.
356 Grossman, *Yellow Wind*, 103.
357 Yosef Tekoah, *In the Face of the Nations: Israel's Struggle for Peace*, 89.
358 For a recent history of the United States' position on Palestinian statehood, see Clyde Mark, *Palestinians and Middle East Peace: Issues for the United States*, Congressional Research Service Issue brief for Congress, 25 January 2002.

Chapter 11: Divine Assessment and Promised Restoration
359 Goiten, *Jews and Arabs*, 217.
360 Jerome Murphy-O'Connor, *The Holy Land*, 86; cf. Marius Baar, *The Unholy War*, 146–47.
361 *Qur'an*, Sura 3:171.
362 *Qur'an*, Sura 2:125–35.
363 Goiten, *Jews and Arabs*, 66.
364 Shipler, *Arab and Jew*, 181–222.
365 See Chapter 2, note 4.
366 Seth N. Klayman, "Who Was a Jew, Who Is a Jew?" (senior honors thesis, The Ohio State University, June 1998), 106.
367 Ibid., 105.
368 Rabbi Yechiel Eckstein, *What Christians Should Know About Jews and Judaism*, 276.
369 Pragai, *Faith and Fulfillment*, 154–55.
370 Eckstein, *What Christians Should Know*, 306.
371 Samuel Sandmel, *A Jewish Understanding of the New Testament*, 279.
372 Donald A. Hagner, *The Jewish Reclamation of Jesus*, 46 ff.
373 Herbert Danby, *The Jew and Christianity*, 3.
374 Ibid., 25–28; Eckstein, *What Christians Should Know*, 263.
375 Pichas Lapide and Ulrich Luz, *Jesus in Two Perspectives*, 114.
376 Samuel Sandmel, *Anti-Semitism in the New Testament*, 134.
377 Eckstein, *What Christians Should Know*, 267; Hagner, *Jewish Reclamation*, 214.
378 Samuel Sandmel, *We Jews and Jesus*, vii.
379 Kaufmann Kohler, *Jewish Theology*, 88.
380 Kac, *Spiritual Dilemma*, 35.

381 Dean McBride, "The Yoke of the Kingdom," *Interpretation* (July 1973): 273–306.
382 Kohler, *Jewish Theology*, 86.
383 Ibid., 428–29.
384 Ibid., 89–90.
385 Francis Brown, S. R. Driver, and Charles A. Briggs, *Hebrew and English Lexicon of the Old Testament*, 25.
386 Kohler, *Jewish Theology*, 91; cf. Kushner, *When Bad Things Happen*, 72–73 (as a liberal alternative allowing for evolution, i.e., God and animals producing man).
387 Kohler, *Jewish Theology*, 336, 413; Eugene Kaellis and Rhoda Kaellis, *Toward a Jewish America*, promote mass conversion to Judaism.
388 Ibid., 417.
389 Eckstein, *What Christians Should Know*, 321.
390 Ibid.; see also Sandmel, *Anti-Semitism*, 138 ff.
391 Eckstein, *What Christians Should Know*, 317.
392 Ibid., 321.
393 Sandmel, *Anti-Semitism*, 165.
394 Arthur W. Kac, *The Rebirth of the State of Israel*, 52.

Appendix B
395 Charles C. Torrey, *Jewish Foundations of Islam*, 89–90.
396 Walter Laqueur, *The Israel-Arab Reader*.
397 Ibid., 16.

Select Bibliography

Books

Anderson, Sir Norman, ed. *The World's Religions.* Grand Rapids, Mich.: Wm. B. Eerdmans Publishing Co., 1980.

Applebaum, Morton M. *What Everyone Should Know About Judaism.* New York: Philosophical Library, 1959.

Arberry, Arthur J., trans. *The Koran Interpreted.* New York: Collier Books, 1955.

Atherton, Alfred L., et al. *Toward Arab-Israeli Peace: Report of a Study Group.* Washington, D.C.: The Brookings Inst., 1988.

Avishai, Bernard. *The Tragedy of Zionism: Revolution and Democracy in the Land of Israel.* New York: Farrar, Straus, and Giroux, 1985.

Avnery, Uri. *My Friend the Enemy.* Westport, Conn.: Lawrence Hill Co., 1984.

Baar, Marius. *The Unholy War: Oil, Islam, and Armageddon.* Trans. Victor Carpenter. Nashville: Thomas Nelson Publishers, 1980.

Bauer, Yehuda. *The Holocaust in Historical Perspective.* Seattle: Univ. of Washington Press, 1978.

Beatty, Ilene. *Arab and Jew in the Land of Palestine.* Chicago: Henry Regnery Co., 1957.

Beaty, John. *The Iron Curtain over America.* New York: Gordon Press, 1980, 1951.

Begin, Menachem. *The Revolt: Story of the Irgun.* New York: Dell Publishing Co., 1977.

Bein, Alex. *Theodore Herzl.* Philadelphia: Jewish Pub. Soc. of America, 1956.

Ben-Gurion, David. *Israel: A Personal History.* Trans. Nechemia Meyers and Uzy Nystar. New York: Funk & Wagnalls, Inc., 1971.

Brandeis, Louis D. *Brandeis on Zionism.* Washington, D.C.: Zionist Organization of America, 1942.

Brown, Francis, S. R. Driver, and Charles A. Briggs. *Hebrew and English Lexicon of the Old Testament.* Oxford: Clarendon Press, 1907.

Bruno, Leon. *Why Is the Middle East a Conflict Area?* (Opposing Viewpoints Pamphlet). St. Paul, Minn.: Greenhaven Press, Inc., 1982.

Buber, Martin. *A Land of Two Peoples.* New York: Oxford Univ. Press, 1983.

Burrows, Millar. *Palestine Is Our Business.* Philadelphia: Westminster Press, 1949.

Chakmakjian, Hagop A. *In Quest of Justice and Peace in the Middle East.* New York: Vantage Press, 1976.

Chapman, Colin. *Whose Promised Land?* Ann Arbor, Mich.: Lion Publishing Company, 1983.

Chase, James, ed. *Conflicts in the Middle East.* New York: H. W. Wilson Co., 1969.

Cohen, Aharon. *Israel and the Arab World.* New York: Funk & Wagnalls, 1970.

Cohen, Avner. *Israel and the Bomb.* New York: Columbia University Press, 1998.

Cohen, Jeremy. *The Friars and the Jews.* London: Cornell University Press, 1982.

Cohen, Michael J. *Palestine and the Great Powers, 1945–1948.* Princeton, N.J.: Princeton Univ. Press, 1982.

Colbi, Saul P. *A History of the Christian Presence in the Holy Land.* Lanham, Md.: University Press of America, 1988.

Cooper, Anne. *Ishmael My Brother.* London: MARC Europe STL Books, 1985.

Cragg, Kenneth. *The House of Islam.* Belmont, Calif.: Wadsworth Pub. Co., 1975.

Dall, Col. Curtis. *Israelis' Five Million Dollar Secret.* Reedy, W.Va.: Liberty Bell Publications, 1977.

Danby, Herbert. *The Jew and Christianity.* London: Sheldon, 1927.

Dawidowicz, Lucy. *A Holocaust Reader.* New York: Behrman House, 1976.

Dimont, Max I. *Jews, God, and History.* New York: Simon and Schuster, 1962.

———. *The Jews in America.* New York: Simon and Schuster, 1980, 1978.

Dodd, Martha. *Through Embassy Eyes.* New York: Harcourt, Brace and Co., 1939.

Dunlop, D. *The History of the Jewish Khazars.* New York: Schocken Books, 1967.

Dyer, Charles H., ed. *Prophecy in Light of Today.* Chicago: Moody Press, 2002.

———, ed. *Storm Clouds on the Horizon.* Chicago: Moody Press, 2001.

Eban, Abba. *My Country: The Story of Modern Israel.* New York: Random House, 1972.

Eckstein, Rabbi Yechiel. *What Christians Should Know About Jews and Judaism.* Waco, Tex.: Word Book Publishers, 1984.

Edersheim, Alfred. *The History of the Jewish Nation.* Grand Rapids, Mich.: Baker Book House, 1956.

Eidelberg, Shlomo. *The Jews and the Crusaders.* Madison, Wis.: Univ. of Wisconsin Press, 1977.

Elder, John. *The Biblical Approach to the Muslim.* Toronto: Fellowship of Faith for the Muslims, 1965.

Elon, Amos. *The Israelis: Founders and Sons.* New York: Penguin Books, 1971.

Epp, Frank H. *The Israelis: Portrait of a People in Conflict.* Scottsdale, Pa.: Herald Press, 1980.

Fernea, Elizabeth and Robert. *The Arab World.* Garden City, N. Y.: Doubleday, 1985.

Finegan, Jack. *Discovering Israel.* Grand Rapids, Mich.: Wm. B. Eerdmans Publishing Co., 1981.

Finkelstein, Louis, ed. *The Jews, Their History, Culture, and Religion.* 2 vols. New York: Harper and Bros., 1949.

———. *The Pharisees.* Philadelphia: The Jewish Publication Society of America, 1938, 1962.

Fisch, Harold. *The Zionist Revolution: A New Perspective.* New York: St. Martin's Press, 1978.

Fishman, Hertzel. *American Protestantism and the Jewish State.* Detroit: Wayne State University Press, 1973.

Ford, Henry, Sr. *The International Jew.* (Abridged from orig. 4 vols. in 1919). London: G. F. Green, 1948.

Forrest, A. C. *The Unholy Land.* Toronto: McClelland and Stewart Limited, 1971.

Friedman, Thomas L. *From Beirut to Jerusalem.* New York: Anchor Books, Doubleday, 1995, 1989.

Fromkin, David. *A Peace to End All Peace: The Fall of the Ottoman Empire and the Creation of the Modern Middle East.* New York: Avon Books, 1989.

Frydland, Rachmiel. *When Being Jewish Was a Crime.* Nashville: Thomas Nelson, 1978.

Gabrieli, Francesco. *Muhammad and the Conquests of Islam.* New York: World University Library, 1968.

Gade, Richard E. *A Historical Survey of Anti-Semitism.* Grand Rapids, Mich.: Baker Book House, 1981.

Gallagher, Wes. *Lightning Out of Israel (The Six-Day War)*. New York: The Associated Press, 1967.

Gatje, Helmut. *The Qur'an and Its Exegesis*. Berkeley: University of California Press, 1976.

Gilbert, Martin. *Atlas of Russian History*. New York: Dorset Press, 1972.

———. *Jewish History Atlas*. New York: Macmillan Publishing Co., 1969, 1976.

———. *The Arab–Israeli Conflict: Its History in Maps*. 4th ed. Jerusalem: Steimatzky, 1984.

Goiten, S. D. *Jews and Arabs: Their Contacts through the Ages*. New York: Schocken Books, 1964.

Goldberg, Louis. *Turbulence over the Middle East*. Neptune, N.J.: Loizeaux Brothers, 1982.

Graetz, Heinrich. *History of the Jews*. Reprint Edition. Philadelphia: The Jewish Publication Society of America, 1967.

Grossman, David. *The Yellow Wind*. New York: Farrar, Straus, and Giroux, 1988.

Gulston, Charles. *Jerusalem: The Tragedy and the Triumph*. Grand Rapids, Mich.: Zondervan Publishing House, 1978.

Hagner, Donald A. *The Jewish Reclamation of Jesus*. Grand Rapids, Mich.: Zondervan Publishing House, 1984.

Halabi, Rafik. *The Westbank Story*. New York: Harcourt Brace Javanovich, 1982.

Harkabi, Yehoshafat. *Israel's Fateful Hour*. New York: Harper and Row, 1988.

Harris, Wm. H., and Judith S. Levy, eds. *The New Columbia Encyclopedia*, New York: Columbia Univ. Press, 1975.

Hart, Alan. *Arafat: Terrorist or Peacemaker?* London: Sidgwick & Jackson, 1984.

Hazleton, Lesley. *Jerusalem, Jerusalem*. Boston: Atlantic Monthly Press, 1986.

Hersh, Seymour M. *The Samson Option: Israel's Nuclear Arsenal and American Foreign Policy*. New York: Random House, 1991.

Hertzberg, Arthur, *The Jews in America*. New York: Simon and Schuster, 1978.

———. *The Zionist Idea: A Historical Analysis and Reader*. New York: Meridian Books, Inc., 1960.

Herzl, Theodor. *The Jewish State (Der Judenstaat)*. New York: Herzel Press, 1970.

———. Sylvie D'Avigdor, trans. *The Jewish State: An Attempt at a Modern Solution of the Jewish Question*. London: H. Pordes, 1967 (orig. 1895).

Herzog, Chaim. *The Arab-Israeli Wars: War and Peace in the Middle East—From the War of Independence through Lebanon*. New York: Random House, 1982.

Hilberg, Raul. *The Destruction of the European Jews*. Chicago: Quadrangle Books, 1961.

Hillel, Marc, and Clarissa Henry. *Of Pure Blood*. New York: McGraw-Hill, 1976.

Hillel, Shlomo. *Operation Babylon*. Trans. Ina Friedman. New York: Doubleday, 1987.

Hirschmann, Ira. *Red Star over Bethlehem*. New York: Simon and Schuster, 1971.

Hitler, Adolf. *Mein Kampf*. New York: Reynal and Hitchcock, 1939.

Hitti, Philip K. *History of the Arabs*. New York: St. Martin's Press, 1970 (orig. 1937).

———. *Islam: A Way of Life*. Chicago: Regnery Gateway, 1970.

Hull, William L. *The Fall and Rise of Israel*. Grand Rapids, Mich.: Zondervan Publishing Co., 1954.

Hussein, King, of Jordan. *My "War" with Israel*. New York: William Morrow and Co., 1969.

Jackson, F. J. Foakes. *Josephus and the Jews*. Grand Rapids, Mich.: Baker Book House, reprint 1974.

Jeffery, Arthur. *Islam, Muhammad and His Religion*. New York: Bobbs-Merrill Co., 1958.

Josephus, Flavius. *The Wars of the Jews*. London: J.M. Dent & Sons, Ltd.; New York: E.P Dutton & Co., 1928.

Kac, Arthur W. *The Rebirth of the State of Israel*. Chicago: Moody Press, 1958.

———. *The Spiritual Dilemma of the Jewish People—Its Cause and Curse.* Grand Rapids, Mich.: Baker Book House, 1963, 1983.

Kaellis, Eugene. *Toward a Jewish America.* Ed. Rhoda Kaellis. Lewiston, N.Y.: E. Mellen Press, 1987.

Kateregga, Badru D., and David W. Shenk. *Islam and Christianity.* Grand Rapids, Mich.: Wm. B. Eerdmans Publishing Co., 1980.

Keil, C. F., and F. Delitzsch. *The Pentateuch.* Grand Rapids, Mich.: Wm. B. Eerdmans Publishing Co., n.d.

Kessler, Martha N. *Syria: Fragile Mosaic of Power.* Washington, D.C.: National Defense University Press, 1987.

Kiernan, Thomas. *Arafat: the Man and the Myth.* New York: W. W. Norton and Co., 1976.

Klausner, Joseph. *Jesus of Nazareth.* New York: MacMillan, 1943.

———. *The Messianic Idea in Israel.* New York: MacMillan, 1955.

Kohler, Kaufmann. *Jewish Theology, Systematically and Historically Considered.* New York: The MacMillan Co., 1918.

Korting, James. *An Outline of German History from 1890 to 1945.* Toronto: Forum House, 1969.

Kushner, Harold S. *When Bad Things Happen to Good People.* New York: Schocken Books, 1981.

Lambert, Lance. *Israel: A Secret Documentary.* Wheaton, Ill.: Tyndale House Publishers, 1975.

Lapide, Pinchas, and Luz Lurich. *Jesus in Two Perspectives: A Jewish-Christian Dialog.* Trans. Lawrence W. Denef. Minneapolis: Augsburg Publishing House, 1985.

Lapp, John A. *The View from East Jerusalem.* Scottdale, Pa.: Herald Press, 1980.

Laqueur, Walter, ed. *The Israel-Arab Reader: A Documentary History of the Middle East Conflict.* New York: Bantam Books, 1969.

Leone, Bruno. *The Middle East.* St. Paul, Minn.: Greenhaven Press, 1982.

Lewis, Bernard. *The Arabs in History.* Revised ed. New York: Harper and Row, 1967.

Limburg, James, ed. *Judaism: An Introduction for Christians.* Minneapolis: Augsburg Publishing House, 1987.

Lorch, Netanel. *The Edge of the Sword (Israel's War of Independence, 1947–49).* New York: Putnam's Sons, 1961.

Maalouf, Tony. *Arabs in the Shadow of Israel: God's Plan for Ishmael's Line in Prophecy.* Grand Rapids, Mich.: Kregel, 2003.

Magnus, Lady. *Outlines of Jewish History.* Philadelphia: The Jewish Society of America, 1890.

Mansfield, Peter. *The Arab World.* New York: Thomas Crowell Company, 1976.

Margolis, Max L., and Alexander Marx. *History of the Jewish People.* Philadelphia: The Jewish Publication Society of America, 1927.

Meinecke, Friedrich. *The German Catastrophe.* Boston: Beacon Press, 1950.

Meir, Golda. *A Land of Our Own.* Ed. Marie Syrkin. New York: Putnam's Sons, 1973.

Memmi, Albert. *Jews and Arabs.* Chicago: J. Philip O'Hara, Inc., 1975.

Menuhim, Moshe. *The Decadence of Judaism in Our Time.* New York: Exposition Press, 1965.

Ministry of Foreign Affairs, Information Division. *Facts About Israel.* Baltimore: Art Litho Co., 1985.

Morse, Arthur D. *While Six Million Died.* New York: Hart Publishing Co., 1968.

Murphy-O'Connor, Jerome, *The Holy Land: An Oxford Archaeological Guide from Earliest Times to 1700.* 4th ed. New York: Oxford Univ. Press, 1998.

Neusner, Jacob. *The Incarnation of God.* Philadelphia: Fortress Press, 1988.

———. *The Oral Torah: The Sacred Books of Judaism.* San Francisco: Harper & Row, 1986.

O'Brien, Conor Cruise. *The Siege: The Saga of Israel and Zionism.* New York: Simon and Schuster, 1986.

Parkes, James. *A History of Palestine from 135 A.D. to Modern Times.* London: V. Gollancz, 1949.

——. *The Conflict of the Church and the Synagogue (A Study in the Origins of Anti-Semitism).* Philadelphia: The Jewish Publication Society of America, 1961.

——. *Whose Land? A History of the Peoples of Palestine.* Baltimore: Penguin Books, 1970.

Peretz, Don. *Israel and the Palestine Arabs.* Washington, D.C.: Middle East Institute, 1958.

Perlmutter, Amos. *Israel: The Partitioned State: A Political History Since 1900.* New York: Charles Scribner's Sons, 1985.

Pippert, Wesley G. *Land of Promise, Land of Strife.* Waco, Tx.: Word Books, 1988.

Pragai, Michael J. *Faith and Fulfilment.* London: Vallentine, Mitchell and Co., 1985.

Prager, Dennis, and Joseph Telushkin. *Why the Jews?* New York: Simon and Schuster, Inc., 1983.

Rausch, David A. *Legacy of Hatred.* Chicago: Moody Press, 1984.

Reich, Walter. *Stranger in My House: Jews and Arabs in the West Bank.* New York: Holt Rinehart and Winston, 1984.

Rejwan, Nissim. *The Jews of Iraq: 3000 Years of History and Culture.* Boulder, Colo.: Westview Press, 1985.

Roth, Cecil. *A History of the Jews.* New York: Schocken Books, 1961, 1970.

——, ed. *Encyclopaedia Judaica.* Jerusalem: Keter Publishing House, 1972.

——, ed. *The Concise Jewish Encyclopedia.* New York: New American Library, 1980.

Rudin, James A. *Israel for Christians.* Philadelphia: Fortress Press, 1983.

Runes, Dagobert D. *Concise Dictionary of Judaism.* New York: Greenwood Press, 1966.

Ryan, Michael D., ed. *Human Responses to the Holocaust.* New York: Edwin Mellen Press, 1981.

Sachar, Abram Leon. *A History of the Jews.* New York: Alfred A. Knopf, Inc., 1964.

——. *Redemption of the Unwanted.* New York: St. Martins/Marek, 1983.

Sachar, Howard M. *A History of Israel: From the Rise of Zionism to Our Time.* New York: Alfred A. Knopf, 1976.

——. *A History of Israel: From the Aftermath of the Yom Kippur War.* New York: Oxford University Press, 1987.

Sandmel, Samuel. *A Jewish Understanding of the New Testament.* New York: University Publishers, Inc., 1956.

——. *We Jews and Jesus.* Reprint edition. New York: Oxford University Press, 1973.

——. *Anti-Semitism in the New Testament.* Philadelphia: Fortress Press, 1978.

——. *The Several Israels.* New York: KTAV Pub. House, 1971.

Schonfield, Hugh J. *The Passover Plot.* New York: Bantam Books, 1966.

Segev, Tom. *One Palestine, Complete: Jews and Arabs under the British Mandate.* Trans. Haim Watzman. New York: Metropolitan Books, Henry Holt and Company, 2000.

Shakir, M. H., trans. *The Qur'an.* Elmhurst, New York: Tahrike Tarsile Qur'an, Inc., 1985.

Shapiro, Delilah. *Israel: Triumph of the Spirit.* New York: MetroBooks, Friedman/Fairfax Publishers, 1997.

Shipler, David K. *Arab and Jew.* New York: Times Books (Random House), 1986.

Shlaim, Avi. *Collusion across the Jordan.* New York: Columbia University Press, 1988.

Silver, Abba Hillel. *Messianic Speculation in Israel.* Boston: Beacon Press, 1959.

Singer, Isador, managing ed. *The Jewish Encyclopedia.* New York: Funk and Wagnalls, 1901.

Smith, Huston. *The Religions of Man.* New York: Harper and Row, 1958.

Speight, R. Marston. *God Is One: The Way of Islam.* New York: Friendship Press, 1989.

Taylor, Alan R. *Prelude to Israel.* New York: Philosophical Library, 1959.

Tekoah, Yosef. *In the Face of the Nations: Israel's Struggle for Peace.* New York: Simon and Schuster, 1976.

Ten Boom, Corrie. *The Hiding Place.* Grand Rapids, Mich.: Zondervan, 1971.

Torrey, Charles C. *The Jewish Foundation of Islam.* New York: KTAV Publishing House, Inc., 1967.

Uris, Leon. *The Haj.* Garden City, New York: Doubleday and Co., 1984.

Vital, David. *The Origins of Zionism.* London: Oxford University Press, 1975.

Von Rad, Gerhard. *God at Work in Israel.* Nashville: Abingdon, 1974 (in German), 1980.

Walvoord, John F., and John E. Walvoord. *Armageddon: Oil and the Middle East Crisis.* Grand Rapids, Mich.: Zondervan Publishing House, 1974.

Ward, Richard, Don Peretz, and Evan M. Wilson. *The Palestine State: A Rational Approach.* New York: Kennikat Press, 1977.

Watt, W. Montgomery. *Companion to the Qur'an.* London: George Allen and Unwin Ltd., 1967.

Weizmann, Chaim. *Trial and Error: The Autobiography of Chaim Weizmann.* New York: Schocken Books, 1966.

Whiston, William, trans. *The Works of Flavius Josephus.* Grand Rapids, Mich.: Baker Book House, Reprint, 1974.

Wilkins, Ronald J. *Religions of the World.* Dubuque, Iowa: Wm. C. Brown Co., 1979.

Wilson, Marvin R. *Our Father Abraham: Jewish Roots of the Christian Faith.* Grand Rapids, Mich.: Wm. B. Eerdmans Publishing Co., 1989.

Yadin, Yigael. *Masada.* London: Wiedenfeld and Nicolson, 1967.

———. *Bar-Kochba.* London: Wiedenfeld and Nicolson, 1971.

Yaseen, Leonard C. *The Jesus Connection: To Triumph over Anti-Semitism.* New York: Crossroad Publishing Co., 1986.

Periodicals

Agha, Hussein, and Robert Malley. "Camp David: The Tragedy of Errors." *The New York Review of Books,* 9 August 2001.

Anderson, Jack, and Dale Van Atta. "Intefadeh Leaders Dismiss Killings of Arab Informers." *The Oregonian,* 7 June 1989.

———. "Rival Foresees Assassination of Arafat." *The Oregonian,* 8 June 1989.

Bar-Illan, David. "Simplistically Blaming Israel." *New York Times,* 31 December 1987.

Chafets, Ze'ev. "Fear and Loathing in Israel." *U.S. News & World Report* (10 July 1989).

Charen, Mona. "Films on Palestinians Mug History." *The Oregonian,* 11 September 1989.

Chesnoff, Richard, with David Kuttab and David Makousky. "Distrust and Dissension in the West Bank and Gaza Strip." *U.S. News & World Report* (10 July 1989).

———. "Peace in the Middle East." *U.S. News & World Report* (10 July 1989).

Coad, Thomas. "Converging Sides May Find Mix for Mid-East Peace." *The Oregonian,* 7 June 1989.

Collins, Frank. "Why Palestinians Kill Palestinians in Israeli-Occupied Territories." *Washington Report on Middle East Affairs* (November 1989).

Eban, Abba. "Shared Interests May Form Peace Basis." *The Oregonian,* 30 May 1989.

Fisher, Allyn. "Sharon to Form Hard-Line Faction in Likud Bloc." *The Oregonian,* 15 February 1990.

Geyer, Georgie Anne. "Intefadeh Has Settled into Routine." *The Oregonian,* 12 December 1989.

Hamilton, Canon Michael. "American Churches Are Speaking out on Palestine and Israel." *The Washington Report* (January 1990).

Ibrahim, Youssef M. "Abu Nidal Followers Kill One Another." *The Oregonian,* 12 November 1989.

Kaidy, Mitchell. "Rising Discrepancy Between Intifada Events and U.S. Media Reports." *Washington Report on Middle East Affairs* (November 1989).

Kaufman, Asher S. "Where the Ancient Temple of Jerusalem Stood." *Biblical Archaeology Review* (March/April 1983).

Kennedy, Charlotte T. "Israelis Can Follow Lead of S. Africa." *The Oregonian,* 15 March 1990.

Klayman, Seth N. "Who Was a Jew, Who Is a Jew?" Senior honors thesis, The Ohio State University, June 1998.

Kohl, Manfred Waldemar. "Towards a Theology of Land: A Christian Answer to the Hebrew-Arab Conflict." *International Congregational Journal* 2 (August 2002): 165-78.

Krauthammer, Charles. "Palestine's Misery." *San Francisco Examiner,* 11 January 1988.

Levin, Jerry. "Creeping Transfer—Israel's Newest Weapon Against the Intifada." *Washington Report on Middle East Affairs* (November 1989).

Lewis, Anthony. "Time Is Right for Palestinians to Accept Peace Bid." *The Oregonian,* 7 June 1989.

Lowenheim, Francis L. "Israel's Recognition Didn't Come Easily." *The Oregonian,* 8 December 1989.

Mark, Clyde. *Palestinians and Middle East Peace: Issues for the United States.* Congressional Research Service Issue brief for Congress, 25 January 2002.

McBride, Dean. "The Yoke of the Kingdom." *Interpretation* (July 1973): 273–306.

Meir, Golda. *Life* (3 October 1969): 32.

Morrow, Lance. "An Intifadeh of the Soul." *Time* (23 July 1990).

Piper, John. "Land Divine?" *World* (11 May 2002).

Ritmeyer, Kathleen, and Leen Ritmeyer. "Reconstructing Herod's Temple Mount in Jerusalem." *Biblical Archaeology Review* (November/December 1989).

Rose, Emanuel. "As Supporters of Israel, We Must Decry Brutality." *The Oregonian,* 23 February 1988.

Sanders, Eli, and Bobbi Nodell. "Two Peoples, One Land: Understanding the Israeli-Palestinian Conflict." *The Seattle Times,* 12 May 2002.

Sella, Yaacov. "The Palestinian Tragedy." *Consulate General of Israel* (January 1988).

Shasheen, Jack. "Lawrence of Arabia: Memorable for What It Is, Regrettable for What It Might Have Been." *Washington Report on Middle East Affairs* (November 1989).

Spring, Beth. "Palestinian Christians: Caught in a War of Two Rights." *Christianity Today* (18 April 1986).

Toameh, Khaled Abu. "PA Population to Double in 19 Years." *Jerusalem Post Internet Edition,* 9 January 2003.

Toynbee, Arnold, and Solomon Zeitlin. "Jewish Rights in Palestine." *Jewish Quarterly Review* 152 (1961–62).

Walz, L. Humphrey. "Evangelical Church Issues Statement on Israeli-Palestinian Conflict." *Washington Report on Middle East Affairs* (November 1989).

Will, George F. "White House Ready to Dance with PLO." *The Oregonian,* 17 September 1989.

Index